BAITING THE TRAP

BAITING THE TRAP

One Man's Secret Battle
To Save Our Wildlife

Tony Saunders

SIMON & SCHUSTER
A VIACOM COMPANY

Author's Note

Some names have been changed on legal advice; in all other respects,
everything in this book is true.

First published in Great Britain by
Simon & Schuster UK Ltd, 2001
A Viacom Company

1 3 5 7 9 10 8 6 4 2

Simon & Schuster UK Ltd
Africa House
64–78 Kingsway
London WC2B 6AH

Simon & Schuster Australia
Sydney

A CIP catalogue record for this book is available
from the British Library

ISBN 0-7432-0747-5

Typeset in Garamond 3
by Palimpsest Book Production Ltd,
Polmont, Stirlingshire
Printed and bound in Great Britain

For my mother and in
memory of my father

ACKNOWLEDGEMENTS

I would like to thank Ken Connor for getting the ball rolling and his valuable advice. Also Gordon and Neil for their excellent work and Sir Ranulph Fiennes for his kind words. Special thanks go to Denise, Kerry & Terry for putting up with so much. To those Special Operations Unit colleagues past and present who endeavoured to enhance the professionalism of the unit and, in particular, to Don Balfour for his past support. The Police Wildlife Office, Specialist Units, Customs and Excise have all provided me with excellent support over the years. Billy for being a good friend and helping me out so many times. Last but not least, the RSPCA for giving me the chance to fulfil my ambition and do my bit for animal welfare.

CONTENTS

An old man was walking along the beach at dawn when he noticed a young woman picking up starfish and throwing them back into the sea.

Getting closer, the man asked her the reason for her actions.

She replied that if the starfish stayed on the sand until the morning sun rose high, they would then all die.

'But the beach goes for miles and there are starfish as far as the eye can see,' observed the old man. 'Why do you bother?'

The young woman looked up, and then down at the starfish in her hand. Then she threw it out to sea.

'For that starfish,' she said, 'it makes all the difference.'

Antoine de Saint-Exupéry

PROLOGUE

To: Chief Superintendent Don Balfour, RSPCA
    Special Operations Unit
From: Chief Inspector Tony Saunders

Tape based on information received from Morgan
Connor, junior gamekeeper, of Ribblesdale, Lancs.

*Hello, Don. I'm recording this for you in a hotel bedroom. I'll write
it up as a report later but I thought you should hear it straight
away, pretty much as it was told to me. The lad Connor had no
idea what he was going to see and was completely devastated by it,
which was why he went to uniform, and so to me. It's strong stuff,
Don. Here goes.*

The arena, maybe eight feet by four, stood inside a dark and
dusty hut, deep in the woods. About twenty men stood
shoulder to shoulder around it – young men, working men,

country men. This particular bunch lived and worked in the Pennines, but as you know, you find them all over rural Britain, the kind you might see driving a tractor, a JCB, a Land Rover or a 4WD, the kind who like a pint and a bet on the horses, a bit of hare coursing, rough shooting, or lamping rabbits. They like to see some sport, these men.

As yet they could see very little, just the bare wooden floor enclosed by a wall of hay bales. Then one of them, a game-keeper called Geoff Verril (not his real name), a stocky, powerful-looking type of about thirty, climbed over the bales into the arena. He wore an old combat jacket with the sleeves rolled up and, unlike most of the others, he was bare-headed, his fair hair cropped to the millimetre. Verril was the leader, the master of ceremonies.

A hessian sack stood in a corner, tied at the top with baler twine. Verril signalled to one of the others to open the door wider, letting in more light, then he grabbed the sack with a hand like a pit shovel and lifted it. Whatever was inside was heavy. The veins and muscles stood out on his bare arm as he reached for a sheath knife at his belt. This was no ord-inary knife. This was Verril's trademark, his highly prized US Marine K-bar, well used and sharpened, and it slit the plastic twine as easily as a surgeon's scalpel slices skin.

The spectators tried to get closer, somehow, straining to see more clearly into the gloomy rectangle with its boarded floor and walls of dead grass. Verril took the sack by its bottom corners and shook it.

Something fell out with a thump. Whatever it was looked dead. For perhaps thirty seconds nothing happened. Then four or five men pulled the rings on their beer cans and the rapid sequence of pops and hisses seemed to invigorate the heap on the floor. It twitched.

Verril stepped back over the hay wall and joined the others.

Slowly the animal uncurled. There was a ripple of satisfaction around the arena as the men, expecting a fox, realised they had a much more entertaining time in prospect. Instead of Reynard, vicious but lightweight and, ultimately, a coward, here was a badger – Brock, the doughtiest gladiator of them all.

At first the black and white striped face of the sow badger showed nothing. A few seconds passed in silence. Then she realised she was in enemy territory, well behind the lines. Her natural instinct was to run and hide. She scrabbled and scurried round the bales, back and forth, unable to believe that there really was no chance of escape.

Verril smiled and slipped outside the hut. There was the bang of a car door and he returned holding a Lakeland terrier. He dropped the dog into the arena.

With a string of piercing, screaming barks the little brown terrier launched itself at the badger. She immediately rolled herself back into a defensive ball.

On home ground, of course, in the narrow tunnels and chambers of a sett, the badger would have been favourite to win, or at least to force a draw. There the dog would have been forced to head straight towards the badger's teeth.

Here, in the open, the dog had the edge. It could come at her from any direction, and duck and dive. The badger's options were limited and, for the moment anyway, her thick, rubbery skin offered the best defence.

The terrier ripped and tore at the badger's hind quarters for a good ten minutes, occasionally breaking off to try a snarling thrust elsewhere but careful not to get too near her jaws. It danced in and out of range like a skilful boxer fighting a heavier and stronger man. After each little foray it went back to attack the hind quarters.

Its bark changed in pitch when it tasted blood. Blood, and

victory. Intoxicated with success it changed its line of attack and tried to get a grip on a softer place, further up the badger's body.

This was what its prey had been waiting for. In a blur of movement she uncurled and struck upwards, jaws closing on the terrier's unguarded throat. Very few animals have a bite as powerful and tenacious as a badger's. Her jaw locked solid, and she held on.

The terrier screamed in agony and tried to shake itself free. The badger's grip only tightened, her determination strengthened by this sign of weakness in her opponent. The terrier's manic efforts to save its own life seemed likely only to hasten the end. The badger's jaws were immovable; with every twist and turn the terrier was ripping itself apart. In among the blood and chocolate-brown hair the watching men could now see the dog's windpipe, white and red. How long would it be before the badger shifted her grip by an inch and bit right through it?

The spectators started to mutter. The mood in the hut had changed. This was not the way things were meant to go. They lunged forward, leaning over the bales, screaming abuse and obscenities. Verril ran outside and brought in his lurcher, which itself was something of a one-off, looking like it had a lot of bull terrier in it, mixed with collie. Its coat was mainly grey with blue flecks, its broad head came to a muzzle on which there was very little hair, only scar tissue, and the powerful front legs were covered in small round wounds where the hair would never grow back. This dog was no stranger to combat.

Verril scrambled over the hay bales, dragging his dog behind him by the scruff of the neck. His eyes bulged and the veins stood out on his forehead as he threw the lurcher into the fray.

The dog didn't react straight away. While the terrier's insane bravery made it discount all options but immediate attack, the lurcher's collie brains were maybe telling it not to take things at face value, to look before it leaped.

Verril had no patience with that. He stepped towards the badger and gave her a savage kick in the flank with his steel-capped boot. Everybody heard ribs break and sensed the rupture of internal organs.

Grievously hurt, the badger let go of the terrier. Blood trailed across the floor of the arena as the little Lakeland fighter slunk away, beaten — for the moment at least — and in a bad way, a hospital case. Or, in Verril's eyes, nothing that a few stitches wouldn't fix.

The lurcher now had the situation cracked. The badger, half its size, was badly wounded, probably fatally. The dog took the poor sow in its jaws and, with a mighty heave, shook her like a rat. But where a rat would have died instantly, its neck or back broken, the badger lived on. The lurcher dropped her, pausing before its next move.

Verril wasn't prepared to wait. He pushed the dog aside and stamped his foot down, across the old girl's neck, with all his strength.

The badger dredged up her last shreds of defiance and made a final attempt to break free. She flapped and wriggled and heaved like a salmon on a river-bank. Of course, she had no chance. Verril did what the crowd wanted. He pulled out his knife and thrust its blade between the badger's ribs. There was a small squeal as it sliced tissue and grated against bone, then silence.

Stabbed through the heart, the badger was dead. Badger muck mixed with blood on the circus floor while Verril wiped his knife on her coat.

*   *   *

Well, Don, I told you it was strong stuff. But I'm afraid there's no possibility of a prosecution at this stage. Nobody who was there, not even young Master Connor, would ever give evidence in court. But we'll get the bastard one day. Now I'm going to bed. It's half past two and I'm due up at five. See you.

1

—

Uncle Tony was famous in the family, legendary even, for the stories he told. I was about four years old when I first heard the one about the crocodile.

I was on the couch, a small boy between two men who seemed very large to me, my dad and my uncle. For some unknown reason Uncle Tony was telling my dad about Nile crocodiles. You know how your childhood mind takes photographs that never fade? Mine made a permanent recording of that conversation, and it changed my life.

'They only feed once or twice a year, you know, and they lay an ambush to catch their dinner,' said Uncle Tony, all confidential. 'Such as a zebra. A zebra makes a very good dinner. The croc will hide in the shallows, in the mud, waiting. Then, along comes the zebra for a drink. Talking of which, I wouldn't mind a drop myself.'

Dad went to get some beer out of the pantry. I know I was staring at Uncle Tony's face. My mouth and eyes couldn't open

any wider. I expect, looking back, that the dramatic pauses
were for my benefit.

With the pale ale poured, the men settled back in the couch.

'So there's the croc, invisible. In the mud. He – or it might
be a she – is merged into the surroundings. And, here comes
the zebra. It's hot. It's scorching. That zebra must have a drink
of water if it's the last thing it does. Very nervous, the zebra
is, and it has every right to be. Life is hard on the banks of
the Nile. You might be as big as the rag and bone man's pony
and a lot faster, but that's not much defence against the jaws
of the crocodile.'

I was mesmerised by this entirely new idea, that there lived
an animal that thought it normal to have the rag and bone
man's pony for its dinner.

'The croc, though, has a problem. If he catches the zebra,
what's he going to do with it? His jaws are for gripping, not
chewing. And he doesn't have a knife and fork. Anyway, we'll
cross that bridge when we come to it, because here's the zebra,
stepping carefully through the mud towards a shallow pool
of cool, clear water. It sniffs the air. Its eyes flick this way and
that. Satisfied, it bends its noble head to the surface of the
pool, takes the first delicious slurp, and . . . BANG!'

Uncle Tony clapped his hands together and I nearly jumped
through the window.

'The zebra, kick and squirm as it might, is caught in the
croc's jaws. There is no escape. Soon, the zebra is dead and
. . . do you know what happens next? The croc wedges the
zebra, nice and tight, under a submerged tree root, or a fallen
trunk. Then, he takes a bite. Then, he spins. That's what he
does. He spins. He takes a bite of zebra, holds it firmly between
his teeth, and, being a crocodile, that's about as firm as can
be, and he spins his whole body until the meat tears away and
he can swallow it. Sometimes two crocs even do this together,

one holding the carcass while the other spins. Now, what do you think about that?'

I had never heard anything so extraordinary. From that moment I was a pest, asking my dad, my uncle and anybody who would listen for more and more information about crocodiles, zebras and everything else that lived and breathed in the wild. I was hooked. It didn't matter if it was butterflies in Tibet or a mouse in the house. From that moment I had the call. I lived and breathed animals, and I have been like that, consumed by the call, ever since.

As soon as I was old enough to go out alone I spent my every waking moment searching for wildlife. I grew up in the fishing town of Hull, close to the docks. A passer-by might have thought the only wildlife was the trawlermen in the pubs at night, but nothing could be further from the truth. There was wildlife everywhere, if you knew where to look, and half the pleasure was finding those places. Take the old railway sidings on the docks. They were full of all sorts of rare flowers and butterflies. Great crested newts, or horse newts as we called them, were quite rare, but I knew where I could discover them. I soon knew every feature of the wildlife that existed within a half day's walk of our house.

It was fifteen miles to Spurn Point but that didn't matter, because there I could find lizards. Even further away, there were grass snakes on a disused bombing range at Aldborough, living among the frogs and toads in the ponds that gathered in the shell craters.

Now I know how damaging such careless enthusiasm can be to endangered species and their habitats, but in those days I was blissfully unaware of any moral or conservation issues. All I saw was something that interested me. If I could catch a newt or a butterfly as well as watch it, so much the better. I wasn't alone in my youthful ignorance: Gerald Durrell and

Bill Oddie both spent their early years collecting animals and Bill even had a collection of birds' eggs.

My friends, like most boys, were interested in things that lived in ponds, streams, woods and the sea, but they weren't as keen as I was. They didn't want to spend so much of their time looking at wildlife when there was cricket and football to play in the street or a game of rugby league to go and watch. I liked all of that too, but the wildlife came first and so, usually, I went out on my own except for my very best pal, a whippet-cross dog called Skipper.

Skipper couldn't come when we went for pigeons. This was a dangerous exercise for us boys, which few sane adults would have undertaken unless it was for a large bet. We were after squabs, nestlings that were just about fledged but not yet flying, the offspring of the many, many feral racing pigeons that lived among the timbers of the great wooden jetties. There were grain silos nearby to provide food, and, hidden below the jetty platforms with only the sea beneath them, the pigeons were perfectly safe from all predators except us.

We needed a team of two. Daniel usually came with me, a pale, skinny lad with straggly blond hair. If any of us ever thought we were badly off, we only had to look at Daniel to feel better about it. His family was always on the breadline, and the usual way he got clothes was by waiting for me to grow out of mine. The only things he really had of his own were head lice.

We would walk the jetties, looking down between the planks until we saw a nest, then Daniel would stay at that point while I went back to the shore to start my climb back towards him from below, up the supports and along, navigating by his calls. If the tide was out I could climb at a less nerve-racking, low level among the massive wood stanchions, but my ways were covered in slippery seaweed and mud. If the tide was in, I had to start much further away and climb much higher, but the route was clearer.

In either case it was a miracle that none of us lads ever fell. With the tide out it was actually more dangerous. I was a good swimmer so I didn't mind being high up if I had the water underneath me. I knew that if I fell at low tide, into the bottomless clinging mud of the Humber estuary, it would have swallowed me and a thousand more small boys without leaving a sign. Not that such a thought bothered us in the slightest.

Once we reached the nest we took the squabs from inside, stuffed them down our shirts and headed back. We kept the best to stock the pigeon loft, bringing them up as our own and racing them between ourselves. Pigeon fanciers paid a lot for their birds. We had ours for nothing, and better than nothing because we sold our surplus to Mrs Skilbeck.

Mrs Skilbeck was an old and frightening woman. Although she no longer had a pigeon loft, she'd painted the walls of her back yard with white strips, mimicking the white slats on the front of the loft that the pigeons used as a homing beacon. It was always jam-packed with pigeons. They perched on every window sill, downpipe, gutter, door handle, you name it, they were all over the spot. We thought she ate the birds too, but she always had plenty around.

She had a special method of getting rid of their homing instinct, which would have made them fly back to the docks. She held their little heads under a running cold tap for several minutes, which, she said, brainwashed them. Her other way was to put a pigeon's head in her mouth and close her lips around the neck, also for three or four minutes, which had the same effect.

We tried it, of course, but it never worked for us. We had to use the traditional method of keeping them in for several weeks. We wondered what her secret ingredient was, and, behind her back, in whispers, referred to Mrs Skilbeck as the Pigeon Witch.

Acquiring pigeons was a year-round activity. There would be some mating and nesting every month of the year, including the winter, and the act of getting pigeons became more important than the prizes themselves. When a February gale was blowing and anybody with any sense was at home in front of the fire, we'd be out there, me swinging around over the icy Humber, the only UK estuary with a full-time permanent lifeboat on duty, and Daniel above on the decking, telling me to hurry up because he was freezing.

The next really significant turning point in my life came through a lad I otherwise kept well clear of. This was John Mann, called Manny, big at over six foot, the bodybuilder type, a couple of years older and as hard as nails. His reputation was fearsome, as the best fighter around and as someone with a really mean, violent streak.

I was up a hawthorn tree looking at a blackbird's nest with chicks in it. They were quite well grown and not far from flying. Skipper was at the bottom, his ears pricked, watching my every move, when I saw Manny down below. My first thought was to get away from the nest; if he saw me up there, he'd know what I'd found and want to destroy it. But he'd spotted me and stood waiting at the bottom of the tree.

'What's in the nest?' he asked when I reached the bottom.

'Nothing,' I said, but Manny gave me that look. I thought: he'll be after the eggs anyway, and I'm too young to die. I told him.

He had a duffel bag slung over his shoulder. He put it down with some care and started to climb the tree.

I shouted up to him. 'There's no point going up there; there's no eggs in it, only chicks.'

He took no notice. He grabbed the chicks, stuffed them in his pockets and climbed back down the tree.

If I couldn't believe what I'd already seen him do, my mind was stretched to near snapping by what happened next. He opened the duffel bag and put his hand inside. I heard a loud noise, 'Click, click, click,' like slow castanets. Carefully and with great pride, like an amateur magician whose trick has finally gone right, he pulled out a grey and brown ball of feathers. I recognised it instantly from my wildlife books, even though I'd never seen one before. It was a young tawny owl.

The tawny is the owl that looks like a slightly comical, rather portly judge. It has huge black eyes and, rather than the red or yellow irises that make other species of owl seem so fierce, it has a red marking around the eyelids like a line of crimson mascara. With the white stripes on its head and its rotund body shape, it looks so serious and pompous it makes you want to laugh.

This one looked very serious indeed. It clicked and clicked and dug its talons into Manny's arm. He pulled one of the blackbird chicks out of his pocket. The chick was nearly as big as the owl's head but the tawny opened its mouth wide, flung its head back and swallowed twice. One of the blackbird's feet still stuck out from the side of the tawny's beak. On the third gulp it disappeared.

I stood amazed. All had been revealed. I had seen the light. I knew that, whatever else I did in life, I had to have an owl.

I threw caution to the winds and asked where he'd got it. He said there had been two in the nest and he'd got both of them. I pleaded with him to let me have one but he wouldn't hear of it so, for the whole of the rest of that day, I followed him about as he went looking for more nests to feed the insatiable appetites of his owlet twins. My first offer was ten shillings, a fortune to anyone like us at the time, but he wasn't interested in cash. It was probably lucky for me; I had nothing like that amount.

'What about a swap, then? My fishing rod for one owlet. No? All right, my fishing rod plus my new rugby ball.'

He drove a hard bargain. As young as he was, he was shrewd enough to recognise desperation when he saw it, and I certainly wasn't clever enough to play it cool. I added my sheath knife to my side of the bargain, but still it was no go. I didn't have much left to barter with.

'Right,' I said. 'My fishing rod. My rugby ball. My sheath knife. Half a crown to be paid in five weekly tanner instalments. And . . .'

I was almost choking. The one thing I prized above all else in my tiny collection of worldly goods was my air pistol, my Webley .177.

'And,' I said, 'my air pistol.' I had reached the limit. I had nothing more to give. Manny probably knew as much but he still went through the process of thinking about it for a while. Then he gave me the nod.

I ran home, collected my entire wealth together and ran full tilt to Manny's house. There we did the deal. I had my owl. He had all I possessed. That was thirty years ago, and it still ranks as one of the three or four happiest days of my life.

I couldn't get home fast enough. The pigeons were unceremoniously evicted from one of the smaller lofts and the owl, by now called Tal, was installed. Using a book about falcons as a guide, I made my owl some jesses – leather anklets, which are supposed to have a swivel fitted to attach the training line. I didn't have a swivel so I used a small keyring; I wasn't going to train him to hunt, just give him the freedom of the back yard on a line.

Tal became a local celebrity. People came from miles around. He'd perch on the back wall and swivel his head three-quarters of the way round, bobbing up and down and watching the dogs and cats as they passed by underneath him.

Feeding him was hard work. Every morning I'd get up at the crack of dawn and jog down to the nearest piece of waste ground, beside an old railway line about a mile and a half away. This was my hunting territory. Here I was the lone trapper, finding food for my family. My equipment was fairly rudimentary, a dozen Little Nipper mousetraps that I set six at a time, hidden in the brambles and baited with sweet biscuit or, if I could get my hands on some, chocolate.

Every morning I'd gather in the previous day's catch, usually one or two shrews or field voles and a field mouse if I was lucky, and put them in my blazer pockets along with the used traps. I had already learned that the wild rodents won't go near a trap that smells of blood, so I had to take the traps home and get rid of the scent by suspending them in the smoke of the coal fire.

I'd cross a wood yard to the railway line, knowing that every day a timber train slowed down for the junction. I'd leap onto the back of one of the wagons and get a free ride to within half a mile of the school gates.

This all went well for a few weeks until there was a spate of thefts at school. My form teacher decided on an impromptu search of everyone's satchels and pockets. I refused to turn out mine, so Mr Jones thrust his hands into both blazer pockets at the same time. His face was a picture. He had no idea what he had hold of but he knew it wasn't very nice, and when he pulled out a couple of dead shrews he squealed like a schoolgirl. The word must have got about the staff room, because I was never searched by anyone again.

I must have been stretching the regenerative capacity of the local vole population to the limit, because my catches for Tal began to thin out. I had to move further and further afield, which made me late for school more often than not. I was starting to get into deep trouble. With nowhere to turn, I let it be known that I was ready to trade.

Before long there was a steady stream of lads with pockets bulging with furry and feathered corpses. I traded my entire bird's egg collection for road accident victims and titbits recovered from the jaws of neighbourhood cats.

It took me a while to realise this wasn't the same as making friends. All I cared about was feeding Tal, my very own owl. If nobody wanted to come with me on my expeditions, so what? I was happy enough, setting my traps and turning over rocks and railway sleepers looking for voles' nests, or taking a full day to walk to Spurn Point looking for common lizards and grass snakes.

Unfortunately children don't really like anyone who is different, who doesn't conform to the rules of the tribe, and I soon became a target for bullies. After school and during weekends and holidays I was joyously occupied, doing what I wanted to do, out and about exploring, discovering more about wildlife. This seemed acceptable at primary school but the tribal laws grow stricter as you get older. A solo wildlife enthusiast at junior school isn't a funny little eccentric, he's someone to tread on.

This meant that for every hour of happiness I had in the open country, I had an hour of misery at school. Three main bully boys started off with jeers and taunts and, after a few weeks, delivered the first severe beating. They came at me together after school, broke my nose, knocked me to the floor and gave me a good kicking. I got them back individually for that and they left me alone for a while. Everything was fine until they closed our school and we were all moved to another one, which had its own bullying regime already established. My old bullies teamed up with some new pals, and from then on it was hell. There seemed to be no end to it. I was beaten up virtually every day.

I don't quite remember how it happened, but I changed schools again. I was transferred to Southcoates without putting in a request myself and, before I knew it, I was being taken through a spelling test by my new headmaster. He seemed pleased with me, even if I couldn't spell 'ceiling', and there I was.

At my new school I embarked on a new philosophy. Attack was my best means of defence. I would get my retaliation in first. I became a feared figure, a solitary gunslinger with a huge chip on his shoulder, taking on anyone who crossed my path. It was my way of ensuring I was left alone.

I don't quite know which side of me would have won eventually had it not been for the third of my great formative experiences. After the crocodile story and John Mann with his owls came another incident, one which still gives me bad dreams.

By now I was fifteen. Tal had been released into the wild, I didn't bother with pigeons any more, and I was a bicycle owner. My range was thus extended by thirty or forty miles, but one of my favourite things to do on Saturday mornings was cycle the six or so miles to a nature reserve, known locally as Little Switzerland.

It was the spring of the year, the sun was rising over the Humber estuary and Little Switzerland was like paradise to me, a group of worked-out, flooded chalk quarries rich in pond-life, including great crested newts, frogs and all sorts of birds. There were rocky parts where lizards lived, and wooded areas with a host of different species. It was my own private national park, and I knew it better than any warden ever did.

I had recently acquired a powerful pump-action air rifle, a .22 calibre that could knock down rabbits and even wood pigeons if you hit them right. With my gun I was the Man, creeping silently through the jungle towards the snake-infested swamp as I walked quietly down the footpath to the chalk quarry. There was no one about.

The silence of the early morning, after the dawn chorus, was broken by the beautiful, melodic tune of a song thrush, a sound more thrilling and more moving than any orchestra. There he was, silhouetted on a branch at the top of a beech tree, singing for all he was worth and telling me that this sector of the wood was his and his alone.

I can't even remember raising the gun or pulling the trigger but I do remember the sickening thud as the pellet hit the thrush and the song stopped.

The bird fell backwards, lifeless, from the top of the tree and wedged on a small branch about ten feet from the ground. I dropped my gun and rushed forward. As I reached the tree the thrush toppled from its resting place and landed at my feet. I picked it up and held it in my hands. I felt the warmth of its life, and I stared at it. Blood trickled from beneath its wing along its speckled chest.

I felt a profound sadness, an emptiness inside, followed by utter disgust at what I had done. I had silenced one of the marvels of the British countryside. I was responsible for a death that could have no possible justification. Even if I could scarcely believe that it was actually me who'd lined up the little silhouette in the sights of the air rifle, that it was me, Tony, the great wildlife expert, who had squeezed the trigger, there was nobody else. I was the guilty one.

I made the most solemn promise to myself that I would never again deliberately harm any living creature, but that didn't wipe away what I had done. In my mind I could still hear the silence when the song stopped, and I could still see that thrush tumbling through the branches. I still can.

2

When I left school in 1974 my career was mapped out. It was a family tradition. My brother was in the forces; father and grandfather had been in the forces. I would leave school at sixteen, join the navy and see the world and all its wildlife. As soon as I could I went down to the navy careers office to enlist as a trainee diver. It was a natural thing to do. I had always excelled at swimming, and had every award that was available, and I looked forward to a life of adventure, over and under the sea.

I'd finished my training at HMS *Raleigh* at Tor Point in Devon and had had my first shore leave when I met a girl at a dance. I really fell for her and arranged to meet her under the church clock at seven the following Saturday. Most of that afternoon was spent preparing my number ones for the occasion, pressing the bell-bottoms with the regulation seven creases, one for each of the seven seas, and bulling my boots till I could see my face in them. I looked absolutely immaculate.

I was full of myself and couldn't have been any happier as I walked to the gate to hand in my leave pass. The petty officer on duty must have been having a bad day.

'Where do you think you're going, laddie?' he said.

'On leave, sir,' I said. 'Meeting a girl. A nice girl. My pass, sir.'

'Now there's a funny thing,' he said. 'Meeting a nice girl, are we? And there I was, thinking we were down for cleaning the urinals.'

'Oh, no sir,' I said, beginning to feel a bit uneasy. 'I'm on leave.'

'Are we saying I don't know what I'm on about, laddie?' There was menace in his tone. 'I'll see about that, shall I? Laddie?'

Within fifteen minutes I was in number eights – fatigues really – and scrubbing the urinals and WCs with a tooth-brush. I am sure that discipline is a cumulative process and that there is a long established point to such things, but frankly I failed to see it at the time. I also couldn't under-stand how anyone, even one as exalted as a petty officer, could rearrange my own free time for me. I knew nothing about the girl except her first name, so that would be that.

My navy career ended there and then, after less than a year. On the way home I rang up and asked my dad if it was all right to come back. I felt ashamed that I had let the side down and broken a long tradition, but I couldn't hack it. My parents were astonished that I thought it necessary to ask permission to come home, but that was the way I felt.

For six months I moved from job to job. Nothing could keep me motivated or interested for more than a few weeks at a time. One day, I was sitting on the floor next to my dad in the living room, explaining that I couldn't do these ordin-ary jobs because I was desperately keen to find work with animals. He mentioned that a distant relative by marriage, a guy called Jack Hartley, was manager of the local RSPCA animal shelter in Hull. I was flabbergasted. I couldn't believe he hadn't said so before. I rang Jack and made an appointment to go and see him.

Jack was a legend in Hull, Mr RSPCA for thirty years. He was in his late sixties with a shock of grey hair, massive calloused hands, a grip of steel and an infectious enthusiasm for the job. He explained that the only post available at the time was kennel maid. He'd never employed a male for the position. To me it was the first rung on the ladder; I didn't care what they called me. I wanted that job.

The kennels were our holding pens. In those days when stray dogs came in, we looked after them, and after a few weeks they went one of two ways – to a new home, or to be put down. The implications of this were fairly obvious to me. The cleaner the kennels, the better looked-after the dogs, the more likely the public was to take one home.

It was hard, dirty work with a relentless routine. I was in charge of twenty kennels that had to be scrubbed out twice a day. I had to prepare the food, feed and water the dogs, exercise them and, when the public came round, practise my rapidly acquired skills as the dogs' unofficial advertising agent. The pressure was really on when the kennels were full. If a new dog came in, the oldest resident – proved by its long stay to be unattractive to all callers – would take the lonely road to nowhere, so I was always praising such animals to the skies. I used to make up stories about the ugliest and least appealing dogs to try and convince someone to take them home.

As a kennel maid, or kennel hand shall we call it, I was on the bottom rung of the RSPCA ladder. I enjoyed it, it was non-stop, but I didn't want to be doing it for the rest of my life. I looked above me and saw what I believed to be the most exciting job imaginable at that time: animal ambulance driver. These people were called out to emergencies – road accidents, rescues of all kinds. That was my next goal.

I did have one slight problem. I couldn't drive, nor was I likely to for some time. I was just seventeen, I had no money for driving lessons, and my brother-in-law could only be press-ganged into taking me out in his car when he was free, which wasn't often.

Out of the blue one of the drivers left and there was a vacancy. Such positions were rare and I might not get another shot for a long time, so I told Jack I was taking my driving test next week and I'd like to apply. I booked a day off for it, and also arranged my real driving test for as soon as I could, in two months.

Jack was so delighted when I said I'd passed my test first time that he never bothered to ask to see my licence, and the two months' practice in the ambulance must have been extremely helpful, because when I came to take the test I really did pass first time.

I did that job for four months. I was still kennel-maiding during the day but on certain evenings I was on call, the duty driver, my own boss. Whenever the police or the public called me out, I drove off in my van and had to cope with whatever accident might have occurred. Despite a lack of obvious attractions, like any money at all, I spent my other evenings trying to persuade one particular girl that she should look at me in a favourable light.

Denise was fifteen and still at school. She had blonde hair that hung down to her waist and a smile that caused grown men to drop down in a dead faint at two hundred yards. She also had a younger brother to look after and I could help with that. Eventually, even though I can't have looked like much of a prospect, Denise agreed to be courted by a male kennel maid. Things were looking up.

Denise must have had an inkling about her new boyfriend's obsession with animals, because my idea of a date was to sit on the quay for ten hours waiting for a vixen and her cubs to come out from their concrete earth in the dockside. Instead of taking my girl for a cruise around in a convertible with the top down and the Beach Boys on the radio, I took Denise out in my RSPCA ambulance rescuing cats and dogs. I thought I could not have been happier. If Denise had reservations about my one-eyed outlook on life, she didn't say so.

One fateful day I was asked to get a kennel ready 'for the inspector's dog'. I didn't know who the inspector was, and imagined him to be a superior being, like the headmaster or the magistrate or the Lord Mayor. Whoever the inspector was, he would have a dog with him and I was going to be responsible for it.

In fact the Hull RSPCA inspector had resigned just before I arrived at the kennels, and here at last was his replacement. When I saw him I knew immediately, without any reservation, that I was looking at my future. His van was fitted with two-way radio, animal rescue equipment and all sorts of interesting gear. I asked him a thousand questions in the first ten minutes, as I was putting the dog he'd brought in as a cruelty case into the kennel.

Everything he told me about the job seemed too good to be true. He was provided with free accommodation by the RSPCA, a vehicle he could use in his own free time and, as far as animal welfare went, he had his own patch, and he reigned supreme.

From then on every spare weekend I had, or day off during the week, I volunteered to work with the inspector. I followed him round like a little lapdog.

*   *   *

Three years went by. Denise was getting used to me. I couldn't wait to be an inspector. Jack retired and his place as manager was taken by Ann, the assistant manager. Everybody else also moved up one rung, except me of course. The man who took over from Ann was Cyril, previously head of the ambulance drivers and not someone I got on with terribly well, mostly because I thought he was in the wrong job.

He was in his early forties then, a thickset chap with a round, red face, a wart on the end of his nose and a remarkable set of goofy teeth. These particular features meant that people stared at him a lot and I think he developed an automatic dislike of everyone as a result. We used to bet – behind his back – that he could eat the meat off a pork chop through a tennis racquet. I couldn't understand how he could be so moody and unpleasant and still have his job.

Politics comes into everyone's life, and it was about to enter mine. Head office lowered the minimum age for the post of inspector from twenty-two to twenty. I had recently turned twenty and I applied. I passed through the early stages easily. My Hull inspector, who knew me well by now, gave me a report which glowed so much it was embarrassing. The regional superintendent interviewed me, and that went all right. Now there was only the formal interview at HQ in front of a selection panel, plus my reference from my current place of work. Reference writing was always the responsibility of the assistant manager, in this case my friend Cyril.

I filled in the weeks before my interview in a gloomy frame of mind. One day I went to a part of the premises that was generally avoided because it was where the humane destruction of the animals took place. It was also where they kept the bin-liners and occasionally I had to venture in to resupply my kennels with plastic bags.

I'd seen Cyril go in ten minutes before with the biggest Alsatian I had ever set eyes on. It was extremely hairy and looked more like a timber wolf than a dog. People often brought animals to be destroyed, and Cyril used to take on this responsibility with some glee.

Nowadays, animals are put down by a humane lethal injection, but in those days it was common practice to destroy dogs with a contraption called an electrothanator, a box similar in appearance to a greyhound racing trap. The lid lifted up and there was an entrance at the back. The dog was taken in and tied up facing the front, and a wet metal clip on a wire was put on each ear and a back leg. The box was closed and a switch flicked, which sent a current through the dog's head and rendered it unconscious. The dog fell to the floor and then a second switch was flicked, which sent a current through the dog's entire body, stopping the heart. Thankfully these machines have been obsolete for some years, but back then they were considered perfectly humane – if used correctly.

Not long after Cyril had gone in with the Alsatian I heard a lot of shouting and commotion so I thought I'd better see what he was up to. As I walked into the room I saw that he had managed to get the Alsatian into the box and had secured it by its leash to a hook at the front. He was trying to put the electrodes onto its ears but every time he went near the dog started to growl. It was an impressive animal, too big for the box, and its head was out over the top.

I was busy pretending to collect plastic bags when I heard the dog yelp in pain. I turned to see Cyril with a length of wood, about to hit it over the head for a second time. In my entire RSPCA career it was the only time I ever witnessed the slightest cruelty by any RSPCA employee. I stormed over to him and told him, in no uncertain terms, that I would do to him exactly what he had just done to that dog.

He effed and blinded, threw the wood into the corner and paced around the room, ranting and raving and spitting and frothing. I told him that if the dog had to be put to sleep I would put the electrodes on, to make sure it was done humanely. I was terrified. It meant putting my fingers within inches of the dog's mouth. After much trepidation and several minutes I succeeded. I left Cyril to put the last electrode on its back leg.

As he threw the first switch all hell broke loose. One of the electrodes must have come off, and there was this terrible screaming. The electrophanator cabinet lid flew up, the back door sprung open and the whole thing rocked from side to side as the dog struggled to get free. All the time it was giving out bone-chilling howls in true timber wolf fashion.

Cyril panicked. Before the dog could get loose he was out of the door, shutting it behind him. With one almighty heave the dog had the cabinet over onto its side and there it was, free, on the concrete floor. I didn't have time to exit the way Cyril had. I backed, slowly but as fast as I could, and climbed onto a table in the corner.

The dog looked even bigger now as it circled the room. It was the first time in my life I had been frightened of an animal. I thought it would carry out some terrible retribution for what it had gone through, and my heart was thumping and my mouth went dry as I frantically looked for a way out of the room. Then an incredible thing happened. The dog raised itself up on its hind legs, put its front paws on the table, sniffed my face, and licked me. Thinking about it now, twenty years later, I still get a lump in my throat.

I put the dog on the lead and took it to one of my kennels. I persuaded Ann to let me try to home it. Within two days I had found it a great place with a family, but my trouble had only just begun. Cyril hadn't written my reference yet.

I confided my worries to my inspector and the regional superintendent. They had a quiet word with Ann, who told Cyril that, since he was new in the job, she would write the first reference to show him how it was done.

In those days the actual interview was an intimidating event. The selection panel of eight consisted of the great, the good, the high and the mighty, and each one of them gave me a thorough grilling. Somehow I got through it and in 1978 I was taken on as a trainee, starting with six months at HQ, in Horsham in Sussex. I didn't want to be away from Denise for all that time, but I looked on it as a necessary investment in the future.

I have to say that I found those six months both boring and frustrating. Four months consisted of classes in legislation – necessary, but not very exciting. There was a lot of material on animal welfare too, but the law classes seemed three times as long. The other two months were spent on active service with a chief inspector, which was a much better way of passing the time, but the effect on this particular keen young lad was to make me want to get out and on the job even more.

With my training completed I was given my first posting, to Doncaster, one of the worst areas in the country for animal cruelty. When I heard the news I was delighted. Here was a big challenge and a chance to show what I was made of. On second thoughts I realised that a major part of my very attractive intended marriage proposal to Denise would now have to include the promise of a new life in Doncaster. Well, it was not too far from Hull and there were some nice parts to it. You just had to find them.

We had been living together in a small bedsit, so the next step of matrimony may have looked like a formality to some. They didn't know about the animal burdens I was already laying on Denise, like Toby the crossbred Alsatian, brought home by me from the RSPCA kennels to save it from being put down, then left with Denise while I went off to Horsham. The landlord of our bedsit lived on the ground floor and he had a very strict no-pets rule, but Toby had to be taken for walks. The only way was for Denise to wait until the old boy was asleep in bed, then carry the animal past his door. This same exercise was repeated first thing in the morning, before the landlord was awake.

Denise's care and devotion came to nothing. The dog picked up gastroenteritis and died.

If Denise were to make a forecast of our potential years of married life, how many times could she expect this sort of thing to happen? Was I going to be worth the aggro? I had good cause to be worried.

Later that year, 1978, much to my grateful relief, Denise agreed to say 'I will', so I had to buy a suit. The local tailor, Southwells, had a sale of blue pinstripe. Very cheap, it was, so I had my wedding whistle made of that. The next problem was what we could afford at the reception. The choice was between porridge and beetroot sandwiches until Denise's nana stepped in with a modest budget. We booked the banqueting room of the Goat and Compasses in Greatfield, Hull, and looked forward to the day.

I arrived in my new suit to find that the bride's father and at least three uncles had also been recent customers at South-wells' sale. Never mind, Denise was radiant and we were wed. The buffet was a home-made affair, with a sandwich upgrade to ham, and the music for the evening party was provided by Nana doing her impression of Winifred Atwell. The taxi back to Denise's place was her brother-in-law's Transit, which was handy, because we were able to take all the presents with us in the back.

We moved to Donny in 1979 and began the next phase of

life. I was still a probationer, under training, and it was on a training secondment that disaster struck. Standard procedure then was for all new inspectors to take a horsemanship course at the Household Cavalry barracks in Kensington. I was grooming one of the big drum horses when I started sneezing. My nose began to run, my chest tightened up and my eyes were streaming with tears. I went to the doctor and was confined to bed for two days.

After all this time being surrounded by animals, I was suddenly allergic. Something had clicked in and I was instructed to stay away from horses – only it wasn't just horses. Within a few months of taking up my Doncaster posting I was having similar reactions to any hairy or furry animal. It didn't matter if it was a hamster or an Irish wolfhound, I was allergic. Cats and dogs, the staple of all RSPCA work, were the worst. The effects soon developed from severe hay fever into quite bad asthma, and I could be stricken with either or both at any time.

It was grotesquely funny in a way. I had achieved the summit of my ambition but was instantly rendered incapable of fulfilling it. The whole objective of my job, to care for animals, was the single cause of my being disabled. I couldn't see an animal without breaking out into sneezes and snorts and being rendered unable to run twenty metres to save my life. Unless the entire population of Doncaster traded in its animals for goldfish, I had to give up and do something different. At least, that is what everybody thought, except me. The RSPCA senior management wanted to relieve me of my duties, until I convinced them I could still manage. I could not contemplate giving up. I didn't care what miseries I went through, somehow I would do the job I wanted more than anything in my life.

Each morning I would fill the glovebox in the van with a dozen clean handkerchiefs and a spare inhaler – I used to get through one every two days. Modern hay fever drugs weren't available then so the only stuff I could take to combat my symptoms was also liable to send me to sleep. I was on a course of desensitising injections that were so powerful I had to be in hospital for them in case I had a bad reaction. I couldn't see any noticeable improvement. I still can't. The problem continues to the present day. While doing covert filming of a Mafia-run slaughterhouse in Italy where thousands of horses were being killed for meat, I sneezed so constantly that the videotape later had to be edited to remove the noise.

If my personal life was a constant battle against an allergy, my professional life was superb, however. I worked every hour God sent and was having great success, recording more rescues and prosecutions than had ever been seen in that area.

The life of an RSPCA inspector then was something similar to that of the village bobby. You were a part of the community. You had a brass plaque on the front door, you were in the phone book, everybody knew who and where you were, and there was a more or less constant stream of people coming to you with sick animals.

I was out most of the time – Denise claims I was only home for five hours in twenty-four but that can't be right – and so, like the bobby's wife, she had to answer the phone and deal with all sorts of inquiries, injured birds, stray tortoises, the lot. It went on around the clock. If the locals didn't provide enough animals to crowd us out, I was sure to bring a few home.

Our daughter Kerry was born in 1981 soon after we arrived in Doncaster, and young Terry came along two years later. Still I expected Denise to bottle-feed seven baby hedgehogs, or look after half a dozen injured guillemots. There was one point when we had foxes, badgers and deer all in the garden at once, and even a seal in the bath for a couple of days, until it could be safely released back into the wild. And that was without our own pets, which we acquired in much the same way and which made me sneeze in the same way, except they stayed.

I picked up Stodge, our Jack Russell cross, one morning on a routine call and spent the rest of the day on cruelty complaints. The little pup was so quiet in the back that I forgot all about her until I came home and opened the van door. Out she jumped and sat on the driveway, looking at me. I was indecisive. She was a bonny little dog, white with black splodges and an eyepatch, but we couldn't give a home to every dog we found. She got up, brought me a stone, dropped it at my feet, wagged her tail and looked up again. Not getting the reaction she wanted, she pushed the stone towards me with her nose. Well, that was it.

Stodge was with us thirteen years, a constant companion for us and for my next acquisition, Ben the Rhodesian ridge-back, unwanted, the last of the litter. He died of old age, outlasted only by Ziggy the cat, who died aged fourteen, and Willie the cat, who is still with us, aged twelve. I found Ziggy stuck in a garage cavity wall having kittens. Willie was a stranger case, a feral cat caught in a trap and listed to be put down. I didn't have the heart so I took her home and let her go in the garden. She made a life there, but it was two years before we could pick her up, and that was at her instigation. She was giving birth to kittens and having some trouble with a big one when she came up to the back door. Denise helped her deliver and after that the cat was amenable to being petted. She still wouldn't come in the house, though. We've moved house twice with her, and she still will not cross the threshold. The most comfort she will accept is the garden shed, where she comes and goes through the window.

This was everyday life for Denise – me not there, animals, kids, hassle. There were also a few memorable incidents by way of variety. She was eight months pregnant with our daughter Kerry when the police knocked on the door to say I had been involved in an accident, and would she come with them to the hospital? They didn't know how I was doing and didn't appear to have any means of finding out. Denise naturally assumed I was dead and was certain she was going into labour. The police driver put his foot down and turned the siren on. He hadn't had much training in delivering babies.

I'd been called out, by the police and the environmental health office, to assist with the removal of twenty dogs from an upstairs flat. A woman and her daughter lived in this little place and they were like a miniature RSPCA, taking in dogs from anywhere and everywhere. Athough they loved them, the whole enterprise was out of control. The flat was a health hazard, flea-ridden, with dog muck and urine seeping through the floors into the neighbours' flats below.

A court order was obtained and the dogs had to go. We found the place almost empty except for the woman, the girl, the dogs and a gas stove. There didn't seem to be any furniture at all in the living area. We got the dogs out, amid much protesting and abuse, and as I picked up the last one the daughter grabbed a saucepan off the stove. It had been steaming away there but nobody had paid it any attention until the girl, under orders from her mother, threw the boiling water in my face. I put my hands up instinctively and the skin just peeled off.

They rushed me to hospital, where I was being treated when Denise ran in to find me alive. She burst into tears on the spot. I like to think that they were tears of relief but she always teases me and insists they were tears of disappointment.

She hadn't had long to dry them when the police came back saying that they needed to move my van but there was a huge Alsatian dog in it. This great animal had come from the flat but had now taken personal charge of my van, pending my return, and it was going to guard it with its life. The police dog handler couldn't get the Alsatian to come out. I had to rise from my sick bed, deal with the dog, and return to hospital.

After two days of such inactivity I'd had enough, so I discharged myself and went back to work. I got a rocket from HQ for reporting while unfit, a complaint rung in from a member of the public about my blistered appearance, and another sigh of long suffering from Denise. Later I heard that the water-throwing girl had been given two years' probation.

The volume of possible work in Doncaster seemed inexhaustible, and I could not clock off. The longer I kept going, the more the work kept coming. I was breaking so many records that I was top of the RSPCA hit parade, the all-time greatest hitter. There was no end to it except that nobody could maintain a rate of work like that for ever.

We had our holidays, of course. There was the log cabin in north-west Scotland, where I was told I would see pine martens, and the tent in the New Forest, looking for honey buzzards.

After five years the stress became so bad that even I noticed it. There was a vacancy in Bridlington, a rural posting that would surely have a less gigantic workload and give me a better chance of doing something about my allergy. I applied, got the job and in 1984 we moved to the seaside, not very far from where I grew up. I looked forward to a new life of obscurity, no longer in the *Doncaster Star* every week and no longer top of the RSPCA charts, and, with any luck, no longer a martyr to hay fever and asthma.

The first bit I got wrong was the obscurity. Someone found out about the story of the RSPCA man who was allergic to animals and, instead of being in the *Star*, I was in the *Sun* with two Page Three girls. Luckily, they had taken their fur coats off.

Likewise I was wrong about the allergy. Five years of sea air and less frenetic action did not do me a ha'p'orth of good. Also I was witness to endless cruelty; its unchanging nature could get me down. One case in 1987, related by the local paper under the headline 'They Claim This is Sport' shows what I mean.

A badly mauled terrier whimpers in agony after its callous owner pitted it into a vicious underground battle with a badger – 'for sport'. The Humberside police photographs reveal how the dog was left with terrible mouth wounds after the struggle at Fridaythorpe, near Driffield.

Beverley Crown Court agreed that Driffield magistrates were right to convict the dog's owner and two other men – all from Leeds – for offences related to badger-baiting. A panel of three headed by Judge Nigel Fricker turned down the men's appeal against conviction. Judge Fricker said: 'These offences were so serious that two of you must go to prison.'

Mr John Jones, a veterinary surgeon based at Driffield, told the court that a 'roughcoat' terrier had a severe wound to its mouth and muscle damage after being forced down a badger sett at Gritts Farm, Fridaythorpe on 30 December, last year.

A black 'roughcoat' – a trained working dog worth £450 – was left with huge bites on the right side of its face, blood oozing from its mouth and cuts to the inside of its top lip. Mr Jones said the two dogs also had bruising and swelling following the fight, plus scars from previous wounds.

The two dogs and another terrier taken on the badger-baiting outing from Leeds were all exhausted, filthy, dishevelled and shocked when discovered on the farm.

Sgt Keith Abel said two of the dogs were underground when he and farmer Mr Henry Watson found the defendants, along with two other men, huddled around the badger sett in a copse on Mr Watson's land.

Sgt Abel told the court he saw fresh diggings which appeared to be man-made at the sett and two spades and canvas sacks nearby.

RSPCA Inspector Tony Saunders said the dogs had injuries consistent with head-to-head confrontation with animals underground.

Change the names of the people and the location of the magistrates' court and that story could have come from Doncaster years before, when I started as an inspector, or at any time since. It could be in any local paper tomorrow. I had run down hundreds of individual cases in that time but nothing had changed fundamentally. Looking on the bright side, I could say that I had made a small difference in each of those hundreds of cases, that I had stopped cruelty and prevented people from doing it again, for a while anyway.

If I looked on the black side, I could say that, since the cases kept coming, the fines got no bigger and it was just a different person with a different dog. I was making no progress whatsoever. Denise used to tell me that I shouldn't expect to change human nature. I should do what I could and nobody could do more. She was right, but that didn't stop me feeling depressed and frustrated at times.

In addition a couple of incidents with the children made me realise that my single-mindedness could be both selfish and dangerous. In our garden at Bempton – we lived there, by Flamborough Head, because of its proximity to the bird reserve – I was rehabilitating an injured buzzard. I had it on a bow perch and a leash. Kerry was in the garden, playing, when the buzzard suddenly launched itself at her and buried its talons in her face. Kerry screamed, I ran and somehow prised the buzzard off, and rushed my daughter to hospital. A talon had gone through her right lower eyelid. As the surgeon pointed out in the middle of the very severe bollocking he gave me, a fraction of a fraction more and the eye would have been lost.

Denise fainted as they began to stitch. Although Kerry got away with just a tiny scar, we were all more shaken than we'd ever been by the sheer unpredictability of wild animals.

They don't have to attack you to put you in danger, either, as we found out with a kingfisher's nest that was too far down the bankside for me to see if it was occupied. I persuaded little Terry to let me dangle him by his feet so he could look inside. Just as he was peering into the hole there was a flash of brilliant blue and the bird shot out, past the end of his nose. Terry jumped and bucked with surprise and left me holding his wellies while he fell into the river. He went under, came up, and floated downstream, bobbing below the surface and crying out. I ran like a madman, plunged in and grabbed him. He promised not to tell his mother, which lessened the short-term impact but did nothing to improve my general state of mind.

After ten years as a uniformed inspector, plus three more as a kennel hand and ambulance driver, I was past thirty. I didn't think I was superintendent material and, more importantly, I don't believe the RSPCA thought I was superintendent material. I was too keen on the job, too anxious to be up and at 'em. I could never be a management type, politicking and manoeuvring. I had no patience for all that. So what was I going to do next?

A part of the RSPCA I'd hardly heard of, which at that time was called SOU, or the Special Operations Unit, based at RSPCA headquarters, in Horsham, Sussex, was looking for a new boy. Investigating abilities were of prime importance and were judged by your record in the field. Since I had achieved one of the highest levels of convictions in RSPCA history I stood up well to that criterion and was accepted on my first application, a quite unusual feat.

Special operations, obviously, meant undercover work. I liked the sound of that, so much so that I decided to start doing it, off my own bat, in the time between my being accepted and being posted for duty. There was a lot of animal cruelty in the countryside, organised cruelty some of it, conducted on the quiet by closed circles of those in the know. Perhaps I could do something about it now, in my new capacity as special investigating agent.

It was a risky endeavour that I was contemplating. I was in uniform during the week, a public person you might say, sometimes photographed in the *Yorkshire Post* or the *Evening Press* with court appearances, sometimes on Yorkshire Television and the local radio, and then I was expecting to mix in with hard cases on a Saturday night.

These were men (always men, never women) who owned shotguns and who cared so little for human sentiment, the law and everything else, that they could carry on ruthlessly with their cruelty and enjoy it. Trying to be one of the boys with this lot would be a mind-shaping experience, to say the least. If they accepted me, I would have to go along with all sorts of stuff I hated and had spent my life so far trying to stop. If they found out who I was, I didn't think they'd be exactly congratulating me on my fine acting and buying me a pint to show no hard feelings.

Risky or not, I was desperate to get on with my new job officially and to show them what a good undercover operator I could be, so I needed some practice. Over the years I had become something of a national expert on badgers. I'd helped start the North and East Yorkshire Badger Protection Group and I tended to receive quite a few titbits of information about badger diggers and badger baiters. One such I'd been hearing

about for a year or so, and he lived in Hull. This was outside
my Bridlington patch, so I wouldn't be so well known as an
RSPCA man, and it was home country to me and I had a Hull
accent. I decided it would be a good place to start my undercover career.

With combat jacket, dirty jeans and heavy work boots I
had the uniform about right, and I borrowed an old, beaten-
up car, but that was where my preparations stopped. I had no
recording equipment, nobody to back me up, and nobody to
tell where I was going.

My man, called Pete, lived on a council estate in a part of
north Hull that had a reputation for being a very rough area.
My plan was to knock on his door and say I was looking to
buy a terrier pup. Quite what I was going to do after that
hadn't been worked out in detail, or at all.

When I reached the house it was fairly obvious he had
terriers. The garden was full of holes, all sorts of sizes and
depths, and the wood of the front door was almost through,
having been worn thin by dogs scratching it.

I had an inkling of what to expect when my man came to
the door. I had heard he was a tough customer and not a pretty
sight, but I wasn't ready for the monster who answered my
knock. He was huge, over six foot and at least eighteen stone,
in his late twenties, with a shaven head and tattoos covering
both massive forearms. His T-shirt was torn to reveal a vast
expanse of hairy belly and his jeans had more rips and spotty
white skin than denim. He was like a professional wrestler,
only more horrible. His general air told me that he liked
policemen, RSPCA inspectors and other representatives of
authority, but only for breakfast.

Keeping up appearances, I said I was looking for a terrier
to work and I'd heard he had some pups. Pete never ques-
tioned where I might have acquired this information but

invited me in, explaining that he didn't actually have any pups at the moment but that he did have a young bitch, nine months old, that he was thinking of selling.

We went through the house to the back yard, a shanty town in miniature, a totally haphazard collection of little sheds and home-made hutches with a small square of concrete in the centre. From the noise and the turmoil of little dogs vying for Pete's attention and warning me off, it seemed as if there were a hundred of the creatures in that yard. Looking at my new friend, I doubted very much whether the neighbours would have had the courage to complain if there had been a thousand. Doing a quick count, I reckoned there were actually eleven, mostly black Patterdale types but with a couple of chocolate Lakelands as well.

The menagerie was completed by a polecat ferret in a hutch in the corner. It was slinking up and down, patrolling rest-lessly as they do, but unusual in that it had to cope with a very low ceiling to its hutch. This was not so much because of a lack of generosity in construction but because it had to stand on a thick layer, six inches or more, of decomposing rabbit parts mixed with mouldering ferret crap. All ferrets and polecats are naturally clean animals, and why some people insist on keeping them in such filth is beyond me entirely.

Pete bent down to one of the shanty kennels and pulled out a Patterdale bitch, which he held aloft by the scruff of its neck. 'Look at that!' he cried, showing me how its fangs were all displaced and its neck and bottom jaw were covered in scar tissue. 'And that. Look there. She's a fighter, this one. Show me any fox and she'll nail it. Show me any badger and my money's on this little girl. Famous, she is, for badgers. She's killed more badgers in her few months than most terriers do in a lifetime. Fifty quid.'

That would have been a fair price then, if I'd really been

in the market. A week's wages for a renowned badger killer? What a snip.

'That sounds all right,' I replied. 'I haven't got it on me, like.'

'Wouldn't matter if you had,' he said. 'I'm not letting this little beauty go without you seeing her work. I've got my reputation to think of. Sunday morning. Be here at half five. We'll go and nail a few foxes.'

The emotions I was going through could not be described beyond saying they combined fear, dread, loathing, fury at my own stupidity, and a complete lack of activity in the thinking department.

'No, no, that's okay,' I said, with what I hoped was a light and careless laugh. 'I'll take your word. No need for a demo. Your reputation, as you say. I'm sure she'll be . . .'

'Not a chance, mate. I'm known, I am, for breeding the best terriers in the East Riding. Or whatever they call it now. The very best. I'm not going to let a dog go unless I am one hundred per cent satisfied that the client is a hundred and ten per cent satisfied. Get me?'

'I'm away this weekend,' I said. 'And I was hoping to have the terrier for my own work the following week. So I don't see that I can. I'll call in tomorrow with the fifty quid. How's that?'

It came on to rain, heavily. I pulled up the hood of my jacket while he stood there in his shirt, getting wet and not noticing.

'Tell you what,' he said. 'I'll show you how hard she is. You watch this. An automatic killing machine. The terminator terrier.'

He started searching around, between and under the hutches. To my utter dismay he began calling out. 'Here, puss, puss. Here, pussy, pussy. Come to Uncle Peter. Puss, puss, puss, puss.'

I could not believe the mess I was in. Here I was, on my first undercover operation, and my only way out was going to be to blow my cover. If he found the cat, that was.

I prayed that the cat had learned a few survival techniques while it had lived here. If it had any sense right at this minute it would be running as fast as it could into the next county. Pete was on his belly on the wet ground, careless of whatever muck there might be on it, scrabbling under one of the hutches. He gave a grunt of triumph and produced a tortoiseshell cat, a kitten really. I'd say it was eight to ten weeks old.

I had no ideas. My only option, apart from digging out my ID card from underneath my right sock, where I'd hidden it in my attempt to be the true undercover man, was to jump the back gate and run like stink. Seeing as I'd been clever enough to park my car smack outside his front gate, Pete would no doubt be there, waiting for me, when I got to it. What an incredible balls-up.

Here was Pete the Beast, against whom I would have little chance in a physical struggle, about to set a terrier onto a cat for my amusement. My feelings were a terrible mixture of horror and indecision to the point of freezing. Above all I most earnestly wished that I had never come here in the first place.

'Watch her nail this cat,' said Pete. Nailing was obviously his favourite spectator sport. He held both animals up by the scruff, one in each hand. They both hung there, resigned to whatever fate Pete had in store for them.

I bent down to my shoe to get my warrant card. I doubted if Pete would take very kindly to this and I fully expected a good kicking for my trouble, but I couldn't see what else I could do. At that moment, the rain stopped and a magic switch put a light on in Pete's brain.

'No. Better hadn't,' he said, with regret and, almost, embarrassment. 'I gave this cat to the kids. I'll be in it up to here if I kill their present. Life wouldn't be worth living. The wife would go mad, the kids would go mad. You got any kids?' he said, as he put the terrier back in its box and threw the kitten to wherever it might land.

I nodded, pretending to scratch an itch on my ankle.

'You'll know what I mean, then, eh? Sorry about that. Haven't got anything else here to demonstrate on, only Popeye my ferret, and I don't want to lose him. It'll have to be Plan B.' Then, he had an even more brilliant notion, an absolute cracker.

'Tell you what. Why don't I come with you next week? What a good idea. You come down tomorrow, pay me half, take the terrier and I'll go out with you when you first work her. If you're not a hundred and ten per cent happy, I'll take her back and give you your twenty-five quid. How about that?'

'Yeah, excellent, Pete,' I said. We shook hands. I was very pleased to get my hand back. He opened the back door for me and showed me through to the front. 'Thanks, Pete,' I said. 'A lot of people wouldn't bother. I'll see you tomorrow. Thanks again.'

'Jesus wept,' I muttered to myself back in the sanctuary of my car. It was raining again and it rained all the way home. By the time I was coming through the outskirts of Brid I had rationalised the situation perfectly. I was an amateur bungler. I had jumped in at the deep end without any idea of how to swim. Never mind. Put it down to experience. I was about to join the RSPCA Special Operations Unit, where I would learn the skills of my new trade. I would pass on the tip about Pete to one of the more experienced officers and he would deal with the tattooed hairy beast while I studied the arts and crafts of undercover work at the feet of the masters.

My first day was induction. I was lectured on the work of the department and I was astonished to find that undercover work had absolutely no part in it. They didn't do any, and they had no intention of doing any. They hadn't even thought of doing any.

The Special Operations Unit, I was told, had been created by senior RSPCA personnel as a direct development of a big campaign of ours called SELFA – Stop the Export of Live Food Animals – and that was the main item on the agenda, the live animal trade between the UK and continental Europe. The campaign was out to persuade government and industry to change 'from the hoof to the hook', to slaughter the animals in this country and export them as meat. To expose the reasons for the campaign and to move public opinion, we needed to gather evidence of the excesses.

This usually meant following lorries full of farm animals across Europe. I soon found out what these dramatic-sounding words really meant. We often had to stay with a lorry for several days and nights without being detected and the drivers were wary and always on the lookout. We were there to make them unemployed, after all. Following a vehicle at a suitably covert distance, between half a mile and a mile away, for sixty hours almost non-stop, was an incredibly taxing and draining thing to do, mentally and physically. You couldn't pull in for a meal when the driver did, because he would spot you the second time, and you couldn't do it when he was motoring along or you'd lose him. Same with sleep. You couldn't sleep for long because you didn't know when he was going to be up and off again. My favourite way of keeping awake was to pinch my earlobes. Others favoured the interiors of their nostrils, which does give a short, sharp alarm call.

The practice we were trying to stop was long-hauling live animals without giving them the rests, food and water that they were due by any humane standard and that were required under the law. Usually the wagon driver was no farmer and knew nothing about farm animals. He simply wanted to get to the destination as rapidly as possible and his cargo was nothing to do with him. At the end of his journey he had to sign a declaration that he had rested, fed and watered the animals according to the regulations. Any signature would be false, and we could have him if he was working for a UK firm. If not, we passed our evidence to the European Commission.

Sometimes journalists came with us. They would confront the driver with a camera and expose him and his employers that way. Sometimes our investigations went further. For instance, in Spain and Greece there were some very dodgy slaughterhouses that didn't obey the rules. They didn't stun the animals first, and generally mistreated them in all kinds of ways. There was little we could do about it apart from inform the local authorities, who probably knew anyway and were turning a blind eye. We were in a foreign country with no more status than an ordinary British tourist – in fact, I did a slaughterhouse investigation while we were on a family holiday in Greece, much to my children's disgust and Denise's disbelief. The results were well worth it, though. Stung by the popular outcry over the cruel methods of slaughter that my colleague Eddie and I had exposed, the Greek government closed down 300 slaughterhouses.

The export of live animals is still a significant part of the duties of the SOU and will remain so until this unnecessary and cruel trade is stopped for good.

Just before I joined the department there had been an addition to the brief, because of the rapid and worrying increase in organised dogfighting, but that was the entire remit – two avenues of investigation only.

After a few of those marathons across the continent, I started talking to my new bosses, Chief Superintendent Morrison and Superintendent Balfour, about badger digging and other forms of wildlife crime. Wildlife was something entirely new to their thinking, which until then had been exclusively focused on farm animals and domestic pets. I explained that the very nature of wildlife crime demanded that you oppose it undercover. Wildlife crime was invisible, hidden away, perpetrated by experienced, cunning and watchful country people who knew all about keeping themselves and their activities secret and could spot a stranger a mile off. You couldn't barge around openly as the RSPCA, even in plain clothes, and expect to get close to these men. You had to infiltrate, become their trusted friend and ally. To catch a badger digger, you had to pretend to be one.

My bosses could see my point but were unsure about whether we should be involved or how we should go about it. Therefore, logically enough, they were not keen on such a radical initiative. I found it very hard indeed to persuade them to let me have a go but I kept at them. I think eventually they saw an opportunity to nip a potential problem in the bud by telling this troublesome newcomer to go away and do something. If I knew so much about undercover work, I had better get it sorted. And so I became the RSPCA's first ever undercover operative. I was the pioneer, doing something nobody in the UK had done before. At the time, I didn't realise that nobody anywhere else in the world had done it either.

Being a pioneer is a fine thing in some respects. Everyone likes the idea of doing something new, of boldly going where no one has gone before. The downside of it is there is no support, no back-up, no one to ask, no one to help, no procedures, no manuals, no experience, no *anything*. The unit was as geared up for undercover work as a motorway service station is for repairing jumbo jets. We belonged to an allied trade, but that was all.

I started by reading everything I could get hold of about undercover work, particularly material on the special forces in Northern Ireland. This was where the arts and sciences of undercover operations were developed and refined to their most advanced forms. For practical help I could only go and ask, and I did. I asked everybody – regional crime squads, SAS, Intelligence Corps, everybody. I knew nothing. They knew it all.

For instance, the course run by ex-members of 14th Intelligence Corps was all about urban surveillance: how to observe without being observed, how to get into your observation post without being noticed, the art of remembering every detail of what you see, how to work at night. There are tricks to every aspect of this trade, and we had none of them.

The Regional Crime Squad ran another course, about surveillance on foot. Our trainer acted as the subject we were to observe, and I and the two official police trainees followed him to this house. He went inside and stayed there. After two hours in the rain, one of the lads persuaded the lady living opposite that he was on a course and needed to watch over the road from her place. She let us in but chucked us all out when she saw my ID was different from the others. Meanwhile, our trainer/subject had emerged and set off down the street. We started after him, only for three squad cars to screech to a halt beside us. Eight coppers got out and we were spread-eagled and handcuffed in seconds. Down at the station they had us for a professional gang of bogus police, but they let us go eventually.

That night, in the pub, the two police, especially the one from the Met, showed no mercy about my Mickey Mouse ID, which had caused all the bother. Not so, said our trainer when he turned up a while later – he'd just been on the phone to the woman to apologise, and she said she'd thrown us out and called the police because 'that Cockney one looked so shifty, like he was going to steal the silver'. That shut him up for a while.

It was seven years after I started with SOU before the RSPCA began its own official training of any sort in my kind of work, and even then it was mostly on covert rather than undercover ops. It's important to understand the difference. Covert surveillance simply means you are watching people without them realising it. You are hidden, in plain clothes, at a distance, using special equipment, whatever. Undercover operations mean you are posing as one of the group you are investigating, or as a professional associate or someone who can do them some good. When you are undercover, you are actively involved, in among it.

In Ireland a British soldier would pretend to be a member of the IRA or the UVF. If he or she was exposed, there was little doubt about what would happen. My undercover life wasn't played for such high stakes, although it might have its moments. The army agent could expect execution; I could expect a heavy beating, or even to be shot at by gamekeepers. By arming myself with all the expertise I could, I hoped to avoid the beatings and the shotgun pellets and halt the work of some cruel men.

The building up of this body of knowledge didn't seem anything peculiar at the time, but it's clear now that as I was the only one doing such work I must have been the animal world's leading expert at any given moment.

For twenty years I've been completely dedicated to the job, as uniformed inspector and then undercover. I have lived and breathed my work and the price I have paid is that I've never really had a proper social life. If I'd had a wife with anything less than a super-tolerant attitude, I wouldn't have had a family life either. And we still haven't had a honeymoon.

My son and daughter are grown-up now but when they were very small I had left the house before they got up, and when I came home they were invariably in bed. It wasn't the job that made the demands. I could do as little or as much as I wanted, but I didn't know when to stop. There was always another catalogue of horrors to face.

When I returned home I wanted to try and switch off from it. I never did, because I was always working things out and planning the next job, going over the day's events. Had they latched on to who I was? Would I get a surprise next time I visited them?

Denise stopped putting social engagements in the diary. She used to invite somebody home or we'd be asked out for dinner, but I'd have to drop out at the last minute and let everybody down. After a while people gave up. Our circle of friends grew smaller and smaller and it was easier not to bother.

I couldn't explain to friends or strangers that I needed my telephone with me all the time in case some scumbag badger digger rang me up. I had to make up some pathetic excuse that I was on call. They looked at me as if to say, 'Sad bastard, can't switch off from his job, hoping his little pager will ring and prove he's important.'

One thing makes you stop, and that's time. A forty-some-thing badger digger is as rare as rocking-horse droppings, so my days as an undercover officer are limited. I hope Denise will be pleased. I know she'll be relieved. My family have had to put up with a lot. I've never lost my rag at work, but I have tended to bottle up my tiredness and frustration, ready for release at home. I can regret not spending more time with my children as they grew and, if I'd had another sort of job, I would have done. But I didn't, did I? My job always came first. I saw being a husband and father as the ordinary, normal side of things. I wanted my life to make a difference.

3

——

Usually, when animals are mistreated it's by people who don't know better. Though few in number, uniformed RSPCA inspectors are very good at dealing with such matters.

But there is another kind of cruelty to animals, the kind that brings delight and satisfaction to its depraved enthusiasts. It is widespread, often highly organised, deeply secretive and just about impossible to detect in the normal way.

Luckily for us the natural reaction to organised cruelty – repulsion – is not confined to 'nice' people. Some very shady characters are repulsed by it too, and they need to tell someone about it. One such is Darren, who lives in the north-west of England. I was up that way on a surveillance job, and I'd checked in at a hotel I'd never been in before, the Trafalgar, near Preston. It's a fairly plush three-star and its normal tariff was well beyond the RSPCA allowance but, as ever, I'd negotiated hard on the price of the room.

Hotels were a problem for me. I needed the freedom to

come and go, and the facilities of a good hotel, but I couldn't afford much more than boarding house prices. I always booked on the phone rather than in person, because often I didn't look like the kind of guest any decent hotel would want. If I was working on operations against badger diggers at the time, say, hiding in a bush all day long, I wasn't necessarily the person a receptionist might want to walk up to her desk. And after covert surveillance in the rain and mud until the early hours of the morning, it wasn't uncommon for me to spend only three or four hours in the hotel and be off again before breakfast.

On this occasion, with the surveillance job still to come, I had arrived from nowhere more disreputable than the motorway. I'd been into town to get a meal – we don't stretch to hotel dinners, I'm afraid – and I was getting ready for bed when the mobile went. It was Darren.

'I've got something for you,' he said, sounding his normal ebullient self. 'Meet me at Forton services on the M6.'

'How did you know I was up here?'

'You told me, Tony.'

'Oh, right. Make it after breakfast. Meet me at nine.'

Darren had come to us after watching a programme about badgers on the television. He knew so much about it I always thought he was an ex-digger himself, but I never asked him outright.

If you saw him in the street you'd think he was designer National Front, the best-dressed football hooligan of the year. He was a big lad, certainly, six foot and broad with it, and he obviously kept himself in shape, and he had a shaven head, tattoos, the lot. Subtlety was not his middle name.

I got to Forton before him on a fine summer's morning and found a patch of grass where I could top up my tan while I was waiting. His arrival, a few minutes later, was something to behold. Darren lived every minute of his life as if he was going for the try line in the rugby league cup final. He didn't look up, or to right or to left. He just went for it.

He drove a Sierra Cosworth, so it was perfectly natural for him to drive it around the service station as if he was doing a getaway for the local godfather. He screeched round the corner of the car park, spotted me, squealed to a halt near my sunbathing spot, jumped out and swaggered towards me.

Great, just great, I thought. I was undercover, anonymous, discreet, considering my next move on at least three different difficult cases. I was taking time out to meet Darren but I wanted a quiet meeting. I did not want him behaving like he was a pop star's bodyguard.

To make it worse, he looked like he'd been up very early and done some hard hours on the muck spreader. Everybody else around Forton services was in summer clothes – shorts, bikini tops, straw hats, shades, sandals, shirts with palm trees. Normally Darren was the one you went to if you wanted to know what Jean-Paul Gaultier was up to this week. I think he spent more money on clothes than I spent on my mortgage, but today, to go with his dramatic entrance, he was in combat jacket and trousers with army boots. To complete the look he was covered in what I hoped was mud. He'd have stuck out less in that service station if he'd been a streaker.

Oblivious to the effect he was having on several dozen sunny M6 travellers taking a break, he swung a black plastic bin-bag up and down in one hand. A stream of dark fluid was dripping steadily from one corner.

'There you are, Tony,' he said, plonking it down beside me. 'Don't say I never give you anything.'

'What's this then, Darren?'

'Told you I'd get you in on something good, didn't I? Have a look.'

I peered inside the plastic bag. I could see the white eye stripes of a badger.

'For Chrissake, Darren. What the hell are you doing?'

'I've been out with this real bastard today,' he said, with some feeling. 'And I mean a real bastard. A gamekeeper, a thickset, skinheaded bugger. I thought it was to do some foxes but then he went for this billy. He put the terrier in, dug the badger out, whacked it with the spade and chopped its head off. He said he was going to have it mounted on a plaque as a trophy, then he realised he'd cut it too close and there wasn't enough skin left. You need a good bit of skin, you see, if you're going to be able . . .'

His voice faltered as he saw my expression. Even Darren could sense that his triumph wasn't being received with the expected cheers and rose petals — but he was Darren, so he ploughed on a bit further.

'Well, yeah, with his trophy being no good for the sitting-room wall, he carried on to try and get another. When he gave up he buried the body but forgot about the head, so I went back later to pick it up. I thought you'd be pleased.'

I stared at him. We'd been together, in a manner of speaking, for a few years now. What he lacked in wisdom and under-standing of serious matters was made up by his enthusiasm and willingness to put himself about. He was something of a villain but he hated animal cruelty in his heart and above all he hated the badger men.

I had always known that Darren could be a gross liability at times but I had thought he'd learned a few rudiments along the way, which would have made him think twice before handing me a badger's head in a motorway service area having first made sure that everybody in Lancashire was watching.

'Why didn't you tell me what you were doing?' I managed to say. 'We could have had some people there. We could have got a result and done the job properly.'

'I didn't know they were going to dig badgers, did I? I thought it was foxes. I thought we were going cubbing. Come on, Tony. I didn't mean . . .'

'Darren, listen to me,' I said. 'Please, go home, away, out of my sight. No, leave the head. I'll deal with it. Thank you. And Darren? Don't call me. I'll call you.'

So powerful was this rebuke that Darren drove off like one of those old men in a Lada, the ones who always have a hat on. He must have gone all of fifty yards before he recovered, dropped down a gear and shot away like the car chase cop his image demanded he should be.

I stared at the bag he had left behind. That head was from a sow, which might well have been feeding cubs. I felt my fury rise. I raged, silently, at the diggers for their barbarity and at Darren for his stupidity. I'd told him over and over again exactly what to do if something like this came about. Instead he'd ignored his instructions and ended up on an illegal dig, accessory to killing a badger. He'd played no part in the actual killing, but he was still liable.

I'd have to keep the head as evidence in case we managed to prosecute, though I was sure the defence would claim entrapment. In any event, I couldn't ask Darren to give a witness statement. It would put him in danger and you don't do that to your informants. It's nothing to do with compassion. It's purely practical. Compromise the safety of an informant and the word would soon get around our small world of gamekeepers, poachers and pet-shop owners. We'd never recruit another.

To catch the badger digger we needed a professional, airtight, stainless steel court case without the tiniest crack for a slippery lawyer to wriggle through. Otherwise the target would be away, killing again. I knew of diggers who went out twice a week throughout the year and killed at least one animal every time.

It's perhaps hard to understand, but there are literally hundreds of these guys in the UK, killing thousands of badgers. According to research carried out by Professor Harris for the National Federation of Badger Groups, digging accounts for a conservative estimate of 15,000 badgers a year out of an estimated UK population of 300,000. They try to justify it with reference to the disease the animals are supposed to carry, and the damage they allegedly cause. Some farmers believe that badgers spread tuberculosis in cattle, others don't; the case is not proved either way. Badgers do suffer from TB, and so do cattle, but the link is simply not established beyond doubt. I know dairy farmers who are happy to have badgers living in their woodland, and I know of others who look the other way when the diggers drive along the back lane in their 4WDs with searchlights on the roof.

Badgers are also blamed for taking poultry, but they say the only time a badger will come down into a village, or any inhabited area, is if he's an old brock who has been turfed out of the family residence by a younger one. Then, if he's too old and weak to fight his own kind, he'll often be too old and weak to fend for himself. Answer: a ready-meal in the chicken hut, but it's the last hurrah for the old boy. He won't survive long.

In any case, a smallholder losing a hen once every blue moon and the suspicion that badgers might spread disease have nothing to do with the blood-lust of badger diggers and baiters. These men are killing for killing's sake, for the perverse thrill it gives them. In short, they're scum.

We have many of their names and addresses on file but it might as well be a Christmas card list. Nobody has the resources to tackle it. It's a secret society of bad bastards. They know how to move about without being seen and they know the countryside they're operating in. No copper in a uniform in his panda car is ever going to catch a badger digger except through sheer luck, and no senior police officer is going to authorise putting CID undercover to catch somebody who's only killing a few wild animals.

It's left to the RSPCA, but resources are limited there too and, as well as the badgers, there are all the other species that are tortured, maimed and killed in their thousands. Foxes, deer, birds, all sorts of living creatures are targets for these maniacs, but there's no one thing you can do, no grand gesture you can make, that will stop them. You have to deal with it case by case. There is no other way. You are only scratching the surface of the surface; but you keep scratching or you give up, turn your back and pretend it doesn't happen. I wasn't going to do that.

Sitting on that service station grass I asked myself, not for the first time, how men who presumably loved their wives and children and sent cards on Mother's Day could be enthralled by the possibility of beating the life out of an animal that had never done them the slightest wrong.

As I picked up Darren's bin-bag, still dripping blood, and walked to my car, I swore to myself that I was going to get the man who'd done this. He didn't know it yet, but he was a marked man.

I stopped to buy a roll of bin-liners and some string, and wrapped the badger's head in three more bags, and parcelled it up tightly. There was no more blood seeping into the carpet in the car boot, but it didn't solve my main problem. The weather was still hot and there were two more days before I could get home to put it in our freezer. A stinking, fly-blown badger head in my car boot was not an option I was keen on, but I couldn't just bury it somewhere; it might be needed in evidence.

I headed back to the Trafalgar. The girl on reception was the same one as earlier, very pretty, in her early twenties, with long blonde hair right down her back, which is always fatal for me. She gave me the hundred-megawatt smile and I hoped that my grin conveyed friendliness and good will, rather than betraying the fact that I had a severed head in my hand luggage.

'Er, miss, I'm staying here . . .' – the smile again – 'and, er, I've been out and come back, you see, because I couldn't remember if I'd forgotten to say this morning, that is, whether or not I might not be back tonight, but I will be back tomorrow . . .'

'I have made a note of it, Mr Saunders.'

'. . . and, er, I wondered if you . . . do you think you might do me a favour?'

'If I can, Mr Saunders, of course.'

I decided that attack was the best means of defence. Rejecting my original ploy, which had been to say that I'd bought a frozen leg of pork at the market, I went for it.

'See this bag? It contains a consignment of smuggled tigers' private parts that the woman at the Lotus Blossom takeaway in Bury is going to make into love potions. Do you think you could put it in the freezer for me?'

'No problem. What shall I write on the label? Private parcel, or parcel of privates?'

As she disappeared in the direction of the kitchen I thanked her and tried not to think about what would happen to her if the chef found a badger's head in his freezer. Now, time for the rest of the day.

My information was that a gamekeeper called Geoffrey Verril, a man known to us, was going to lead a badger dig somewhere up country not far from Clitheroe, sometime tonight or tomorrow. I had good directions to a vantage point.

Everything went well with the set-up. I had a very good spec, I was hidden in the bushes, and there was even enough cover to allow me to indulge the calls of nature, a luxury I was not always afforded. It was a bit muddy but not too bad, and I had nothing to do but watch and wait.

I watched and waited all that night, all the next day, and most of that evening. Verril wasn't coming. Either he'd had a tip-off or the information was wrong in the first place. I gave in. Back to the Trafalgar.

I hadn't slept, my eyes were bloodshot, I had two days' growth of beard, and my camouflage outfit was completed with bits of twig stuck in my hair and soil splattered all over me. As I walked from the car park I saw through the windows that the bar was buzzing with people dressed in their best dickie bows and evening dresses, and more were rolling up by the minute. It looked like a charity dinner, or an annual ball, attended by the cream of Preston society.

I came through the door following a particularly bejewelled, mink-stoled woman and her beautifully tailored husband, and stopped at the desk. The receptionist was one I hadn't seen before. Just my luck. She looked at me as if she'd found a cup in the fridge with a mouldy egg yolk in the bottom.

'I was here the night before last,' I said with a smile.

'Really.'

'I said I might not be back for last night, but I would be back for tonight.'

Silence.

'I was in room 142, I think it was. Or was it 124? Anyway, they said they'd keep me something.'

She looked me over as if to say the Salvation Army hostel's a couple of miles down the road, and scrolled through her computer screen.

'Sorry. We have no rooms.'

It was looking like I was going to have to sleep in the car when one of the managers walked by. He did a double take then recognised me from two days ago.

'Problem?' he said.

'I don't think we have any rooms,' the receptionist said, 'for this . . . gentleman.'

'Put him in 59,' the manager said, taking the key off the board and handing it to me before she could argue.

I should have gone straight to bed but I fancied a nightcap to help me unwind, and my social sensitometer had switched off. As I made for the bar through the well-groomed revellers, I intercepted a few shocked looks. They hadn't paid a fortune for their tickets and got dressed in their finery to rub shoulders with a mud-covered vagrant.

At least the barman was amused. He poured me a large Jameson's. As I downed it in a couple of gulps, I heard somebody mutter about sending for the manager. I turned to walk back the way I'd come and saw a trail of muddy footprints leading from the reception desk all the way to the bar. Trying not to make any new prints, I retraced my steps and headed for a long hot shower. In the shower a thought suddenly struck me.

'Darren,' I said into my mobile moments later. 'The badger digger. The one who cut off the head.'

'What about him?'

'Did you say he was well built and a skinhead type?'

'That's him.'

'How did you know he was a skinhead?'

'Because, Tony, he didn't wear a cap.'

'How old?'

'Mid-thirties?'

'Did he have a bloody great sheath knife, US Marines sort of job?'

'Yes, he did. How did you know?'

'I've got to go back down south tomorrow, Darren, other-wise I'd be with you. Until I see you again, keep a special eye on your man. Remember what he does. He's a bastard, Darren, a right bastard. His name is Verril, Geoffrey Verril.'

4

It was yet another in a long series of heat wave mornings. I was staring out of my Horsham office window, enviously watching the sunbathers in the park and trying to ignore the mound of long overdue paperwork on my desk, when the phone rang.

'RSPCA. Special Operations Unit.'

'Hello? Tony?' It took me a minute to place the voice. Then I had it: a contact in Customs and Excise, one of my friends at Heathrow on the Animals Team, illegal imports.

'Barry. How are you doing? Found any unicorn smugglers lately?'

'No unicorns, Tony, but it's the next best thing. Ivory. Some antique dealer in Lancashire's been on the phone, with a mad story about some ivory. So I naturally thought of you.'

'Ivory?' I said. 'This is the RSPCA, Barry. You know, dogs and cats.'

'Ivory, Tony boy, ignorant northern git that you are, comes

from elephants. Elephants are animals, Tony, which is what the A stands for. Did you know that? And, if somebody is selling ivory, somebody is killing elephants to get it.'

'How do you know it's not from before the ban?'

'Because all that ran out yonks ago. This has to be new ivory, from a recently dead elephant. But if you're not interested, I'll call the local plod.'

'Don't do that! Barry, yes, of course I'm on to it. It's something I've been wanting to do for years. Give me the number.'

It turned out that this antique dealer, a chap called Nigel, had been sitting in his shop in the old Lancashire mill town of Darwen a couple of days before. He was wondering where his next customer was coming from when a woman turned up at the door with a pram. He knew her vaguely but was a bit surprised by the pram because she was well past childbearing age.

'I thought you might like to see this,' she'd said. When Nigel looked in the pram 'this' wasn't a baby but a four-foot elephant tusk. He expressed some vague interest and the next day an Arab arrived at the shop. Nigel recognised him too. He had the kebab takeaway in Darwen behind the bus station.

The Arab apparently behaved like the stereotype, all gestures and spread hands and lifted shoulders. He moaned about times being hard and the kebab business being slow.

'This ivory I sent my woman with,' he said, 'has always been in my family, but . . .' The gestures came again. This time they said that, regrettably, even family heirlooms have to be disposed of when necessary.

Nigel showed interest but said he needed to talk to a colleague first. The Arab told him he could get plenty more ivory, as much as he wanted.

'How many ancestral elephant tusks can there be in one family?' I said.

'That's what I thought,' Nigel said. 'What are you going to do?'

Good point. What was I going to do? I made my desk look as tidy as possible, took a deep breath, and walked over to the far side of the office to have a word with my boss.

Chief Superintendent Don Balfour was the head of the Special Operations Unit. Approaching retirement age, he was a sharp dresser with steely grey hair and that rugged, weather-beaten look that seafarers have. In fact he'd never been on a boat in his life and owed his great outdoors appearance to pottering in his garden and a holiday in Florida every year.

I got on well with Don. His knowledge and commitment to the unit were without equal and the respect in which he was held truly reflected that. He was a real character, broad Yorkshire, but exhibiting two of the major personality flaws that have given we Yorkshiremen such a bad name. One was that he was a pessimist, or miserable sod as we might say. In Don's view, every job we ever undertook was doomed to failure. It made him a good devil's advocate at the planning stage, but it was irritating at times and his negativity ground some people down.

His other fault was thriftiness. Yorkshiremen are Scots without the generosity. While we defend this trait as a virtue, pointing out that if you look after the pennies, the pounds will look after themselves, some of our tribe do take it a bit far. I was sitting in the car with Don one time, doing surveillance. He had a box of Tic-Tacs and, incredibly, offered me one. When he shook the box, two of the tiny sweets fell into my palm. Before I had the chance to react he pounced on the second Tic-Tac like a striking cobra and put it back in the box.

Don proved particularly reluctant about this ivory business. We argued about it for a quite a while but in the end he gave in.

'Well, you'll do it anyway, whatever I tell you,' he said, 'so you may as well bugger off and get on with it.'

Next morning I was on my way out of Sussex and heading for Darwen. It was another hot one and after five sweaty hours in the car I reckoned I was due a break. Perhaps I could find a spot to indulge in my favourite sport: sunbathing. I also enjoy running, swimming, backpacking and watching wildlife, but the suntan's the thing.

The moors above Darwen and Blackburn are not so wild and bleak as some but they are quiet and, through Belthorn heading towards Pickup Bank, I found the perfect place. I parked the car off the road and settled down for half an hour's R & R: repose and rays.

Feeling braced, I then drove on through a pretty village and stopped on the next hilltop looking down on Darwen. The most obvious objects in view were the strange tower on the opposite summit, looking like some kind of medieval folly, and the massive mill chimney in the valley below. It belonged to the India Mill, still a place of work if not quite as originally intended. The mill workers in their clogs were long gone but, from my vantage point, I could see that the rows of back-to-back terraced cottages were still there.

So, this was Darwen, ivory-smuggling hotspot. I couldn't imagine it, somehow. There would probably be a few punch-ups on a Saturday night after the pubs chucked out, but that, I thought, would be it for the local crime scene.

I drove down the hill into the town, not looking for the police station. At the start of something like this, we never tell any other agency, not even the police, that we're on their patch. Uniformed police and CID alike are not trained undercover operators and it's too easy to commit an unwitting indiscretion that can alert a target.

I'd learned that lesson the hard way when trying to catch

a gamekeeper who was using dead pheasants as poisoned bait for goshawks. He gathered up the casualties, usually ones that had been shot but not retrieved, injected them with strychnine and strewed them about. The goshawks would come, and that was that.

A colleague hid in a bush for three days watching this man, sometimes from no more than four or five yards away. He picked up the dead birds, sure enough, but he simply put them in a sack and carried on walking. It was a completely wasted operation. It turned out that the original informant, an underkeeper on the estate, had also told the local policeman about the poisoner. The policeman had let a word drop somewhere, innocently, to someone he trusted, and it had got back. So, when entering Darwen, I made sure nobody knew I was there.

As in all the old mill towns, the India Mill was by the river in the bottom of the valley with the ranks of terraced mill workers' cottages surrounding it, running straight up the hill sides. Many have been gentrified and are now owned by young professionals. They have fresh paint, PVC windows, newly pointed stone walls and a 4WD parked outside on the cobbles.

My first call was on Nigel's antique shop. We had a coffee and a good chat. I was keen to see if he was the right type. His background wasn't all antiques, I found out. He'd also been in the forces and I hoped enough of the military discipline remained for him to carry out his part of the job.

I needed him with me to make the initial introduction and it took a lot of guts for him to do it. For one thing, people involved in activities like ivory smuggling tend to be rough and rather careless with those who get in their way. For another, Nigel lived in the same town and, like all small towns, everyone knew everybody else's business. He had been there for years and expected to continue living there. Yet despite the risk if things went wrong, he was prepared to help me if he could.

People like Nigel, members of the public, could easily stay quiet and avoid any threat to themselves but they have a strong feeling about what is right. What is harder to understand is not that they're willing to stand up, but that the need for them to do it continues to rise. You would think that TV wildlife programmes and the increased awareness of animals and the environment would mean that the RSPCA's job would be getting easier. Not at all. The number of cruelty complaints varies greatly from year to year. The most recent year's figure was 126,000, but it has been as high as 150,000 and in general the trend is upward.

Very roughly, we get 1,500,000 phone calls a year, about all sorts. There's a duck in the office car park, I've just seen some fool of a walker feeding Coca-Cola to a sick lamb, there's a pig in my garden, my parrot's escaped. And, maybe one in ten, the man next door beats his dog, locks it up and never feeds it.

During a year we'll pick up 150,000 animals and get 3,000 convictions, and half of those will be for cruelty to cats and dogs. Most of the rest will be farm animals and just a small proportion, less than 10 per cent, will involve the much less visible, more secretive, better organised cruelty to wildlife. Up to the point where I met Nigel, nowhere in the RSPCA records had any success ever been logged against the international criminals of cruelty.

These are the people who rip horns from rhinos and tusks from elephants while they are still alive, the people who, for the sake of a few coins, will kill a mother and leave the young to the hyenas and the vultures or to a slow and painful death by thirst and starvation. These are armed bandits. They are poachers, but not the sort who walk by night to catch a pheasant for supper. They are ruthless killers, impoverished, desperate men whose only hope of a few dollars is ivory.

Against them are the rangers, who similarly are not as we imagine – driving about the Peak District in Land Rovers checking on car parks and quad bikers. The African wildlife ranger is a trained soldier. He shoots the poachers because if he doesn't they will shoot him.

There is an argument that if the ivory trade were legalised and controlled it would stop poaching. This is nonsense. It would increase poaching, because if there is legal ivory on open sale it would nowhere near satisfy demand. As the system has not yet been devised that can tell an illegal from a legal piece of ivory, the poachers would be out in ever increasing numbers against a few underpaid and demoralised rangers trying to cover thousands of square miles of country.

All this is for the sake of satisfying the foul market for aphrodisiacs and decorative trivia. Such trifles are judged to be worth the deaths of innocent and magnificent wild animals.

Nigel knew that killing elephants for the sake of their tusks was not right and he was willing to do his bit to stop it. Here in Darwen, he was obviously nervous, but he was dealing with the situation pretty well.

'I don't really understand why there's still such a market for ivory, though,' he said. 'They don't make piano keys and billiard balls out of it any more, do they?'

I'd been doing some research so I knew the answer.

'No, and not knife handles either, or chessmen, or hunting horns. It's all decorative stuff now, which is worse, really – jewellery, ceremonial things, statuettes, sculptures, carvings in relief – a lot of it's religious, but always it's for the beauty of the object. Ivory has special qualities, it's been carved for thousands of years, and some people don't see why it should all stop just because there aren't so many elephants these days.'

We got in the car and headed off. As we turned into the road leading to the target house I kept chatting to Nigel, trying to keep him at his ease by rabbiting on about ivory buddhas and riding crops. All the time I was doing my automatic checks: how easy or difficult would surveillance be from the road? Was the area busy with traffic and passers-by? Where were the blind spots and good parking places? Were there nosy neighbours – twitching curtains, people sitting out on the steps or loitering on corners?

Gentrification had definitely not yet reached this part of town; the houses looked shabby and down at heel. We pulled up outside the target house. It didn't look like the sort of premises an international ivory smuggler would choose, although it had one perfect quality. It was totally anonymous, the same as all the others in the street.

My back-up, Paul Goldston, was already in place. I'd been giving him updates over the radio, telling him our expected time of arrival, and his silver Mondeo was parked a good hundred metres past the house. With luck, if he was only there for ten or fifteen minutes nobody would give him more than a passing glance. He was smartly dressed and had a clipboard on the passenger seat. While he innocently filled in forms, as any rep might while out on his rounds, he listened and watched.

Paul was born in Lancashire but I'd never held that against him. He served in the police for a while before joining the RSPCA as a uniformed inspector and now had ten years' experience. He'd only been with the Special Operations Unit for eight months but he was a solid, reliable guy and a really quick learner.

We were a similar height and build but otherwise were complete opposites. I was a black-haired, sun-tanned liberal, Paul was a pale, blond, blue-eyed right-wing reactionary, but as far as the job went I knew that if I got into a tight spot any time he would be there to back me up and that was all that mattered.

I didn't even glance in his direction as I got out of the car. We tried to be very thorough, leaving nothing to chance. Normally there would have been covert surveillance for several days, building a profile of the target's movements and contacts, but this job had gathered speed so quickly that there hadn't been time to do any such background work.

I'd done what I could to prepare – plan, plan and plan again is our motto – but compared to our usual undertakings we were operating pretty blind. In essence the main tactic was straightforward: impersonate a crooked ivory dealer. First impressions are everything, so I'd given the clothes I was wearing a good deal of thought. I'd decided on a pair of good quality shorts, Nike sandals and a smart but casual short-sleeved shirt, leaving the tattoos on my forearms exposed. I'd acquired them in my teenage years when I joined the Royal Navy and I'd often thought about having them removed, but they were such an advantage during undercover operations that I left them alone. People seeing a man with tattoos automatically assume that he cannot be any kind of official.

You had to have the psychological upper hand on these operations, and the clothing you wore was only a part of it. Everything else had to look right too – your demeanour, your way of talking, the vehicle you drove – and the smallest thing out of place could blow your cover.

Police and other officials are accustomed to being obeyed and often carry a subconscious sense of authority that can be disastrous in undercover work and, because it's subconscious, can be far more difficult to disguise than, say, an accent. Paul was a first-class, all-round officer, but he did convey that commanding air. Once, when we went to a pub for an after-work pint one Friday evening, a local low-life went straight up to Paul and challenged him. 'You CID? Eff off out of it.'

Paul hadn't said a word but his stance and manner were enough to set the alarm bells ringing in the other man's mind. This aspect of Paul's personality limited his scope in under-cover work. We couldn't use him where he would have to mix with any public bar types who might have a natural antipathy for the police, as badger diggers or dog fighters almost invari-ably had. He was fine with the more upmarket kind of work, though.

I had an electronic bleeper with me, which I could use to signal Paul if I needed help fast, but I wasn't wearing a body mike. It was not unusual to be frisked at a first meeting with a new target. This meant that I had to recall exactly what had been said if the conversation later had to be used as evidence. This was always a primary consideration. We weren't after a sensational story for the press or local radio; what we wanted to get would have to stand up to analysis from magistrates at least and very possibly barristers trying their best to pick holes.

All I could do was make detailed notes as soon after leaving the target's house as possible, but I hoped I wouldn't have to use them. I wanted to get our man by some other route. Appearing in court to give evidence was always a risk to my undercover role and, just as importantly, I didn't want to involve Nigel publicly. Some of these criminals had long arms and long memories.

I looked at my watch. We were ten minutes early, as planned. You never know what you can glean from a slightly unprepared person. As we walked the short distance from the car I tried to keep my movements slow and casual, very aware that, if this was one of the careful class of criminal, I could be under scrutiny from inside the house. I had to expect that the target would be taking a sneaky look from somewhere, seeing if I performed to character. He might be hiding behind the curtains in the bedroom window. If I looked I might clock him; if I didn't he might think I was not taking the ordinary precautions necessary in my business. I snatched a swift glance. Nobody.

I kept my expression neutral as I scanned my surroundings for scraps of information, which might indicate character, standard of living, personal circumstances. Anything at all, from stickers in a car rear window to weeds in the window box, could help to build the picture. Another Mondeo, a blue one, four or five years old, was parked in front of the house. It might be the target's car. The registration number was about the only useful thing I could memorise and that might be somebody else's. Every other feature and detail was exactly as it should have been for a house in a street like this.

Nigel knocked and a woman opened the door. This must be the pram lady, I thought. With the help of Messrs Yardley, Boot and Factor, she was doing everything she could to deny her age – early fifties – but was not being very successful. She was five foot four, skinny, with over-lacquered blonde hair in need of a visit to the dye bottle. She must have been quite attractive when she was young, but life had been hard and the winters long. The jeans were tight, the blouse fresh and clean with one button too many undone, and she would never be able to sneak about, both because of her high heels and because her jewellery in motion made her sound like a team of Morris dancers.

She recognised Nigel and invited us in. We chatted for a minute in the hallway and she looked me over while I did my own, more subtle (I hoped) appraisal of our surroundings. From the atmosphere it would seem that several hundred cigarettes were consumed here daily. The house was neither smart nor particularly scruffy. The furniture was cheap, the decor dull. It was tidy enough but impersonal. It seemed like rented accommodation, run by a landlord who expected nothing from his tenants except the rent. This was a house for birds of passage.

She led us into the front parlour. An open door across the room led into the living room and beyond that was the kitchen in a lean-to built onto the back of the house. From the view into the back yard, through the window over the kitchen sink, I concluded that the residents were not keen on barbecues or patio gardening.

There was no sound other than our voices, and no sign of anyone else in the house, but when the woman ushered us into the living room we found a man sitting in the middle of a green, three-seater sofa facing the window. He wore light cotton trousers and a white shirt, and he was short and very fat for his height – I guessed at five foot six and sixteen stone. Like his girlfriend, he looked to be in his early fifties. His swarthy complexion, moustache and black hair suggested he was Middle Eastern, Levantine, more Arab than Turk. He grunted a greeting and gestured with his hand for us to sit down opposite him in the two armchairs. As arranged, Nigel made the introductions.

'Tony, this is Kefah Almomani. Kefah, Tony is the business acquaintance I mentioned. He looks for animals for taxidermy, skins, horns, and ivory.'

While Nigel was talking, I studied Almomani. He was sweating buckets. Though he kept wiping it away with his shirt sleeve, it made little difference. His shirt clung to him and his string vest showed through the fabric. I assumed that his body's metabolism was trying to shed some of his weight.

The only way to convince someone like Almomani of my credentials was to show that I knew as much about the subject as he did. I had a lifelong interest in animals (to say the least), but little knowledge of the skin and ivory trades, so I'd spent the previous two days doing research. I'd read all the historical data at headquarters and then gone to see Dave Astley, a respected taxidermist in York, who had trained with Roland Ward, one of the major London specialists in big game trophies. I came out of there as stuffed as any of his other work, but with knowledge rather than kapok.

I was fairly confident that I could keep a conversation going and soon had the chance to prove it, though it was more of a monologue. Kefah Almomani, or Fat Al as I was already calling him in my mind, was not going to give me an easy ride. He raised an eyebrow, as if to say, 'Well, young man, impress me if you can,' but said nothing. He just looked, while I had to keep talking.

I had always stressed to any colleague I was training in undercover work that you didn't have a second chance at making a first impression. You had to get the first few seconds perfect. If the target took an instant dislike to you or formed the thought that you might be a fraud or unreliable in some other way, it could prove impossible to retrieve the situation.

I now had those few seconds to convince Fat Al, a man who clearly specialised in deceit, that I was not deceiving him. He would be starting from a position of deep mistrust as a matter of standard policy. I began like someone taking an exam who finds that none of the questions make much sense and so simply spills out everything he knows on the subject, hoping that the general display of learning will be enough for the examiners.

My subject that day was ivory I'd bought and sold, skins I'd imported, dodgy taxidermists I had known. As bonuses I mentioned my new and particular interests in exotic animal parts for Chinese potions and in bush meat – exotic animals for restaurants.

It was a testing experience and grew more so as my fund of knowledge began to run out. Fat Al was no help at all. If I fell silent, he would grunt a two-word question and I would have to get going again. Meanwhile I had to remember any little thing that might be used in evidence, watch the effect I was having on Fat Al without him realising that an actor was inspecting his audience, and keep an eye on Nigel to make sure that he didn't give me away by any inappropriate body language.

Fat Al kept me on the spot for a good twenty minutes, until I was virtually out of fuel, but at last he seemed satisfied. Now it was my turn to take the initiative. I posed the question straight away.

'We've talked enough. Have you any stuff or not?'

I expected him to waver, to dodge, to say maybe tomorrow or the next day. Instead he struggled to his feet and walked past me out of the room, treating me to an overwhelming blast of garlic. I had no idea that a human body had the capacity for enough garlic to produce an effect like that. Count Dracula could not have stayed on the same continent with Fat Al.

He pulled the door half closed behind him but I kept my eye on the gap in the doorframe, looking for a change in the light as he passed to show whether he'd gone left towards the kitchen or right towards the front door. The right-hand side of the door darkened for a moment; he was either going outside or upstairs. I shifted my position slightly so that I could see if he went out of the front door, and strained my ears for the sounds of movement from elsewhere in the house.

I shot a quick glance at Nigel to make sure that he was still okay and wasn't about to faint. I preferred to work alone and it was a real last resort to have members of the public with me on undercover operations. Through inexperience, they were prone to making cock-ups and putting everyone at risk, but Nigel was proving equal to the task. The woman appeared in the doorway.

'Cup of tea?'

She'd left the door open behind her and I could hear movement from further down the hall. Fat Al was doing something near the door, but I couldn't tell what. A few moments later he pushed past her into the room, carrying a four-foot elephant tusk. It was a perfect ivory colour and in such pristine condition that it must have been polished. He handed it to me and stood back, studying my reaction.

I was careful not to show any sign of surprise, at the ivory or the ease and speed with which he admitted to keeping it in his own house. Nothing was impossible in Darwen, it appeared. I'd probably find out soon that the town was the global centre of the smuggled caviar trade as well as having the highest garlic consumption.

As I stared at the tusk I felt a deep nausea growing in the pit of my stomach. What was Fat Al's game? This wasn't ivory. The weight felt about right, but it was too shiny, too flawless. The bloody thing looked like plastic. I took my time, examining the base for the grey lines in the ivory, which are a good indication that it's genuine. I couldn't see anything to convince me, one way or the other. It was either what they call 'hard' ivory, a particularly grainless and dense variety that comes from West Africa, or it was a fake.

I ummed and aahed and stood up to examine it by the window, but really I was going through the motions. It looked like plastic and I didn't have the expertise or experience to say for sure that it wasn't. In desperation I passed it to Nigel. The look of surprise and shock on his face spoke volumes. He balanced and weighed it in his hands, then handed it back to me without making any comment. He knew less about ivory than I did but I needed a couple of seconds to decide what my next move was going to be.

The decision-making process was not helped by a recurring and evil thought concerning the relentless and eternal mickey-taking I would suffer from my colleagues if I spent hundreds of pounds on a four-foot piece of plastic. I could see it all as I stood there. Little plastic models of Dumbo would turn up on my desk for the rest of my career. At the Christmas party I would be blindfolded and, instead of pinning the tail on the donkey, I'd be asked to stick the tusk on the elephant. There'd be giant toothbrushes and heffalump traps and records of 'Nellie the Elephant'. I'd have to leave the RSPCA and join the RAC. I'd be safe there. They don't have undercover RAC men, do they?

'Sod it,' I thought. 'How much?' I said.

'Two hundred quid,' he replied with no hesitation.

The nausea moved from my stomach into my throat. Two hundred was cheap. Very cheap. I'd have said five, maybe six hundred. Either he didn't know the market value of his stock, which was unlikely, or this was another test.

'Will there be more at that price?' I said.

'Two hundred, for that one. Special offer. Introductory. Next time, we start again.'

I'd passed the test. Now I had only two problems. I wasn't sure if I was buying ivory or plastic, and I didn't have two hundred quid on me. I was posing as a big-time dealer in skins, ivory and animal parts, but, like royalty, I couldn't find a few notes when I needed them. I had never imagined I would have travelled so far and so fast with Fat Al. I'd thought it would take several visits before he trusted me enough to start dealing, yet here he was, almost holding his paw out for two hundred pounds, and I hadn't half of that in my pockets. My fob-off line was not one of my most inventive, I have to admit.

'I thought you'd have more than one. I'm not sure if I want to deal in singles. It means the customer I had in mind won't be interested. Tell you what. Let me make a few calls and I'll pop back soon as I can. Okay?'

With luck this would give me time and it would help me find out if he truly could get multiple tusks, or if this was just a single he'd happened across. He didn't seem too put out. He stood up, took the ivory from me and waddled out of the room, this time leaving the door ajar. I saw him stash it in the cupboard housing the electricity meter behind the front door. I now knew where he kept his ivory – not exactly secure accommodation.

It was best to wrap things up quickly, so as he came back in I offered my hand. He seemed surprised at this show of bonhomie but nevertheless managed a limp and clammy hand-shake.

'Good to meet you,' I said. 'I'll be in touch.'

Within a few seconds Nigel and I were out of the door and walking to his car. I glanced to the right and clocked Paul, still there in case anything went wrong. He was filling in his forms and didn't raise his head to look at us but he knew what was going on.

I felt drained as I got back into the passenger seat. This kind of work was mentally exhausting. A short stint of live acting with a target always left me far more tired than a whole week of surveillance.

We drove back to Nigel's shop and Paul joined us fifteen minutes later, having waited so that he didn't arouse the suspicions of anybody watching from Almomani's. By the time he got to the shop, I'd already written up my notes of my conversation with Fat Al. I shook hands with Nigel.

'Thanks for all your help. You can stay out of it now but, if he does call you, make sure you note every detail.'

In case we passed Almomani or one of his associates on the way out of town, Paul and I drove off in separate vehicles and rendezvoused at the Trafalgar Hotel, twenty miles away.

Paul and I were the only guests to have checked in so far that afternoon and we debriefed the job over a pint in a corner of the bar. For security reasons we never used the real names of our targets. We often found out later that they were false names anyway, which could lead to confusion, so we used acronyms, or nicknames describing some physical characteristic. These were invariably derogatory and politically incorrect but they ensured that when one of us referred to a particular target the others could instantly bring them to mind.

Kefah Almomani was already Fat Al. We christened his anonymous partner BB, short for Bony Bet, since she looked like a skinny sister of Bet Lynch, another peroxide blonde incapable of dressing her age.

'Fat Al's trying one on,' I said. 'If it's real, that tusk is grossly underpriced. If it's plastic, which it could easily be, he's making a big fool out of me.'

'Either way, you've got to go back with the two hundred or forget the whole business. What other choice is there?'

I looked at Paul. We both knew there was one major obstacle in the way of that policy: Chief Superintendent Don Balfour.

I thought the world of Don. He was a great RSPCA man and had always been very supportive of me in my work, but when a man was too tight to part with two Tic-Tacs at once, what was he going to think about two hundred pounds of RSPCA money, which he guarded with the same zeal as his own? This was on top of his general attitude that we had enough work on our hands combating animal cruelty at home without worrying about dealers in endangered species abroad.

Exotics were seen as part of the conservation issue, nothing to do with the RSPCA. Illegal international trade in ivory, rhino horn, tiger medicine, endangered species for pets and all the rest of it is second only to drugs in financial turnover. Fancy figures like fifteen billion dollars are quoted as annual sales. In my view, if that was nothing to do with the RSPCA, who was it to do with?

Another pint or two of bitter in the Trafalgar bar with Paul soon restored my optimism and I decided to deal with the Don problem by presenting him with a fait accompli. I would put my card into the nearest hole in the wall, withdraw two hundred pounds, buy the tusk and then tell Don about it afterwards, though I didn't really think I'd ever get the money back. In the RSPCA's expenses system, I doubted very much whether 'smuggled elephant's tusk' had a purchase code.

With that sorted, we did what all Special Operations Unit officers do when they get together over a beer: we moaned about our seniors. Tonight the subject was cars. One of our problems was that the standard issue car for undercover work was often too good for us. A lot of our jobs were in rough areas, in the country or on council estates, where new and newish cars get you noticed. The RSPCA's Mondeos and Orions, new or nearly so, were perfectly unobstrusive in the high street but cause for comment where we were likely to be.

To make it worse, every single one of them had a diesel engine. The decision was mainly based on cost, but when we first went over from petrol engines to diesels, the then head of the RSPCA Inspectorate also did some field research of his own and concluded that from fifteen to twenty feet it was impossible to detect the difference between the sounds of the two engines. We knew he had his faults but until then we hadn't realised he was deaf as well!

The diesels were good for fuel economy but awful when you

were trying to sneak about somewhere in the dead of the night, sounding like a Massey Ferguson coming down a farm track.

When we were on mobile surveillance, we needed faster, larger cars, petrol-driven, two- or three-litre engines. We were constantly chasing up and down the motorways, sometimes doing thousands of miles a week and often having to sleep in the car.

There was also a major security problem. Our cars could all be traced directly back to the RSPCA. By whatever means, it has been known for serious criminals to have access to the police national computer and find out who owns a car. In fact it's equally easy to conceal the true ownership of a car, but our bosses did not understand the risks, the exposure, the need for professionalism, the absolute necessity of taking every safety precaution.

They didn't understand for the simple reason that they hadn't been there and done it. I can't blame them for their lack of experience but we were up against some very hard, ruthless, nasty people.

I still had no idea how well connected Fat Al was, and I didn't want to go back to see him driving a car that could be traced to the RSPCA. It was probably a small risk, but there was no need to take it. Why should I blow the whole thing for the sake of borrowing a car from a mate? Chris, the local uniformed RSPCA chief inspector, had a friend with an old Ford Escort. So I got on the phone to persuade him to borrow it for me.

5

I was up and off for a run the next morning before the sun was too high. After a quick dip in the Trafalgar's pool and some breakfast, I was all set up for the day, starting with the drive to pick up the Escort. It was the perfect vehicle for the job, about five years old, starting to rust in places and one of the doors was sprained and hard to close. I made sure nothing had been left inside that could compromise the image I was trying to portray, that of the shady dealer.

Unlike the young idiots who deal drugs and cannot resist showing off their wealth in flash cars, the older and wiser members of the illegal dealing fraternity like to downplay their own importance. If you're theoretically unemployed with no visible means of support, you don't transport a load of ivory on the public highway in a brand new Mercedes estate car. You do it in a clapped-out Escort. Fat Al would expect no less. He wouldn't trust anyone in a Merc.

I spent an hour driving around getting used to the way

everything functioned. It not only had to look right, I had to be able to drive it without crashing the gears, stalling it, or doing anything else that might arouse his suspicions. The gears were straightforward but the driver's door needed a good slam and I practised it a few times to get the hang of it. When I was happy that it looked like I'd been driving it for ever, I cleansed myself of compromising material. I didn't expect to be searched by Almomani this time but it was by no means unknown for operators to blow their cover by inadvertently dropping something out of their pockets.

Paul was again acting as my back-up and I gave him my wallet, keeping back the two hundred pounds in cash and one credit card that I hid under my foot against the sole of my sandal. I also removed my watch. It was an expensive Seiko and often didn't fit the character that I was portraying, especially when I was involved with badger diggers. It wasn't particularly out of character in this sort of operation but as a matter of routine I removed it. I also took the pager off my belt. Normally it never left my side; I slept with it under my pillow and even took it into the sauna wrapped in a plastic bag.

The major risk compared to the previous day was that this time I was wired up with a body kit to record the conversation. The credit card in my sandal was the only other thing that could give me away.

As soon as I was ready, I set off for Darwen. I drove slowly to give Paul time to get ahead and take up position. Just before my arrival, he did a walk past the address to check that nothing untoward was happening, like a house filling with people in wait for me. As I approached the outskirts, he called to say that everything looked in order.

It was already very hot and I had the windows open in the car. The suntan was coming on well, at least on the right arm that I always had propped out of any vehicle's window. It was a nice golden brown colour and I made a mental note to try to do some jobs as a passenger so that I could get my left arm tanned to match it.

I parked the Escort on the opposite side of the street to Fat Al's. As I crossed over I noticed that the front door and the front windows were open. Ventilation. It could only improve things. As I brushed passed the blue Mondeo parked outside, I let my hand rest briefly on the bonnet. It was cold and obviously hadn't been used within the last half an hour or so.

Before I reached the house Fat Al appeared, blocking the doorway with his bulky frame. As he raised his hand to shield his eyes from the glaring sun he revealed a huge damp patch around the armpit of his shirt. God, I didn't like this guy. He invited me in but remained standing in the doorway so that I had to squeeze past him. Having your back towards a target wasn't the recommended way to enter a building, but there was no way I was going to brave the garlic and sweat zone head-on.

'Right then,' I said, pulling the cash out of the pocket of my shorts. 'Here's your two hundred quid.' He made no move to take it from me.

'Two hundred fifty, that's what I said. Two hundred fifty.'

I stared back at him, my mind racing. What the hell was going on? He'd agreed two hundred. Why had he changed the price? Was this yet another test of some kind? Whatever it was, I had a problem. I didn't have any more money on me.

Sod it. I had wanted this to go quickly and smoothly to gain his confidence, and instead it was all coming apart. It wouldn't look very convincing if I had to leave and get another fifty pounds. I took a deep breath.

'No, you said two hundred.'

'Two hundred fifty or forget it.'

BB came in, dressed to kill, warpaint on, handbag slung over her shoulder.

'Look,' I said. 'I don't carry any more cash than I need when I'm dealing with new people. I've brought two hundred pounds with me. That was the price we agreed.' I waved the notes at him, thinking that if I flashed them in his face and then shoved them into his hand, he might mellow. He wouldn't have any of it. He did his customary shrug.

'Two hundred fifty.'

I made a show of reluctance, knowing that the price was still very cheap, then surrendered.

'I'll have to go to the bank and get some more cash.'

'We're going out now,' Fat Al said. 'We'll take you down to your cash machine.'

'Then you'll have the money and I won't have anything. No, you wait here, my friend, and I'll be back.' I hoped Paul was paying close attention to this conversation. If he wasn't and I went out in the car with Fat Al and BB, it was anyone's guess what he might do. Don't panic, I said to myself. Of course Paul is listening. Keep a cool head.

'I will wait for you,' said Fat Al, 'but you'll have to be quick.'

I found a cashpoint opposite the bus station. It was market day and there were people everywhere, but I pulled over and jumped out.

'Oi. You can't stop there.'

I turned round. Great, something else to add to my problems: a traffic warden.

'I won't be a minute, mate,' I said. 'I'm just going to get some cash from the machine there.'

'If you do, you'll have a ticket when you get back.'

It would be bad enough explaining to Don that I'd drawn

out two hundred and fifty pounds to pay for a lump of plastic without also having to describe why I had a parking ticket.

'The alternative,' he continued, 'would be to park in the designated parking spaces, provided for your use, around the corner.'

Time was passing and no doubt BB was pushing Fat Al to go shopping or whatever they were doing. He hadn't seemed too bothered about the deal anyway. I could see it all slipping away from me. I parked as directed, slammed the Escort door and hurried towards the cashpoint. A teenager with a wispy beard was standing there agonising over how much money to withdraw and two other people were also waiting to use it. I joined the queue, trying to control my impatience at the snail's pace of everyone in front of me.

As I stood waiting my turn, I glanced around me and froze. Fat Al was right across the road from me unlocking the door of his kebab takeaway. There was no reason why I shouldn't be using the one cash machine in Darwen that was smack opposite the kebab shop, but I didn't want the embarrassment. I kept my back that way and at last it was my turn. Fat Al wasn't in sight as I hurried back to the car. I didn't know if he'd seen me but I couldn't do anything about it anyway. I only hoped BB was still at home to close the deal.

Within a few minutes I was back outside their house. The windows were still open and the door was ajar. BB must be in. Before I could knock, she appeared.

'I've got the two fifty,' I said.

'Come in. I don't think he'll be long. He's just popped down to the shop. Want a cup of tea?'

'Don't mind if I do.'

While she was in the kitchen I took another look around the living room. The more I could see of the inside of the house, the better the profile I could build of its occupants.

The telephone was on a shelf behind the door and I checked for an address book near it. There was a sideboard against the facing wall. If there was paperwork, it was likely to be in one of the drawers. The magazines and papers lying about might also give an indication of the type of people I was dealing with.

My next move was to walk through to the kitchen to chat to BB. I have generally found women to be more open and less suspicious than men and this was a good opportunity to find out if she conformed to the rule. I started on the most neutral ground possible, talking about the weather.

'Good, isn't it?' she said. 'I'll be sun-worshipping in the back yard soon as I get the chance.' She fluttered her mascara-laden lashes at me, scattering some tiny flecks of black onto her foundation-caked cheeks. 'Pity of it is, we're so over-looked. No privacy. I can't get the sun to everywhere I want it.' BB was a good ten years older than me and it would have taken a very dim light and ten pints of good ale to make her attractive, but that was hardly the point. Duty called.

I'd noticed that she always referred to Almomani rather shortly as 'him', and the way her lip curled confirmed that their relationship was one of convenience, not passion. This was good news. She might be open *and* disloyal. As we chatted I glanced out of the window, checking the yard for access and hazards in case we had to do any night work around there. The clothes hanging on the line – designer shirts and jeans that wouldn't fit either of the residents I'd met so far – looked like they belonged to a boy or young man.

At the far end of the yard was a wall with a door in it. No problem. Over the wall, or through the rickety door, was the wide alley-way between the two rows of houses. At night cars might be parked though there would be no block to a rapid getaway if it was necessary, but there were always dogs in areas like this. If next door had a wary one, it could easily start off a chorus in the whole street.

BB and I chatted for another fifteen minutes. She kept slipping in the odd double entendre and I kept sidestepping them, but otherwise it was like ordinary, everyday nattering. In among it, I learned some very useful things.

Fat Al made regular visits to the Middle East, flying out every couple of months or so. A Darwen kebab shop couldn't have generated the profits to pay for that. Whatever he was bringing back in his luggage, it wasn't mint and coriander. He was a Jordanian national who had come over to join some friends living in the area and he'd set up in business running the kebab shop.

BB was divorced with a teenage son. She'd gone in for a kebab with her mates after a drinking session one Friday night. Fat Al had chatted her up, they went out a few times, and he'd moved in with her. If she thought then that free kebabs and a fat Jordanian around the house was a tempting proposition, she didn't seem to think so now.

I couldn't push my luck by hanging around much longer. I didn't want Fat Al to find me chatting up his girlfriend or BB to start getting too strong a scent of me. I was just telling her I'd come back later when I heard the slam of a car door followed by footsteps in the house.

BB seemed sensitive to the situation too and disappeared to attend to her washing line as I walked back into the living room. I took charge as soon as Fat Al came through the door, greeting him by waving the two hundred and fifty quid under his nose. He took the money from me and counted it three times. I was glad I wasn't doing a big deal with him or we'd have been there all day. He added the money to an already fat wad of notes secured by a rubber band and shoved it back into his pocket.

He was a cool character – not literally, he was still dripping with sweat – and he showed no emotion. He never cracked a smile and always kept his conversation to grunts and monosyllables. I tried to talk to him about his kebab shop, but he wasn't up for it. He'd got his money, I'd be getting the tusk, no need for aimless chatter. Well, at least you knew where you were with him.

He had to squeeze past me to get to the meter cupboard for the tusk but this time I was prepared and held my breath. I resolved to try and keep upwind of him in future.

He left the tusk on the dining table as he went into the kitchen and returned with some supermarket carrier bags, which he taped around it. It now looked exactly like an elephant's tusk with plastic bags taped around it, but never mind. It was the first piece of ivory any of our firm had ever bought – assuming it was ivory, of course.

I left at once. After half an hour of stale cigarette smoke, BB's perfume and Fat Al's garlic and old sweat, I was mightily relieved to breathe the fresh air of Darwen. Things were getting better all the time. The sun was shining, I had the ivory and I was out of a tense situation.

I'd arranged to rendezvous with Paul at an old cement works about five miles away. As I drove in through the gates the tyres threw up the dust of decades and in seconds the car was covered in a grey film. I tried to wind up the windows to stop the dust being sucked inside as well but by the time I got them closed, there was a good layer all over the dashboard.

Ten minutes later Paul turned up. He had been keeping an eye on Fat Al's after I left, to make sure nothing out of the way happened. We had a quick debrief and then I showed him the ivory. When I removed the plastic bags, he laughed so much he nearly fell over.

'It's plastic, you tosser. You've paid two hundred and fifty quid for a pub decoration.'

'It is not plastic, Paul of little faith. It is hard ivory, minimum grain, from West Africa. You just haven't got the knowledge to tell it from a Formica table top.'

'Well, make sure you don't leave it out in the sun, Tony boy. It'll go flat.'

I had a feeling he was right but I wasn't going to tell him that. He was still having hysterics.

'You'll never live this down, Tony. But look on the bright side – it'll look lovely hanging on the wall behind Don's desk. Which reminds me, he wants to talk to you.'

'I've bought the ivory, Don,' I said as casually as I could when I got through on the phone. 'It's a four-foot tusk.' I took a deep breath. 'Bit of a bargain, really. Market value five or six hundred. To me, two hundred and fifty quid.' There was a silence from the other end of the line.

'I hope you got a receipt.' It was hard to tell if he was joking.

'Smugglers don't do receipts, Don. They're not very keen on paperwork.' I waited for the explosion but none came.

'Oh, right,' he said. 'So what are you going to do now?'

'Head for home. I'll be in the office on Monday for a debrief.'

When I went back to the animal home to drop off the Escort, I showed Chris the tusk. He was the type of inspector who had made the RSPCA. To him it wasn't a career, it was a way of life. His passion for the job was blinding, which sometimes got him into bother, but I trusted him completely. I knew he'd be fascinated by the smuggled ivory.

He barely looked at it. 'What have you done to the bleeding car?' he squeaked.

'I quite like it grey,' Paul said, still giggling. 'Why don't you stick the tusk on the front and it'll look like a rhinoceros.'

'Chris,' I said. 'Do me a favour, would you? Put it through the car wash for me.'

'Oh, don't you worry, Tony. I'll give it a complete valeting. I've got nothing else to do while you're sitting in French restaurants doing surveillance. Yes, no problem. You go back to the Waldorf Astoria and have a sauna.'

He was only half joking. A lot of the uniform lads were envious of us, although Chris never failed to support me when I needed him. I searched my pockets for some coins.

'No, no, don't worry. Please. It's my pleasure. Anything I can do to help MI5.'

'A good job,' I said, 'because I haven't got a ha'penny. Spent all my dosh on ivory.'

'Send me a postcard next time you're up a tree. Now, sod off back to Sussex.'

On the way down the M6 I pieced together everything that had happened and began to plan the next stage. I also devoted a few minutes to Denise's possible reactions on learning we were two hundred and fifty quid light in our bank account.

I kept glancing at the tusk. I had by now convinced myself that it was plastic. There was not an excuse or reason in the world that could prevent my eternal torture at the hands of the gang of satirists and practical jokers I worked with. It was a melancholy journey.

More seriously, there was the thought that my purchase of a large plastic tooth, when news of it reached the upper management of the RSPCA, might do real damage to the cause. Since the early days we had never touched upon exotics or endangered species abroad, and I'd been pushing for us to include them in our remit ever since I'd joined the unit. I needed some successes to convince the RSPCA bigwigs. Instead I'd got two hundred and fifty quid's worth of plastic.

It was very late by the time I got back to Horsham that

night. I'd been away all week and I needed to spend time with my family, but the doom and dread associated with my purchase drove me to my reference books and computer files, trying to find something about a kind of ivory that looked exactly like a plastic imitation.

I chipped a small piece off the base and put it under the microscope. It didn't help, because I didn't know what I was looking for. I tried heating a small piece over a flame. It smelled like burning plastic.

Early on Saturday morning I drove into London, to the Natural History Museum, with the tusk strapped to the pillion seat of my Goldwing motorbike. As I wove my way through the London traffic, I kept reaching behind me to make sure it hadn't fallen off.

I parked the bike in front of the museum, signed in and made my way through the back corridors and storerooms that the public never saw to the office of Daphne Hills, one of the senior curators of mammals and extremely knowledge-able.

I showed her the tusk. She held it up to the daylight and peered at the pointed end, then put the point under a strong artificial light, which showed up a fine, dark grey grain now just visible under the surface, running along the length of the tusk.

'Hard ivory,' she said. 'Elephant, West Africa. Namibia probably.'

I tried my hardest to concentrate on the road as I drove back home. What a relief. This meant so much. My investigation had gone live again and Fat Al was once more in my sights.

I decided to be ten minutes late at the office on the Monday morning, giving Paul time to spread the story that I'd spent the RSPCA's money or, more precisely, my own money, on a lump of plastic. I'd let the mickey-taking go on for a while, and then go and get the ivory out of my car.

It was yet another blistering day. Even at nine in the morning with all the car windows open, sweat was trickling down the back of my neck.

As soon as I walked into the office everyone started to talk about plastic. I was asked if I minded my coffee in a plastic cup. Someone else was wondering about getting plastic windows fitted to his house. Somebody had been advised to buy shares in plastics companies because sales were rocketing. Another said there was a horse called Fantastic Plastic running in the two thirty at Haydock Park.

I was happy. Let them carry on. The more they crowed, the wider my smile. Don, who shared the office with us, cut them short. He rocked back in his chair and folded his hands behind his head.

'Now then, Tony lad, how did you get on last week?'

Don was not the mickey-taking sort. He was too miserable for that, but he also knew what I was trying to do and how much effort I'd already put in. I might not get my money back but he wouldn't have ridiculed me, even if I had bought a plastic tusk. I still wanted to score some points against the others, though.

'Oh, yes, I did all right,' I said and sat at my desk. Don waited in vain for me to continue.

'So where is it, then?'

'The ivory?' I said innocently.

'Of course the bleeding ivory. Where is it?'

'I left it in the car. I'll go and get it.' When I came back, I plonked the tusk on Don's desk.

'Two hundred and fifty quid. Cheap at twice the price.'

Don squinted at it, obviously convinced it was plastic. I went back to my desk and shuffled some papers, very blasé about the whole thing. It took Don a couple of minutes to broach the subject again. He didn't want to tell me what he thought but he couldn't change the habit of a lifetime.

'Are you sure it's the real thing?' he said.

'Naturally.'

'You know,' one of the lads said. 'We had our church fête on Saturday and they served the beer in plastic glasses. I can't stand plastic glasses.'

'They did that at the parent-teacher barbecue,' another said. 'Plastic glasses for the beer. Plastic knives and forks. Even the paper plates were plastic.'

I didn't want to prolong Don's agony too much, but I was getting a lot of pleasure out of this.

'Sorry, Don, I thought you'd know it when you saw it,' I said, going over to the poor old sod. 'See this on the point? Grain. The fineness and the colour of the grain, together with the high polish, show this tusk to be hard ivory, West Africa, probably Namibia. It's more glossy and translucent than the softer sort, from East Africa, which the carvers prefer because it's easier to work, has a more golden colour and is less liable to cracking.' My time with my reference books had not been wasted.

The others were all quiet. Time for the knife to be stuck in.

'Anybody seen that old badger pelt lately?' I said. Suddenly everyone was busy reading reports and tapping keyboards, the reason being a little triumph of mine a few months before. Everybody in the unit except Don and me had taken part in a major investigation into a very active badger digger. They'd raided his house and returned very pleased with themselves after finding a badger pelt pinned to the back of a door. They had all been in the office preening themselves when Don had walked over to my desk and dropped a Polaroid photograph of the pelt in front of me.

'What do you think of that?' he had said.

'Roe deer,' I had replied, handing the Polaroid back.

After enjoying the memory of that moment, I took the tusk back from Don.

'Don't you think you'd better get it looked at, to be on the safe side?'

'I don't need to. I know ivory when I see it.' I don't know how I was keeping my face straight. There was a further silence.

'Look, take it up to London and get it identified. We need to be one hundred per cent sure.'

'Okay, if you're not prepared to take my word for it.'

Don choked on his tea. 'I didn't mean that, Tony. I just think we need to cover ourselves.'

'If you insist,' I said with a great show of reluctance. 'I'll take it now.'

Paul volunteered to come with me. 'No, it's okay,' I said. 'It doesn't take two of us to do it.'

Twenty minutes later I was sitting in a deckchair in my garden, soaking up the rays. I was due for a day off. I left Don sweating until five o'clock, then put him out of his misery.

'I've been to the Natural History Museum,' I said. 'Like I told you. Hard ivory. Namibia. Cheers, Don.'

6

I was due for a trip up north in pursuit of my other sworn target, the badger digger and baiter, Verril. Darren was going to show me the location of the dig that had resulted in the badger's head in the hotel freezer.

We had a license to dig into the sett, issued by English Nature. The job was slightly political in that the site was on private property up towards Giggleswick in the Yorkshire Dales. There are now very strict rules concerning trespass but at the time it was necessary. We had to sneak through someone's land, find the sett and see if we could find more evidence because, for all we knew, badgers were being killed with the collusion of the landowner.

We were hoping to find some remains of that sow badger's body. A bone would do. If we were successful we could match the DNA from the badger's head to the sett and then, if we could make a connection between the sett and Verril, we would have the beginnings of a case.

I picked Darren up from his home and off we went. He was bouncing in the car, as keen to get this bloke as I was. He described the dig to me, and the attitude of the men there – especially the leader, our target, who took such great delight in beating the badger half senseless and slicing its head off while it was still alive. I was going to take enormous pleasure from seeing him in the dock.

We met the local RSPCA chief inspector, Richard Nelson, at a café in Nelson and had tea and a bacon roll. I'd known Richard for some years, from the days when he and I were both uniformed inspectors in Yorkshire. He was a good officer with a special interest in wildlife and a particular leaning towards badgers. He hadn't taken much persuading to come along on this little jaunt.

We drove on northwards, towards the site of the sett. Badgers are secretive creatures and usually live in a very quiet spot. Where we were going had the advantage to us of being isolated, a long way from prying eyes, so we had a good chance of getting there without being seen.

It turned out to be a fairly small sett in a flat grass field. The ordinary passer-by, or the man on a galloping horse, might not have noticed where the diggers had been 'crowning down' as they call it, digging into the chambers from directly above after the terrier has located the prey. Perhaps the landowner wasn't involved because it had all been nicely back-filled to disguise activity, but to the experienced eye there was evidence everywhere. Here most definitely was a sett that had been dug, probably a few times and certainly at least once since the time of the badger's head.

Darren started work with my folding shovel, which hides itself nicely under my jacket. Normally it's used for hiding me when I'm on surveillance in a rural area and need to dig myself in. I make a shallow grave and lie in it so I can see but am less likely to be seen.

Any magistrate in that field on that day would have dismissed all possibility of Darren being a badger digger because in five minutes he was sweating and puffing and panting and asking for someone to take over. I thought I'd show him how it was done. If only the management at head-quarters could see us now, I thought, two RSPCA chief inspectors and an informant from the shady side of the street digging into a badger sett. Well, so long as there wasn't a newspaper photographer perched up a tree with a long lens, or a game-keeper out on his rounds with a twelve-bore and a couple of Rottweilers, or the landowner behind a hedge with a mobile phone calling up the village roughnecks for a stick and boot party, we'd be all right. We took great care to ensure that we only removed the previously disturbed earth.

I lasted half an hour on my excavating shift then passed the spade to Richard. The hole was deep now. Setts on flat land can go down twelve feet or more, or they can be very shallow. The ones on hillsides tend to go in rather than down. Richard was standing up to his waist, shovelling the soil out onto the side, while Darren was surveying the scene around us like a radar scanner, getting more and more agitated every second. I, on the other hand, sensed the possibility of a future wind-up as I looked at Richard in the hole. 'RSPCA Inspector and Family Man Turns Out to be Body Snatcher.'

I had my little sureshot camera that I took everywhere. I gave a quiet signal to Darren, who stepped out of vision, and quickly snapped off a couple of frames. You never know when you might need to extract the Michael and it would be a great shame if the chance came up and you'd not bothered to acquire the wherewithal.

After more than an hour's excavation we reached the bottom

of the hole without success, and it was hard to justify going on. Besides, Darren was getting even more twitchy, and Richard seemed to be catching it from him. We had evolved a cunning plan in case we were accosted, which was to run like hell back to where we had hidden the car, but this seemed less and less appealing as time wore on, the hole got bigger and it started to rain.

We agreed to put the sett back as we had found it and adjourn to a nearby hostelry where we could discuss what to do next. Putting soil back seems a great deal easier than taking it out, and it wasn't long before we were ordering pies and pints in a nice warm pub in Clitheroe.

Richard had been keeping quiet about a few things. He now told us that, having seen the spot and thought about it, he knew the landowner. He was one of those people who should never be allowed to hold land. Good landowners see themselves as the temporary stewards of something that was there long before they were born and that will be there long after they are dead. They see they have a duty to the land, to improve it if they can and at least to pass it on – complete with wildlife – in as healthy a state as they found it.

This owner was one of the other kind, the sort who really believed the land was his personal possession to treat exactly as he wanted, and would commit any environmental vandalism if it was profitable or made things more convenient. He was also well known locally for being very anti-rambler and totally anti-trespasser to the point of taking the law into his own hands.

I thanked Richard for keeping this vital information to himself while we were digging, and pointed out that it was his round. Richard also knew the gamekeeper on this stretch of land, a man called Geoff Verril.

I told Richard how I'd first come across Verril when he was head keeper on an East Yorkshire estate. A young underkeeper called Connor had been invited along to a badger baiting session organised by Verril, and the boy had been so revolted by what he had seen that he'd contacted me. By the time we got proper surveillance going, Verril had been spooked and had moved on.

Now he had resurfaced. The only birds he tolerated were the partridges that bred wild but were looked after as much as possible and the pheasants that he reared and fed. They were so tame and fat that when there was a shoot the beaters had to kick them into the air or they would have walked towards the guns.

Verril also allowed hares to exist, but that was it. Deer were shot because they ate the pheasants' cover. Any predator, be it fox or stoat or weasel, was exterminated. If he could have pressed a button to eliminate every bird of prey and every predatory mammal in the world at a stroke, he would have pressed it – except that it might have taken the fun out of his work. Anything else, like badgers, his mates could come and kill for fun if that was what they wanted.

We yarned a bit about gamekeepers we had known and how commercial pressures were turning them into something different. Their job was always to protect the owner's game, but the traditional respect for Mother Nature was gone as soon as you started charging huge sums of money for a day's shooting. A businessman from overseas who was willing to pay several thousand pounds for a day's shoot was not the sort of chap to smile and say, 'Just one of those things,' if he didn't pot a few brace.

Of course you also had the human predator, the poacher. Poaching in the old days had a kind of romantic aura. The poor cottager, working every hour that God sent for practically nothing, couldn't afford meat for his family. Knowing that the penalties for being caught were severe, he nevertheless took the terrible risk so that his children could have rabbit stew.

It went something like that, maybe. Poaching nowadays is quite different. Times have changed; you can buy pheasants in the supermarket, oven-ready. Ducks five times as fat as wild ones are lying there in the chill cabinet for anyone with a packet of Paxo. Pick up your venison steak and your jar of cooking sauce. But, just as stolen kisses are so much more exciting, stolen meat tastes so much better than the stuff you buy at the butcher's.

Some people, including hotel chefs, like their game well hung. You can't get that in a supermarket, nor can you get fresh-run wild salmon. There's always a ready market for anything out of the ordinary, paid for in cash and made all the juicier by its illicit sources. This is the motivation of the modern poacher and some are ruthless in the pursuit of their prey.

Gamekeepers have different approaches to poachers. While they all try to defeat the commercial poachers, some keepers more or less tolerate the man who's just taking something for the pot. Others have zero tolerance, and Verril was one of the latter.

We had to concede temporary defeat to Verril over the dig. He had won this round, even though he didn't yet know he was in a fight.

Even if he realised that the sett had been disturbed again, there was nothing to link it to an investigation. There was the faintest of chances that he might talk to his mates and put two and two together, spot their friend Darren as the weak link and arrange for a good smacking, but I was sure that the rain would do our camouflaging for us and suspicions would not be aroused. Good. Because next time, Mr Verril, I'm going to get you.

The second phase of my current northern trip was to pay Fat Al another call. This and all future visits would be unannounced, my established and preferred way of working. I might find myself wasting some time, but at least I knew I wouldn't be walking into a trap.

This was always the fear. If you are challenged face to face – if someone recognises you, for instance – you might be able to bluff your way out. If you are in an ambush, where your enemy has sussed you between one meeting and the next, your opportunities are very limited indeed.

I went to borrow the Ford Escort again from Chris, swearing on my mother's soul that this time it wouldn't be coming back covered in cement dust. Even then he was reluctant to let me have it. Some people are born without faith.

Near my sunbathing spot outside Belthorn, I pulled up at the roadside, emptied my pockets into a bag that I hid under the driver's seat of the car, and put on my sound equipment, what we call our covert body kit. The only bulky part is the battery, about the size of two packs of cards. The other parts – earphone, microphone, recorder and wires – are tiny, and the whole lot is fitted with Velcro.

You control it with concealed buttons and pressure pads. You don't need to lift up your lapel to speak, like they do on TV; it picks up everything. It's simple enough to hide your kit under layers of winter clothing or a smart suit, but more difficult in summer when the demands of your suntan require you to wear only a light shirt and shorts. The wires are the danger. One might come loose and drop out somewhere, and there's no normal reason for wearing wires. The only way to be sure is to tape the wires to your body. You simply have to be brave when you're pulling the tape off again; it's a very good way of thinning over-luxuriant chest hair.

I fed the remote switch through a small hole in the pocket of my shorts. Every pair of trousers I possessed had a similar hole cut into the right hand pocket so that I could either transmit on my radio or control the on/off and record switch.

Lastly I put a new tape into the recorder and tested it. Everything was working. I was ready to go.

Fat Al was unlikely to frisk me, so I didn't think my body mike would be discovered. The only disaster I could foresee was an unlooked-for grope from BB. As I pulled up outside Fat Al's house I cleared my head of those thoughts and concentrated on getting myself back into character.

The Mondeo wasn't there, but BB was sitting on the front step, smoking a cigarette. She was wearing shorts and a T-shirt that she'd knotted round her scrawny midriff. She gave me a big smile and greeted me like we'd known each other for years.

'Cup of tea, love?' I followed her into the kitchen. 'He's not in,' she said as she put on the kettle.

I'd worked that one out for myself.

'Gone to Manchester, he has. I don't know what time he'll be back. He may go straight to the kebab shop. You can wait here with me, if you like.'

'I was wondering if he was going to get any more stuff,' I said, thinking that there was no such thing as a free cup of tea. If I waited there with her, I might get some useful information, but what was the price going to be? 'I sold that tusk on. My contact was really pleased and wants some more.'

'Shouldn't be a problem, Tony. He's going to Jordan in a couple of weeks. That generally means he'll be bringing something back.'

I checked the control in my pocket to make sure it was recording and moved closer to her to be certain of the best quality sound. She clocked my move and gave me another big smile. The things I do for animals, I said to myself.

'Never been to the Middle East. You ever been?' I asked.

'One Arab's quite enough for me, thank you. More than enough. Do you do a lot of travelling, Tony? Away from home?'

For what must have been an hour the conversation went on like this, with me trying to drag it back to Fat Al and his Jordan trips without making BB suspicious, and her wanting to talk about anything but. At the end of that tortured period I had somehow extracted a small collection of interesting facts. Fat Al flew from Heathrow. He went down there on the train but BB had to go and pick him up in the car, I assumed because he came back with extra luggage. I could see that BB wasn't finding our conversation exactly fascinating, but I was, and I was determined to be as boring as necessary to find out any little helpful snippet.

'I always fly British Airways,' I said in one of my more scintillating moments. 'If they don't go there, I don't fly.'

'He goes with Egypt Air,' said BB, clearly beginning to wonder if I bored for England.

'Egypt Air?' I said. 'Good Lord. Why does he fly with them?'

'Always stops off in Cairo on the way back. He does the ivory business there and flies home. Do you want another cup of tea?' She rummaged through some papers on the kitchen table. 'Twenty-third's the next time. That's when I pick him up.'

BB had now told me who Fat Al was flying with, where he was flying from, the airport he was returning to, where he bought the ivory, the date he was arriving back and that she was going pick him up. He would have strangled her if he'd known what she was giving away.

I couldn't leave immediately after she'd spilled so many beans, and besides I wanted to keep her sweet. I thought I could disappoint her a time or two more without ruining our relationship. We stayed chatting for another twenty minutes, talking about everything other than Fat Al and his movements and including plenty of flirtatious comments. With luck she'd remember what we'd been talking about last and forget the specifics she'd given away about his Middle Eastern itinerary.

'Maybe I'll go and see him and have a kebab. Where's the shop?' I said, innocently.

'Would you rather see him than me?' she said, doing her best to push herself against me, which was bad news for all sorts of reasons. I said something about business taking precedence over pleasure, for the moment at any rate. With a close encounter avoided and the secrecy of my recorder still intact, I drove away and switched on my mobile phone to check for messages.

The preferred tactic with mobile phones is to have one for each job, so that different groups you are trying to infiltrate all have their own number for you. You know who's calling and there's no danger of slips and embarrassing moments. In the RSPCA we had to cut costs and were stuck with one mobile for everything, which meant that even if you were expecting an important call you couldn't take a phone with you into, say, Fat Al's house, in case somebody else rang on it, like the police, and you were forced into a weird conversation trying to pretend it was your wife.

I parked out of sight of the kebab shop and sorted out my tapes. With the machine switched on, I walked into the empty shop. There was a young, Levantine-looking man behind the counter, slicing doner meat from the rotating spit and putting it into insulated boxes. Quite a big takeaway order, obviously. Why don't they ever put the salad in a separate box instead of letting it get as hot as the meat?

'Is Kefah in?' I said.

He looked blank. Perhaps it was my pronunciation. I thought they understood Yorkshire in Lancashire.

'Kefah?' I repeated, more loudly. Still no sign of recognition.

'Kefah Almomani?'

He shook his head as if he didn't have a clue what I was talking about, and went back to his carving. Maybe I'd got the wrong kebab shop. I started to describe Fat Al to him.

'Ah,' he said and walked into the back. A couple of seconds later Fat Al emerged looking his usual hygienic self and dripping sweat all over his greasy apron.

'Hi,' I said. 'How are you doing?'

He gave me the blank expression, same as the lad. Perhaps this was a Jordanian speciality.

'What do you want?'

Have I been dreaming all this, I thought? I must have made a seriously big impression on this guy. I'd bought a four-foot piece of ivory from him a few days before and he still didn't know me from a bar of soap.

'Well,' I said, trying to maintain my confident air, 'I thought we could have a chat about some business. In private.' I would have had a more understanding reaction if I'd been speaking in Serbo-Croat. 'The commodity you trade in, which I trade in, er, I was hoping we might, that is, if there were to be any more, and you were bringing some more of this commodity back from, er, overseas . . .'

Still nothing and he was getting impatient. I would have to go for it. 'The ivory,' I said. 'I bought a tusk from you.'

At last. He seemed to recognise me. Not that there were any old pals' greetings. This was 'recognise' as in recognising the slug that has been eating the garden plants. I felt a wave of uncertainty pass through me. What had he found out? Fat Al today was not the Fat Al who had freely unpacked his meter cupboard of an ivory tusk and swapped it for two fifty quid. This was Fat Al who felt cheated, betrayed, stitched up, and who was going to show me just how unwise such a thing could be. I very much regretted wearing my wires.

He opened the swing-top counter and beckoned me through without a word. This was the moment. I could turn and run, or I could allow myself to be ushered into the spider's web that, I was sure, had been made especially for me by a very fat spider. I hesitated. He made an impatient gesture. I stepped forward and I was suddenly in the kitchen at the back of the shop.

My mistake was immediately apparent. Waiting for me were two other men, presumably Jordanians, sitting in armchairs drinking tea. Both were solidly built, and one of them looked like he'd been an Olympic weightlifter in the super-heavy-weight division. He had massive shoulders, a moustache and a shaven head. If things turned ugly I could see myself being cleaned and jerked into the Leeds and Liverpool Canal.

Fat Al closed the door behind him and leaned back against it. He said a few words, in Arabic I assumed, and the two men put down their teacups and got out of their chairs. Christ Almighty, the weightlifter was huge, only an inch or two taller than me, but at least twice the bulk, and none of it was fat. He wasn't a weightlifter, I decided, he was an all-in wrestler. He had that strutting walk and a humourless smile, a sort of lip-stretching grimace, which I imagined he had developed while squeezing the life out of his unfortunate opponents.

He did something more horrifying than anything I could have imagined. Instead of grabbing me by the throat and smashing my head against the ceiling he just stood there in front me, staring into my eyes. His stare, pure aggression, said I had as much chance against him as a sick antelope calf against a hungry lioness.

For a few moments I tried to hold his gaze but that contest too was unequal. I cleared my throat and glanced around the room. Behind the wrestler I could see his mate, a lesser threat but still quite enough on his own, searching through a drawer.

It was the drawer found in every kitchen, the one that's full of all the odds and sods of small equipment – the egg whisk, the potato peeler, the old carving knives, the biscuit cutters. He was scratching about trying to find something, lifting out onto the top various items that seemed to satisfy him in some way. These he arranged in a neat line – a carving fork, a serrated knife used for cutting frozen food, a metal skewer, another skewer of a different pattern, and something that looked like a junior hacksaw.

I was really sweating now. Fat Al had found me out and he was going to watch while his two sidekicks gave me a going over, butcher's style. When they found that I was wired up, it wouldn't matter. It would be mere confirmation. They already knew.

The wrestler took a step towards me. I took a step back without any message going from my brain to my feet. I was stiff with fear. There was no artful undercover agent noticing loopholes and planning an escape from impossible danger. There was only a useless, drained, brain-dead human animal somehow staying upright despite his legs no longer working.

Mr Lesser Threat made a small cry, like he'd found exactly what he wanted – a corkscrew, a big one with a bone handle. I have never fainted in my life, but that must have been the closest I ever came to it.

The wrestler stepped forward again and I backed into Fat Al. I wondered briefly if there was any point in doing some damage to Al before I was damaged myself, but I had no time to make up my mind. The wrestler took my right arm in his left hand and, almost lifting me off the floor, guided me to one of the armchairs and pushed me into it. He eyed me, like a hungry man eyes his dinner, giving himself a minute of extra pleasure by postponing the first mouthful.

Behind me I heard a pop, a clink and a glug-glug-glug.

Fat Al appeared in my line of vision with a glass of red wine.

'So,' he said, 'you were happy with the piece you bought?' I nodded, unable to speak for a while. I took three pulls at the wine and it was gone. The Lesser Threat poured me some more.

'Sold it on,' I croaked. 'No bother. Market's crying out.'

'You want more, I get you plenty.' He spoke a few words of Arabic and his two colleagues disappeared through the rear door without a backward glance. They knew they'd done their job.

'Plenty, plenty, Tony,' said Fat Al, all joviality. 'Twenty, thirty tusks. Elephant's head if you want it.' I tried to visualise driving down the M6 with an elephant's head on the back seat.

'A full elephant's head?'

'Of course.' He spread his arms as wide as they would go. I held my hand out for more wine.

'I travel to Middle East soon,' Fat Al continued, pouring. 'I bring tusks through then. If you want, you can have.'

I was feeling better. My brain was working again and I wanted to know how such a thing was done. Tusks are too big and awkwardly shaped to be easily transported. I had to find out how he avoided customs searches.

'If you're prepared to take the risk, I'm prepared to take the tusks. And if quantity is no problem to you, it certainly isn't to me,' I said.

'I bring you three or four personally one trip, another three or four next time, and so on.'

'Personally? You mean in hand luggage? Bloody hell. I wouldn't have thought even Houdini could have done that.'

'Excuse me?'

'He was a magician. An illusionist.' I got an immediate return on my flattery.

'No need for magic,' he said. 'No tricks. I pay certain customs officers at Cairo airport, and perhaps a few people at Egypt Air, and I take ivory as hand luggage. I know exact measurements of overhead compartment and I have special holdall, handmade by close relative. Tusks fit in holdall, holdall fits in compartment. My only risk is being picked up in your green channel at Heathrow.'

'What about the other passengers? Don't they object to you taking up an entire hand-luggage thing?

He did his shrugging hand-spread gesture. This time it asked what bribes were for, if not to ease such difficulties? What had it got to do with me anyway?

'Fair enough,' I said, offering my hand. He looked startled and briefly touched it in his pale imitation of a wet lettuce.

He searched among the mess on the table for a pen while I promised myself never to buy any food that had been near this kitchen. It was filthy. I made a mental note to rip off the environmental health people but it would have to wait until my work was concluded. Fat Al located a pen and jotted his number down on a scrap of paper.

'Give me ring in four weeks' time. I'll have ivory by then.'

'And you'll definitely save it for me?'

He nodded and seemed about to say something, but we were interrupted by the arrival of a weasel-faced white youth at the back door, a dedicated follower of fashion with a Wrangler denim jacket from twenty years back, jeans and cowboy boots. His arms were covered in tattoos, he hadn't put a razor or soap and water to his pock-marked face for a week, and his greasy black hair looked like it had never been combed in his life.

He took a small brown paper bag from the pocket of his jacket and thrust it into Fat Al's hand. They exchanged a few grunts and he disappeared as quickly as he had arrived.

Fat Al stuffed the packet into his own pocket with a furtive look. He could not have looked more suspicious if he'd tried. If he'd just slapped the packet on the table I would have thought nothing of it. Now I would have bet a year's salary and a lifetime's supply of fish and chips that I'd seen a delivery of drugs.

On my way out he insisted on giving me one of his special kebabs. 'On the house. On me,' he said, as if he was buying the whole pub a round of champagne cocktails.

'That's very kind of you,' I said enthusiastically. 'Can I have it wrapped to take out?'

I managed a cheery smile and a thank you. I'm not a particularly fussy eater. I can't be, often having to take food wherever and whenever I can get it, but there are limits. As soon as I was out of the line of sight of the shop, I dumped it in a litter bin.

What I needed was a hot shower back at the Trafalgar. By this time I had developed a special relationship at my second home in the North-West. The receptionists had been highly suspicious at first, thinking I was either dealing in drugs or spying on the nearby British Aerospace factory. As I'd got to know them better, I found out that one, Caroline, an attract-ive blonde, was married to a crime squad officer, which gave us something in common. I felt I could confide in her a little and told her the nature of my work. It paid dividends. After that little conversation I found I could come and go without challenge, and I enjoyed as much security as I could ever expect in a hotel.

This time, I'd been told, a special room had been reserved for me and, however short the notice, they would always keep it for me. It was number 59, the one I'd had when I muddily interrupted the Preston Oddfellows' Ball. It was ground floor, window facing the traffic lights on the Blackburn Road, and I got the room half-price. I thought this was marvellous. How helpful and understanding they were, and how terrific to find a hotel where the staff cared so much about animals.

Later that night the barman let it slip that a man had committed suicide in the room and the chambermaids didn't like working in it. I had been wondering why the lock on the bathroom door was broken – they'd bashed the door down to find the dead man. Since then they never let the room unless absolutely necessary, so they thought it would be nice to allocate it as my private suite. I didn't mind. I wasn't superstitious.

I bought another beer and sat mulling over my next move. Fat Al had already committed one offence by selling me a piece of ivory in breach of the Convention on International Trade in Endangered Species, CITES. The maximum penalty for each offence was two years' imprisonment and/or a five-thousand-pound fine, but I was after much more.

I had enough information to get him pulled at the airport on his way back. Customs would arrest him for smuggling ivory, contrary to every law in the known universe, and we could tag the sale of the one tusk on top. More than that, though, Fat Al was no criminal mastermind. He was a go-between, a fetcher and carrier. He tried to make out he was a big cheese, but I didn't think he had the quality.

Somewhere someone was hiring poachers and arranging for payments, transport and storage, someone who had the power and the connections to commission the deaths of elephants and the transfer of their tusks across international borders to a central marketing point in Cairo. I'd found the last link of the chain in Darwen. I wanted the others, wherever they might be.

7

There are several special difficulties with my kind of undercover work. One is that you can have several jobs going on at once, which means you have to act as a number of different characters, and to slip in and out of their personas. Related to that, you need detailed knowledge of the subject. The terrier man knows his terriers, and the illegal importer knows his exotics, so you have to know them too. Further, as you become more experienced, you can get overconfident. Finally, you have no help if you're psychologically affected by your work.

Police officers, who tend to have fewer and longer undercover operations, have detailed debriefs and sessions with a psychologist to ensure that they don't get so locked into their acting role that they can't readapt to normal policing. It's a potentially serious issue. Some officers have suffered mentally, broken up with their spouses or had their careers ruined. Some have even switched allegiance to the wrong side of the law after forming bonds with criminals they were investigating that were too strong to break.

Debriefs and psychologists were luxuries that the RSPCA Special Operations Unit did not enjoy. We gave our own assessment of what had happened and that was that. It didn't particularly worry me, because I could never envisage any circumstances in which I'd form a genuine friendship with people who took pleasure in or profited from inflicting cruelty and misery on animals. Even my informants were kept at arm's length. None of them knew my surname or where I lived. If I went out of my way to look after them once in a while, it was in the interests of the job, not because we were best mates.

I'd intended to have a quiet couple of days at the office but my best northern informant, Darren, had other plans for me. One of the problems with the Darrens of this world – and there are many, many problems – is that they run with the hare and hunt with the hounds. If they get in trouble, they tend to avoid the normal sources of help, like the police, and come to the only respectable person they know, in this case me. I could hear the panic in his voice as soon as I answered the phone.

'I'm in a lot of trouble, Tony. It could get me killed.'

Darren had been a mixed blessing in my working life. We'd had some notable successes, but I'd also spent months chasing shadows and wild geese. Even so, I took him seriously, and six hours later I was pulling up outside his house. He was down the path before I'd opened the car door.

'You've got to help me, Tony, you've got to help me. I'm really in deep this time.'

This was not the Darren I knew, swaggering about as if he owned half of Lancashire. He was white in the face and his hands shook as he grabbed at my sleeve.

'Hang on a minute, Darren. I've been sitting in the car for the last six hours. Don't I get a cup of tea first?'

'No, no, no. We can't talk here. We'll go for a walk in the park.'

Before I could reply he was off. I bought a couple of cold drinks from the corner shop, we found a bench in a quiet place, and we sat down. I didn't know what to expect but I thought it might be dodgy.

Informers wouldn't be any use if they weren't dodgy, because they have to be able to mix on equal terms with the people the law is trying to nobble. Darren, naturally, was no exception. He could be as dodgy as the best of them, and there was no point in me making value judgements. Also, I suppose, I have to admit I quite liked the man, and today I was a friend and he was in need. I started to make small talk to relax him but he cut me off.

'You've got to help me get out of this one, Tony. There's no one else. And if you don't, I'll be dead by next week.'

'Difficult decision, Darren. Any particular day next week?'

'This is not funny, Tony. There's this guy called Lambert (not his real name). In Manchester. Big-time trader in, er, vegetable derivatives and, er, ironmongery. And because of a favour a pal of mine did for him, which in turn meant that . . .'

Darren's story went round the houses, up the stairs, out the back door and into the next county before its crux finally emerged. Somehow, through this convoluted and unfathomable process, Darren had managed to agree to supply Lambert with handguns and ammunition or, more correctly, to introduce him to someone who was a reliable professional in this specialised area of business. The fact that Darren didn't know such a person hadn't come into it at the time, apparently. Now it had, because time had run out. Lambert was keen to meet and do the deal. Perhaps 'keen' was understating it. Lambert had promised an abrupt and painful climax to the Life of Darren if something substantial didn't materialise in the immediate future.

'He means it, Tony. I know he means it.'

'And you want me to pose as this gun supplier? Are you off your head?'

He was almost in tears as he kept begging me to help him and I kept refusing. This was well out of my league. I was fine with poisonous snakes, both of the serpentine and badger-digging varieties, but armed drug dealers were something else. Of course, he wore me down in the end. Darren was a good informant and I had to do what I could to protect him. I decided not to inform Don what I was up to. I was allowed a certain amount of initiative but it certainly did not include impersonating an arms dealer. If I was found out, the least I could expect was a disciplinary hearing.

'All right,' I said. 'I'll do it. But you will owe me for this. My God, how you will owe me.' The regional crime squad would also owe me, I thought, if I could deliver Lambert into their clutches, which was the sort of debt that could prove handy one day.

Darren was practically doing somersaults of happiness. He called Lambert before I had a chance to change my mind and set up a meeting in a pub outside Preston at two o'clock the following afternoon.

I decided not to mention this particular job to Denise. She already worried enough about the type of undercover work I did. If I told her I was having meetings with non-dumb and tooled-up animals, rather than the usual sort, she might have gone beyond her established practice of reading out the job ads in the local paper. She might have felt compelled to visit the solicitor's office.

That evening, after phoning Denise from the Trafalgar and rejecting the idea of driving an ice-cream van or working in the garden centre, I began thinking about my cover story. I'd been into target shooting with large-bore handguns for a couple of years, so luckily I knew a bit about calibres and the street prices of various kinds of equipment. I decided to say that I'd just come out of the forces and could get guns through my army contacts.

We travelled to the meet in Darren's car. If this guy really was a big-time drug dealer he could have access to the police computer where he could check my registration and I'd be blown, probably literally, before I'd started. We also set off an hour earlier than we needed because, if I really was supplying guns, I'd be very cagey with someone I didn't know. I wanted to do a recce and make sure there was nothing untoward and no one lying in wait for me.

When I'd had a look around, Darren bought me a pint and we sat at a table in the beer garden, well away from the pub, where I could watch the entrance to the car park. Darren was in a right state, visibly shaking and very pale.

Smack on two o'clock a brand new red Porsche pulled in. I made a quick mental note of the number as the driver sauntered over to us with a cool, elegant slouch. He was in his early twenties and nasty-looking, with a head that wasn't just shaven but polished. He was wearing Armani jeans and an Armani shirt topped off with Armani dark glasses, plus a gold Rolex on his left wrist. I had to stifle a smile. He couldn't have looked more like the stereotype of a drug dealer if he'd tried.

Darren introduced us but didn't give my name, saying, 'Lambert, this is my mate,' before scuttling off to get him a drink. We passed the time by discussing the Porsche. I was expecting him to use Jamaican street slang, but he spoke more like a bank manager.

'It cost me over sixty grand,' Lambert said. 'Cash.'

Darren reappeared with the drinks. He didn't seem to be handling the situation too well. Carrying top-ups for us along with Lambert's fancy lager, he was shaking so much that he'd spilt half onto the tray in the short distance between the bar and the table. I thought the best way to distract Lambert's attention was to get straight to the point.

'Right then,' I said. 'What is it you want?'

'As many handguns as you can get.'

It seemed odd that he'd openly discuss buying an arsenal from me without checking my credentials or frisking me first. Then I had the astonishing thought that he must trust Darren. Maybe you do trust people when you are going to kill them if they let you down.

'Darren says you're okay,' I said, 'but I don't know you from a hole in the ground, and I don't do business with people I don't know. So this will be the first and last time you will see me, and any deals that we might do will be done through Darren.' That sounded good, I thought. I must have seen it in a film.

'No problem. So what can you get me, then?'

'Nine-millimetre Browning high powers.'

He raised his eyebrows. 'Excellent, just what I wanted. How much?'

'It depends on how many. Big discounts for bulk purchasers.'

'I can take as many as you can get. Thirty or forty?'

Thank Christ this isn't for real, I thought. Thirty or forty Browning high powers distributed among the drug dealers of Manchester was just what the country needed.

'Two hundred quid each, including a full clip of ammunition.'

'I would say that was expensive. I would say one fifty was nearer the mark, discounted, as it were, for bulk purchasers, wouldn't you?' He took a sip of his drink.

'That's the price,' I said, getting into my role. I gave him a 'take it or leave it, I don't care either way' look.

He sucked his teeth as he thought about it. 'Very well. Two hundred. At least thirty products. Delivery ASAP.'

'I'm out of the country tonight to sort something, give me a week to do the business . . . say a fortnight today. That suit you? I'll check in with Darren when it's all tied up.'

'I'll wait to hear from Darren, then. See you. Or not, as you say.' He didn't bother finishing his drink. Cool, man, Armani cool. And Porsche cool.

Suddenly Darren was patting me on the back, shaking my hand and thanking me. I think I preferred the nervous version.

'I'll see you right for this, Tony, you see if I don't. You saved my life.'

'Only for the next two weeks, Darren.'

'No worries. I'll think of something.'

I passed Lambert's description and car registration to a good friend of mine, Sue Taylor, who used to work in the regional crime squad and still had the contacts there. She called me back later to confirm that Lambert was genuine. He was on file as one of the main dealers in Manchester and had already been implicated in a couple of drive-by shootings. They were grateful for the tip. The squad had been looking for an excuse to turn up the heat and now they had one.

I was always happy to notch up a few Brownie points with my CID colleagues. I only hoped that these particular points were still good for something when I heard, a few weeks later, that Lambert had disappeared and that a person answering his description had been seen frequenting seaside restaurants and lounging around swimming pools in Spain. Perhaps he'd been tipped off about the crime squad interest in him, or maybe one of the other drug dealers had made him an offer he dared not refuse; either way, Darren seemed to be off the hook.

I drove back to Horsham that night, and when I appeared in the office the next morning even Don was impressed by what I'd managed to get on Fat Al. Unbelievably he had also made progress on getting my two fifty back for the tusk, but he wanted to know how I proposed to get a lead on Fat Al's supplier.

The normal course of action to identify associates of a criminal is to obtain information through the police. Trying to identify someone from Egypt through this method was another order of difficulty again. The bureaucracy involved in working through Interpol was bad enough, but the real obstacle was our lack of trust in the Egyptian authorities. If ivory could be smuggled through Cairo at the drop of a banknote, then it was odds on that any suspects we might find would be warned before we could get to them.

I was determined to succeed – think of the publicity for the RSPCA, Don – but he thought the likelihood of finding the supplier was so remote that we should go with what we had, plus a full dossier on Fat Al. I argued for more time, but Don was adamant. I was to set about building up a profile of Kefah Almomani to pass on to Customs and Excise. They would need good photographs and anything else we could find out through surveillance.

I couldn't do the surveillance, obviously, because he already knew me, so the rest of the unit would work on that while I hid in the back of an observation vehicle trying to take pictures. As a rule I didn't mind that job, but the heatwave showed no sign of letting up and the back of the van would be hotter than Fat Al's kebab grill.

Came the day and I was up at three a.m. to prepare the van and test all the surveillance equipment. Paul drove it into position near BB's house at half five, before it got light.

Once on site, movement had to be kept to an absolute minimum. I placed my equipment within easy reach but I had to know exactly where it all was. Even though the van was padded, the noise of something being knocked over might be enough to give me away. Hot drinks were out, because they steamed up the windows, and anything liable to make a noise, like a crisp packet or a plastic sandwich triangle, had to be removed in advance.

Some officers can't stand static surveillance, whether they're stuck in the back of a vehicle or dug into a hillside. I sort of enjoyed it. It was a challenge, and if it needed doing it had to be done properly and professionally. The concentration levels were high, especially if you had a small area of vision, which was more usual than not.

All I had this time was Fat Al's front door. If I took my eyes off it for a couple of seconds to grab a sandwich or take a leak, I might miss him, so everything was done without losing sight of that front door. It takes years of practice to be able to eat your sandwiches or pee into a bottle without looking. There's a game I played at a party once where I had to eat a sugary meringue without licking my lips. Static surveillance is harder than that.

I had a video camera and a stills camera mounted on a tripod, already focused on the front door. The stills camera was on a cable release. If I was lucky, I'd get Fat Al after he'd had his breakfast. If I was less lucky, he'd stay at home for a few hours before venturing forth. If I was really unlucky, I'd have to sit in the van all day and still not see him.

My luck was out. I took up station wearing a T-shirt, jeans and a pair of trainers but by eleven o'clock, with the sun burning down, it must have been forty degrees or more in the back of that van. Very carefully, without missing any door movement, I stripped to my underpants, which made no difference whatsoever. I baked, in a tin oven, and nobody was going to open the oven door until Fat Al appeared.

Every thirty minutes one of the other lads from the unit, parked down the road, would give me a radio check. I was on silent routine and couldn't speak, so I'd give him three clicks for yes. That was my only contact with my colleagues throughout the day and, towards the end of it, three clicks was getting to be hard labour.

I'd only taken two litres of water in with me, and by five o'clock I'd long since finished it and was seriously dehydrating. I had to put up with the discomfort. There was no possibility of any more water being passed through my van window, the sun wasn't going to go behind a cloud and Fat Al would do what he liked. Now I knew what it felt like being a dog shut in a car on a hot summer's day. I was equally helpless, only this wasn't an ordinary hot day. This would have done credit to high noon in Marrakesh.

I expected my ordeal to end at any moment and that was what kept me going. If I had known then how long I was going to be slow-roasted, I might have asked someone to take a small risk to save my life. As it was, since the next minute didn't feel particularly worse than the last minute, I stayed in the oven for the duration, gradually sinking into a torpor without realising it. Air and water are two basic necessities of life, and I was getting very short of both.

I'd seen BB twice but there'd been no glimpse of Fat Al. If he hadn't eventually come when he did, I think I might have been unconscious, but at half past five in the afternoon he finally turned up. I managed to get some good shots of him entering the house and had a bonus three minutes later. A black Ford Capri drove up and a scruffy oik in a brown leather jacket jumped out. Fat Al came to the door and took an envelope from him, went back inside and reappeared with a package that he stuffed into the lad's hand. The lad was off straight away. I'd got him on film and noted his registration number.

Ten minutes later a different youth arrived and the same thing happened again. This was good news and bad news. It confirmed my earlier suspicions that Fat Al was dealing in drugs, but it also meant that I now had to take my evidence to the police; another agency had a chance to get to him before we did.

Sweat was still pouring from me and I'd lost so much fluid I was finding it difficult to concentrate, but it was another half an hour before my carpiece crackled and I heard the message I'd been waiting for. 'Stand down. Stand down.'

All the call signs acknowledged in order. I was the last one and gave the three clicks that showed I had received the message. I began a slow and deliberate check of all the equipment, ensuring that it was securely stowed before the van was moved. I took the SLR camera from its tripod but kept it handy in case anything else developed during the last knockings. My earpiece crackled again.

'Be with you in one minute.' Paul was walking towards the van wearing his covert body kit so he could talk to me. If Fat Al or BB was hanging about as he approached, I'd give Paul two clicks on the radio and he would walk straight past, do a circuit, and somebody else would take his place to collect the vehicle. There was no sign of either of them.

'All clear. Come and get it.'

I heard the front door of the van open and someone get in. 'Good God above,' the voice said. 'It's like an oven in here.' Wait till he feels where I am, I thought. Oven? Furnace, more like.

Still sealed off by the metal wall of the cab, I braced myself for the journey. It was a good ten minutes before we reached my moorland spot. Paul opened the back door of the van and reeled back as the heat hit him.

'Jesus Christ,' he said.

I crawled out, weak, nauseous and light-headed. I'd never been so relieved to get out of anything in my life. The sun had almost set and there was a breeze but it didn't seem to be lowering my body temperature at all. I needed to get some liquid down my neck, and fast.

Paul produced a bottle of water and I gulped half of it down in one go. I felt like John Mills in *Ice Cold in Alex*, when he's been marching through the desert for three days and has a cold beer at the end of it. I poured the remainder of the bottle over my head and down the back of my neck. Even after a drive with the sunroof and all the windows open, it took me two hours and a few more litres of water to cool down properly.

Next day I went to the Darwen police and met a sergeant who reminded me of the one in the old TV series *Hill Street Blues*. I could imagine him saying, 'Be careful out there in Darwen, it's a jungle,' as he sent his men out on to the streets. He'd spent twenty-odd years in the local force and reckoned he'd seen everything.

'It all happens here,' he said. 'We have the complete crime encyclopaedia.'

So I gave him the story about Fat Al and the elephant tusk.

'Never heard anything like that before,' he said. 'But what did I tell you? If it's going to happen anywhere, it'll happen in Darwen.'

Fat Al's drug dealing, however, was no surprise. The police already had some information on him from their Drugs Intelligence Unit, but the three youths making the drop-offs and pick-ups were not previously known.

Darwen police and the RSPCA were not the only ones

chasing him, apparently. Immigration and the Benefits Agency people were also queuing up. This was not what I wanted to hear. We were no different from the other agencies in one respect. We had to get results to justify our existence, and if one of the others pulled Fat Al before I did, my ivory job would be up the spout. And, secretly still hoping to find the missing link back to Cairo, I needed him more than they did. On top of that, he hadn't yet committed the big crime that we wanted to nick him for, walking through the green channel at Heathrow with four tusks in his hand luggage. I could only hope that none of the others would get to him before then.

The other worry was having to hand responsibility for the case over to customs. They had sole jurisdiction over illegal imports and exports. Naturally we resented it, having done the build-up and surveillance and taken the undercover risks only to be pushed aside with no further part to play, but we were also concerned about the risk of conflict and confusion inside the customs service.

We liaised regularly with the CITES – Convention on International Trading in Endangered Species – team, a dedicated group of customs officers based at Heathrow who had a wealth of knowledge about endangered species and the legislation governing their protection, but they were not officially classed as customs investigators. We could pass our information to the CITES team, but they were duty-bound to pass it on to the surveillance and investigative officers at the airport, the CCU – Customs Collections Unit.

I gave a telephone briefing to my CITES friends, so they would be in the know, and said I would be passing the file shortly. It didn't take long before the phone rang. It was Jane Gordon of the CCU, who gave me a hard time for even discussing the matter with the CITES people.

'You had no business talking to them,' she said rather crisply.

'They're our first port of call. You know that. CITES and RSPCA. We go to them and they come to us.'

'I don't care. You shouldn't have discussed it with them. We're the investigators, we're the ones who are on the ground and have the training.'

'Look,' I said, irritated. 'Fine. I'm not interested in your internal politics. You, here and now, are taking complete responsibility for catching our man.'

'Just send me the package you have on him and we'll deal with it.' She was very abrupt, to say the least.

I took a deep breath and counted to ten. 'No, I won't send it. I'll bring it. We've done a lot of hard work on this guy. I'll bring it down to Heathrow and hand it over to you in person.'

The intelligence packet I gave her contained everything we knew about Fat Al, his girlfriend, his vehicle, his background, his associates, his drug dealing, plus details of all the other agencies that were interested in him. There were also detailed descriptions and some excellent head and shoulder photographs of Fat Al and BB.

If best use was made of this first-rate material, I was handing customs one of the biggest, if not *the* biggest, ivory jobs ever on a plate, but their attitude suggested they were doing us a favour. After I'd handed it over I offered to be present when Fat Al arrived at Heathrow.

'We don't need you,' Jane said. 'Thanks for the offer, but we'll manage. We have everything we need.'

I'd given customs my home and mobile numbers in case there were any developments but I didn't expect many calls. Meanwhile the best way to avoid any chance of compromising the job was to stay right out of Fat Al's way.

Jane had promised to ring me as soon as he was pulled, so

the day he was due back in England I stayed at home waiting for the call. I did think about driving down to Heathrow, in case they needed me, but after the reception I'd had last time I didn't really believe it was worth it.

The flight was due to land at 14.20. I watched the clock. Twenty minutes since the flight landed. It would take quite a while to get through the baggage hall, assuming he had a suitcase of clothes as well as the ivory, and up to customs control, but by three o'clock we should be getting a result. At a quarter to four the telephone rang.

'I've got good news and bad news,' Jane said, as if we were playing some sort of parlour game. The lightness in her voice was false. She was going to tell me something terrible and was trying to pretend it didn't matter too much. 'The good news is he landed at Heathrow on the flight you said he would, and at the time you said.'

'And the bad news?' I said, wondering how she was going to phrase it. Was there a good way of rephrasing 'Almighty cock-up'?

'The bad news is that we weren't able to pay him any attention until he'd actually cleared the terminal.'

I realised I was gripping the telephone so hard that I was in danger of squeezing juice out of it. I had this mad picture of Fat Al walking through the green channel with a pair of tusks under each arm, smiling broadly and bowing graciously to Jane as she saluted and waved him through.

'You what?' I said. 'We give you the date, the time, the airport, the airline, a full description, photographs . . . and he walks through customs without you noticing?'

I hardly bothered trying to register her pathetic reasons. Short-staffed, diverted to another incident, the moon was in its first quarter, there wasn't an R in the month. It was a load of vintage cobblers and she knew it.

'You refuse to let us help and then make a complete balls of the whole operation. And you call it good news and bad news? I'll tell you what, Jane the fully trained investigator on the ground, it will be a very long time and under extreme duress before I put any work your way again.'

I hung up the phone with such a bang that it nearly came off the wall. I swore to myself for a few minutes, trying to soothe my disappointment at the waste of all that time, effort and nervous energy. Disappointments were a regular feature in my line of work, but on the Richter scale of cock-ups this took some beating.

I rang Don at home and told him. He took it even worse than me, partly because the more senior you get the more helpless and disillusioned you can feel about ever getting anything important done. The RSPCA has no statutory powers in these sorts of investigations, yet we have all the expertise and all the education.

The Special Operations Unit has been trained to advanced level in mobile surveillance by the police regional crime squads, and in evidence gathering and urban surveillance by Special Branch and ex-members of 14th Intelligence Company. We've also been trained in covert role-playing, rural operations, planning, intelligence systems and observation by ex-members of the Special Air Service, and in interview techniques and general evidence gathering by the CID.

If any other agencies had undergone such broad and intensive training I'd never heard about them. On top of all that we had a huge amount of practical experience.

After Don and I had slagged off customs and moaned about the injustice of it all, I felt a little better. It was time to try and find a way of salvaging the situation. I couldn't see any other first step towards retrieval than going to see Fat Al and trying to buy the ivory he'd just brought through. We would then have a straightforward offence and could prosecute without any further involvement from customs.

There was always the possibility that Jane hadn't told me everything, however. Suppose they had spooked Fat Al in some little detail? Suppose some blunderer had let him see that he was being watched? For all I knew they might even have notified the authorities in Egypt, in which case Fat Al could have been tipped off and come through clean anyway.

There was an additional danger in BB. I hadn't seen her in ages and we had been flirtatious. She might have felt scorned by my ignoring her. She might have decided to stick the knife in me. In conversation with Fat Al over the breakfast table, she might have mentioned all she'd told me, or I'd tricked her into saying, or I'd forced out of her.

Fat Al was no model citizen. He would take unscrupulous revenge on anyone who deceived him, probably assisted by his Olympic wrestler friends, but these were all risks I had to take or we could move no further forward. Fat Al's takeaway it had to be, regardless of who might be sitting in the back room ready to tear me into kebab-sized pieces.

As it happened he was alone in the shop when I arrived there early in the evening. As I walked in he was sharpening his slicing knives. Was it my imagination, or did his sharpening develop a new intensity when he saw me? In any case, he gave me only the briefest of nods. On my previous visit he'd not been the great old buddy at first, so this needn't have meant much, but he should have been expecting me. He had definitely promised to save the ivory for me and, above all, he stood to make a large amount of money. I thought I might have anticipated a warmer welcome.

'How did it go?' I said.

'No good,' he said.

'What do you mean, no good? I've got customers waiting.'

'No good. Couldn't get it this time.' He was still sharpening his knives. 'Maybe next time. Maybe not.'

'I thought we had a deal. I was relying on you. What went wrong?'

He shrugged, very off-hand, took up a different and very large knife, and drew the edge lovingly across the sharpening stone.

'Oh well,' I said, 'I'll keep in touch. I'll want to know when you're getting more stuff.'

'Okay,' he said, meaning 'get lost'.

As I drove back to the Trafalgar my brain was in a knot. Nothing seemed to add up. He was impolite by nature, but we had struck a deal for a lot of tusks in four-tusk deliveries, worth several thousand quid. Since our last meeting some bad weather had turned the milk sour. If it was something I had done or had control over, I could not put my finger on it, but I had lost the psychological upper hand and needed to know why.

With the police, immigration and all the other agencies looking at him, plus the chance that he might have had an inkling about the fiasco with customs, there was a wide choice of yellow and red alerts, but it was no good me going around and around the problem. I didn't know, and on my present information I couldn't know. So sod it, and have a large Jameson's.

It's all very well telling yourself to be logical, but it's extremely difficult to stop your brain working. I must have slipped up somewhere. Whatever it was I'd done, I had very little time to correct the situation. The other agencies were closing in and, if Fat Al had brought in some ivory, in his present frame of mind he wouldn't be sitting on it. The only plan I could come up with was to try BB. Maybe I could get something out of her.

I drove into Darwen at six the following evening and parked about a hundred and fifty yards down the road from the kebab shop. Using a small pair of binoculars hidden in the palm of my hand, I could see the door of the shop and identify anyone going in or out. Fat Al arrived about six thirty, followed soon afterwards by two of his assistants. I gave him another thirty minutes to make sure that it wasn't a fleeting visit, then I drove to his house.

How dangerous this game would prove would depend on how much Fat Al confided in BB. Somehow I thought not a lot, but there was no guarantee, especially if the reason he'd gone off me was because of BB's indiscretions. He might well have mentioned my summary dismissal from the shop the previous night and, being Fat Al and a cunning rat, he might well have arranged a surprise for me should I do the obvious and contact BB.

If there was a trap, either she wasn't in on it or she was a very good actress. She greeted me with a big smile and asked me in like she was Mae West and I was Cary Grant. She was dressed to go out somewhere, and had made a vain attempt to disguise felltop mutton as river-valley lamb – too much make-up, too low a neckline, too high a hemline. Her overdose of perfume, mingled with the ingrained smell of a thousand cigarettes, made her equal last choice in the personal aroma competition with Fat Al's uniquely powerful combination of old spiced goat, garlic and sweat.

She offered me a glass of wine.

'I can't,' I said. 'I'm driving.'

She filled her own glass, right to the brim. If she was trying to get oiled before she went out, was it so she wouldn't have to spend too much money at the pub, or so she could get a head start on the evening?

'I'm off on a girls' night out,' she said.

The thought of BB and a gang of her mates around Darwen made me shudder. No man would be safe. Mind you, I wouldn't have minded being a fly on the wall.

'Kefah not here?'

'No, he's at work. He's always working this time of night.'

'Oh, yeah, I forgot.' I scratched my head. 'I saw him last night and he seemed very off-hand. I thought I must have upset him somehow.'

'Don't you worry about that fat twat.' She paused, watching me. 'Never mind him, Tony. Why don't you come for a few drinks with me?'

'I can't. Like I said, I'm driving.' Bloody hell, she was more frightening than Fat Al and the Jordanian super-heavyweight team, but without her I was stranded with no clues. She was my only route to more information on the ivory smugglers. She mightn't know anything, but if she did I was fairly sure she wouldn't mind telling me. I forced a smile.

'Oh, go on then, I'll have a glass of wine with you. One won't do any harm.'

She poured me a large glass of supermarket Liebfraumilch, nice and warm. I took a sip, forced another smile, and tried to drag the conversation back onto my chosen ground.

'Well, whatever it is I've done, it's a shame. I don't like to lose business this way.'

She didn't reply, plainly bored with the topic and too busy adding another layer of crimson lipstick. Her mind was obviously elsewhere, weighing up the relative merits of an evening with a sober and reluctant me, or getting plastered and no doubt pulling a more co-operative victim. All this was getting me nowhere. I had to accept that the job was totally beyond redemption. I might as well finish my wine and go home, unless . . .

'Right,' I said, draining my glass. 'I'll just use your toilet if I may, and then I'll get off.'

'It's upstairs, top of the landing,' she said, adjusting her bra and pulling her top down in an attempt to reveal some cleavage.

When I reached the landing I saw the main bedroom door was ajar. I glanced back down the stairs. BB was still preening herself in front of the kitchen mirror. Everywhere was quiet, except for the loud, slow tick of the only decent stick of furniture in the place, a grandfather clock on the landing. I presumed it was BB's family heirloom, and found its steady rhythm reassuring.

I quickly checked the other two rooms, making sure nobody else was in the house, then slipped into the bedroom, noting how wide the door was ajar so I could replace it exactly on my way out.

I didn't know what to find there but Fat Al was my first link in a criminal chain, at the other end of which were dead elephants. Somehow he should be able to lead me to the men in the middle.

I didn't have long. Even BB would wonder at me taking more than a minute or two in the loo, then a chance word to Fat Al might result in some orders being issued to the Jordanian Steam Hammer and his mate. I had a feeling that elephants wouldn't be the only dead and dying in such a case.

The bedroom was furnished in plastic-coated MDF-and-hardboard in brilliant white. The matching wardrobes, dressing table and bedside units all had white plastic knobs with gold trim. There was a double bed with co-ordinated mauve velvet headboard and duvet. A pair of cord jeans was hanging over the bottom of the bed and a rather strange baby-doll pyjama outfit in red and black lace with certain parts missing. I had a little smile to myself as I wondered which one of them wore that.

The clock ticked. There was silence downstairs. If BB had already come up to watch me, she was a silent mover. There was very little left to search, my time was certainly up and it looked like the game was lost. I had risked going three rounds with the Amman Strangler for nothing.

A telephone stood on the bedside cabinet and next to it there was an address book. I flicked through it. It only had a few numbers in and they all seemed fairly local. As I was closing it, I noticed a piece of paper inside the front cover. Written on it was a name, Amr Saad, and a telephone number. I got excited as I realised that the number started with 00 20, the code for Egypt. I had no idea whether the name and number were going to do me any good, but I had saved something from the wreckage.

I copied the number onto my own piece of paper and replaced the original. Making sure BB wasn't in sight, I closed the bedroom door to the same position, flushed the toilet in the bathroom and went back downstairs. It had all happened within the space of two minutes or so, and I was fairly sure BB wouldn't have thought anything of it.

'Right,' I said. 'Now I've really got to go. And so have you.'

'You'd have more fun if you came with me. Promise.'

'Yes, well, I have to see a man about a dog. Another time, when I'm not pressed. I always say you need plenty of time to enjoy yourself properly.'

'You are so right, Tony love. I'll see you next time. You and your white bits.'

'I might not have any white bits. I might be brown all over. Must be off. See you.'

She stayed on the doorstep to give me a wave as I walked to the car. Back at the office the next morning I told Don what had happened.

'You're wasting your time,' he said. 'Give it a rest. You can't get anything out of it now, it's dead. Get on with something else.'

Don was probably right. I didn't know how to get back in with Fat Al. I didn't know if he had any ivory or not. All I did know was a phone number beginning 00 20.

8

—

Paperwork. It was the bane of my life. I don't expect that makes us different from any firm, whether it's the RSPCA or ICI.

This particular day was an exception because I was clearing up after an unusually messy but moderately successful court case. Over there on the corner of my desk a mountain of intelligence reports from uniformed RSPCA inspectors and police wildlife officers awaited my attention. I knew for a fact that we wouldn't be able to do anything about 99 per cent of them, so it wasn't a job I was looking forward to. They could wait while I sorted out the file on the Isle of Wight fox-hunters.

Packs of foxhounds invariably have terrier men attached, officially or voluntarily or both, and groups of terrier men sometimes include badger diggers and cockfighters among them. There is also a network of such terrier men, a kind of grapevine, so that badger-digging opportunities are seldom missed.

Our case was against the huntsman of the Isle of Wight pack and a terrier man from a hunt in Essex. It happened that they were especially over-confident, or lackadaisical, whichever and, because we had a particularly courageous and determined informant, we had very little difficulty collaring them. We caught them in the act, digging badgers in a wood on the island, and that was that, we thought. Then the fun really started.

The informant was the first to feel the backlash. Somehow he was identified and then he began to receive threats, had his car damaged and had his life made generally difficult. Despite all this, he stuck to the cause.

Hunting people, like any special interest group, can also stick up for themselves. The difference here was that the hunting people and the followers were also top people, socially and financially. They had the brass and they had the connections.

Terrier men and professional huntsmen are almost always from the lower orders, without the resources to fight a legal battle, but the best lawyers in the business, barristers from London, were hired at huge cost to defend these two worthless rats. Private detectives were also put on the case to gather information that might discredit me and other RSPCA witnesses.

The papers had a marvellous time, with the pro- and anti-hunt lobbies jumping up and down. The problem with the fox-hunting issue is that there is no logic to it but a lot of emotion. Clearly it's a cruel, bloodthirsty, primitive and inefficient way of controlling foxes. If the wild fox population ever got out of hand, a couple of village men who knew what they're doing with a rifle would kill far more more foxes than a hunt ever could.

Similarly if you asked a gypsy or a countryman how he would catch a fox with dogs, he'd tell you. He'd have a scent hound to put the fox up and a sight hound, a lurcher, to run it down. Nobody wanting simply to reduce the fox population would chase them with a load of lumbering, oafish dogs who would probably never catch a fit fox without a lot of help. They only manage to run one down because they're bred for stamina and the long chase – which is the real point. No, the control argument doesn't hold up, and neither does the conservation theory. Hunters say that if they didn't have the hunt farmers would poison and shoot and the fox would be wiped out. It's nice to know that, while they are watching hounds tear a fox to pieces, they are actually thinking about the welfare of the species.

The truth is that certain people enjoy a challenging day's horse ride over the wide countryside but need the excuse of blood, cruel death and all the fox-hunting palaver to go with it.

Once you have established the premise that this is hunting, as opposed to steeplechasing, you then have to get results, and if the hunt wants to be sure of a kill on a particularly important day that's what has to happen. They go to considerable lengths to achieve this, for instance digging up fox cubs, killing the vixen and rearing the cubs in a shed or a dog run. Or they trap and keep foxes in false earths, to be released on the hunting day. The earths are underground chambers, perhaps made of brick or mains drainpipes. Terrier men net a fox or two and imprison them in the earth, giving them food and water and keeping them there for perhaps a week. Early on the morning of the meet, the terrier man takes a fox in a sack and sets it free in a copse that he knows will be drawn. It's daylight, so the fox goes to ground – hides in cover – and what do you know? Here come the hounds. The fox is on strange territory. It's not fully fit after its time in prison. The hunt gets its kill.

Of course hunting people deny this happens, but I have seen it, and I've seen many other things on hunts too, including the brilliant picture of three foxes coming together out of a small wood the hunt was drawing. They appeared to have a conversation about their current difficulties, then shot off in three different directions across open country, never to be found. One of them ran across the lane where I was standing, not ten yards from me. I swear it gave me a wink as it ran past.

Fox-hunting had nothing to with our Isle of Wight prosecution except that it did and does attract badger diggers, as well as those who are willing and able to pay for their defence. This time, though, justice prevailed. All the smooth-talking barristers and private detectives in the world could not break down our case and the two were convicted. With costs and fines together, they each had a thousand quid to pay, and the huntsman emigrated to Canada, where he found a new pack to hunt.

That was that. The file labelled 'Isle of Wight' could be sent to the archives and I could get myself a coffee, allow myself a brief moment of quiet satisfaction, then get on with the pile of intelligence reports. This task always fills me with dismay and frustration. We are supplied with thousands, literally thousands of good leads by our hardworking people out in the field, and we can do almost nothing with them. We don't have the resources to start on any but a few of the most promising, and even then we know that most will fall away somewhere in the process. Today, however, the pile seemed unusually well seeded with practical and attractive prospects.

Here was one about a man in Cheshire who was supplying mutton to Asian restaurants as halal meat – slaughtered in the traditional way according to religious rules by a qualified religious person. The only trouble was that our man wasn't at all qualified, religiously or otherwise. He didn't even have any butchery training. He was buying sheep at auction and slitting their throats himself, inhumanely and in dirty conditions, without any of the proper care and attention, to save the few quid it cost to have them done properly. That looked like the kind of case we could investigate and wrap up in a rapid and economical way. Put it on the possibles pile.

Here was another good one, about a man in Chesterfield who was keeping a seven-foot alligator in his council flat. That was a definite starter for ten.

'David,' I said. 'How's your alligator-wrestling?'

'I taught James Bond, mate,' said our most recent acquisition, David Atkins, ex-REME and Tank Regiment and a Gulf War veteran.

'When I was in the desert fighting the Saracen hordes,' he continued, 'there was nothing we liked better than a bit of alligator-wrestling at the weekend.'

Leaving aside the issue of desert dwelling species of alligator, I passed him the report and asked him to get on to it. Meanwhile, looking at the next report in the pile, I saw that I was going back to the Isle of Wight.

Would this badger-digging issue never go away? Here was a report from Simon Ford, the inspector I'd worked with on the case against the huntsman, saying that a Lakeland terrier had been found wandering about the moors near Sandown. The man who found it while out walking his own dog had handed it in to the police, pointing out that the poor little thing had half its lower jaw missing. The police immediately called in Simon, who took one look and said, 'Badger.' The vet agreed. Such an injury could only have been caused by a badger.

So far this was a run-of-the-mill report, of special interest only because it came from the Isle of Wight, proving that as soon as you lock up one toerag another takes his place. But this time the man moving in to the vacated spot had a special place in my heart. He was none other than Geoffrey Verril. A man giving that name had come to claim the terrier.

'See you, Don,' I called as I headed for the door.

'Now just you hang on a minute, Tony,' said Don. 'Where are you going now?'

'I thought I'd have a few days in the Isle of Wight. It's nice there at this time of year.'

'The reason being?'

'The reason being, Don, that a certain example of the species *Homo illegitimus*, name of Verril, has been spotted with soil in his fingernails.'

'Good luck, my friend,' said Don, with real feeling. 'Bring him back, dead or alive.'

I left a message on the answering machine for Denise, which was about as much notice as she had come to expect. I even had a packed bag in the car, always ready with everything I needed for a few days away, so whenever anything came up I was gone.

A few hours later I was at the door of the RSPCA strays' kennels, which was where the terrier had convalesced and where Verril had picked it up. If it was him. When the kennel maid gave me the description, there was no doubt. It was him all right. I was on the trail again.

He'd spun her some line about how the dog had escaped from his garden and gone off somewhere on its own. The kennel maid was a forceful woman. She wasn't going to swallow that one.

'I wasn't having that,' she told me. 'I could see the Lakeland was no domestic pet. It was a working terrier. It had the scars. It had the conjunctivitis. So I said to this man, "It was a badger did this. Somebody put this brave little dog down a badger sett and it got its mouth torn in half for its trouble."'

'Good Lord,' I said. 'What did the man say to that?'

'He couldn't say anything, could he? He tried. Came up with some load of cobblers about how he knew nothing about that. He was totally ignorant of such things. Of course it was a brave and determined animal. It had been known to pick fights with much bigger dogs. If it had come across a badger sett it must have found a way in and got into a scrap. Well, I looked at him and I said, "I'll tell you what," I said, "I think you ought to take up writing poetry, because you've got a wonderful imagination."'

I looked at her. She was just a slip of a thing but she had more guts in confronting Verril than most men would have had.

'What happened then?'

'He muttered something about thank you very much for looking after him, paid the vet's bill, and off he went.'

I had to admire her, but alarm bells were ringing. I'd already found out that the original intelligence report was a fortnight old by the time I saw it. The kennel conversation was four days ago. The trail, I thought, was getting colder and fainter by the minute.

I met up with Simon Ford for my next visit, to the veterinary surgeon who had carried out two complicated and delicate operations to rebuild the dog's jaw. The vet was in no doubt about the origins of its dreadful injury. The dog's eyes and coat were full of mud. Here was an experienced and war-scarred badger digger's terrier, no question.

I spent the next two days tracking down Verril. Unlike his usual behaviour, he had been keeping his head well down. Nobody knew anything about him – police, badger group, RSPCA of course, nobody. He had been on the island five months and had managed not to come to the attention of anyone.

I found out that he was running a small shoot near Sandown, which was quite a come-down for him. He'd been used to head keeper's jobs on large estates owned by the landed gentry, not managing the kind of set-up he could have sorted with his eyes closed and both hands in his pockets. I wondered if he'd had a domestic break-up. What was he doing on the Isle of Wight of all places?

Verril had to be spotted and followed, so I sat in my favourite disguise, a large gorse bush, about a hundred yards from his tied cottage. There was no sign of life when I climbed into my bush at about seven in the evening, no vehicle, no light on inside, no smoke from the chimney, and there was still none eight hours later. Possibly he was out after poachers. I decided to wait. At seven the next morning I gave up.

Verril was a cautious, watchful, shrewd character. He must have thought about the incident with the kennel maid, and how she'd brought up the subject of badgers with such clear intent. He must have regretted giving his real name, not knowing that was going to happen, and would have put two and two together. If the kennel maid knew, the rest of the RSPCA knew. We would be after him. He'd done a runner.

We needed to know for certain, so I asked Simon to call round. He could say a neighbour had complained about the state he kept his terriers in. Nobody came to the door and a few enquiries quickly established that Verril – and family – had decamped two days previously. The owner of the shoot said he'd found a better job on the mainland, but Simon thought he wasn't quite telling all he knew.

Two days. I'd been on the island in time, but I'd missed him. I briefed Simon on Verril's life history, left him to it, and got on the ferry in a very depressed state. I couldn't blame the kennel maid. She was only showing her emotions up front, attempting to make Verril feel some shame, letting him know that she knew that he knew. Even so, I wished a more timid lass had been on duty that day, or one who didn't know so much about terrier injuries. If he hadn't been spooked, I might have caught Verril this time.

The last word on the Isle of Wight connection came a week later. Simon rang up. The badger group had been through their records and noted that five months before two badger bodies had been found by the roadside. They had looked nothing like a double road accident so a sympathetic vet had had a look at them. They had been covered in dog bites and stabbed through the heart, left side, with a big knife.

My working life has been full of surprises but also depressingly full of predictable people. It was written in the stars that wherever Verril was badgers would be stabbed to death.

Similarly it was never any surprise at all to find that a reptile fancier was heavily built and shaven-headed, with tattoos and earrings, and that where reptiles were traded the name of Blakey was sure to crop up.

The small world of herpetology – reptiles – attracts some strange characters, a few of them fairly reptilian themselves. Those herpetologists with a special interest in venomous snakes are in a bit of a spot because so many of the species they want to study are subject to all kinds of laws and licences. To the genuine people this is no problem, but there are always plenty of opportunities to import and sell illegally.

As is often the way with people who treat live animals as goods and chattels, for sale to any bidder, dealers in the snake market are not famous for the great care they take of their charges. They might be amazingly expert on species and sub-species, able to reel off the Latin name for every snake that slithers, but they don't seem so good at feeding, watering and providing an environment that vaguely resembles home to these creatures, some of which come from the wildest of wild places.

Paul Blakey (not his real name) was one of these, an authority on all things venomous and deeply knowledgeable, but careless of welfare. That made him a target for me. However, partly because he was so well connected in herpetological society, I had a feeling it was going to be troublesome.

During 2000, David came back with a lot of useful information on our latest reptile case, the Mississippi alligator in Chesterfield. He had been using his charms on one of our target's neighbours – bored housewife, David said – and had found out quite a story.

Apparently a few years before a young, newly married couple had moved into the council flat next door to David's informant and, not long afterwards, had called this particular neighbour round to see one of their wedding presents. It was a lizardy kind of thing, she said, yellow and brown. The newlyweds claimed it was an alligator but the neighbour hadn't believed them, not even when the man who'd brought it had given her a lecture on it. This man, the man who'd brought it, looked like a cross between Meatloaf and Mick Jagger, she said.

'Mr Blakey,' I said to David. 'Paul Blakey. Herpetologist extraordinary. One of my life's works.'

David continued. 'Any road up, as I believe you say in the North, everything was fine and dandy for quite a while. The neighbour stopped calling when the alligator, for such it proved to be, went over the metre in length. This didn't matter to the 'gator. It just grew and grew. They gave it its own bedroom, with a plastic paddling pool for refreshing dips, and fed it ever greater quantities of dead rats and rabbits. Then, one day, there was the most awful kerfuffle. Sounded like a triple murder was being committed.'

'Did she phone the police? The neighbour, I mean?'

'They don't phone the police on that sort of council estate, Tony. No, she went round and banged on the door. There was still a lot of shouting, so she banged again, then there was silence. The woman came to the door in tears and let the neighbour in without a word. At first she didn't notice anything, then, on the couch, she saw it. She thought it was one of those cuddly toys you put a hot water bottle in. If it was, it used to be white and the hot water bottle had burst, full of red paint or ketchup or blood.'

'Good God, David, what was it?'

'The neighbour got the clue when her eye caught a little flash of red and yellow tartan. That was the tartan collar the woman's dog wore. The thing on the couch was a West Highland white terrier.'

'Which the alligator had . . .'

'. . . tried to have for dinner. By amazing luck it was still alive. The two women packed it into a laundry basket with blankets all around, got on the bus and took it to a vet, who could not understand the injuries. Never seen anything like it. The women said the Westie had been set on by two Rottweilers, which the vet accepted even if he didn't believe it. One week and seven hundred quid later it was back home and certain ultimata had been delivered, which basically boiled down to a simple choice the husband had to make: the alligator, or his wife.'

I had to laugh. American alligators can live to be fifty years old in captivity, and grow to eleven, twelve feet, or even longer. If our man chose the 'gator over his wife, he had better find a bigger house.

The Mississippi or American alligator is one of the few

conservation success stories. It's not that the Americans had any unique ideas or special abilities, but simply that they did what they said they were going to do without any backsliding, corruption, fudges or turning blind eyes. Conservation programmes are marvellous things, but people often are not.

The alligator first started to get into trouble when farmers began draining the swamps. At the time there was a fashion for crocodile shoes and handbags, for which American alligator skin is perfect. It reached the stage where the species was listed as endangered, and laws were passed prohibiting it being killed. This didn't work entirely, so the trade in the skins was made illegal. No skins could be traded, so poaching stopped. The alligators recovered and are now only listed as CITES Appendix Two to help out with other crocodilian species whose skins are very similar, much sought after and much rarer. CITES Appendix One affords the greatest protection to endangered species, imposing an almost total ban on trade; Appendix Two permits a strictly limited and controlled trade.

Because it's American, from a country with almost limitless resources, the Mississippi alligator is fully protected and very well researched. Just about everything there is to know is known. For example, the mother Mississippi alligator, unlike any other reptile, looks after her babies for up to three years. And both sexes have eighty teeth that replace themselves when they wear out, and they might get through three thousand teeth in a lifetime. Not a lot of people know that. David didn't when I told him.

'So he chose the wife,' said David, ignoring my display of knowledge, 'who by now was a close confidante of the neighbour. He began trying to get rid of the alligator, first by asking the original supplier to buy it back. Blakey came, said he didn't want it, but would take it off their hands if they bought two venomous snakes for fifty quid each. The wife said no dice, matey, so that was that until hubby suddenly said he'd done it. The alligator was gone, sure enough, but he wouldn't tell her where and she didn't believe him. She thought he hadn't got rid, just moved it to a safe place and was carrying on looking after it. Well, that didn't bother her too much. At least it wasn't in the house.'

'And the neighbour doesn't know where it is?'

'Nobody knows, except your man. It's disappeared. It might be dead or escaped, but those women don't think so.'

'Didn't you try following him?'

'The problem is, Tony, he doesn't have a routine. He doesn't work, he doesn't have a car. He might leave the flat six times a day on foot. Paper shop, betting shop, pub, bus stop, alligator. How do you know? He might go to feed Percy – that's what it's called, Percy – early one morning, then not at all for three days, then twice on Sunday, or whatever. You'd need to stake him out full time, with several blokes.'

Our resources were not up to that sort of exercise. My new boss, Robert Campbell, said the alligator was obviously okay for the moment, so we should concentrate on projects with more immediate and practical possibilities.

Over the next few months we kept getting reports from zoos about a man, an anonymous man, trying to sell, then give away, a Mississippi alligator. None of the zoos happened to want one at the time. The first few calls were from the big, famous places, then the wildlife parks, and eventually we had calls from garden centres. This man was getting desperate.

I had another chat with Robert and said it was surely likely soon that the man would release the alligator in a reservoir or something. We had to be more pro-active. He agreed, and we put out the word. The answer was a resounding silence for two weeks, after which we got our break. An informant in the herpetological underground said that he'd heard that a dealer in Ireland had bought a large American alligator from a pet shop, a reptile specialist, in Sheffield. It was to be picked up sometime before the weekend.

That gave us three days. Obviously the pet shop owner had acted as the middleman in a sale. There couldn't be that many American alligators for sale in the Sheffield area. All we had to do was watch the shop. Our man would turn up, with a mate in a Transit. Bearing in mind that all we had so far on him were the tales of the neighbour, some of us would video him at the shop, follow him home and video him there. And some of us would lift the alligator. We would be the pick-up pet shop boys. So long as we got in before the real ones, we'd be fine.

David and Eddie Carlyle, our tame Liverpudlian, would be the surveillance team. I would do the alligator snatching with Andy Jones. Andy was older than the rest of us, late forties, Welsh and the nicest man you could wish to meet. We called him Jones the Volume because he spoke so quietly.

We had the cushier side of the job. We were several hundred yards away in our van, ready to pounce once the beast turned up but not in sight of the pet shop. We could come and go as we liked and suffer no inconvenience. Eddie and David, on the other hand, were in a workmen's plastic hut opposite the shop on the far side of the road on a bit of wasteland. The hut, which wasn't in use at the time, happened to be parked there. They had to go in before daylight and come out after dark and, with their very narrow field of vision, all they could see was the shop door. They took it in turns to watch for thirty minutes; they had to film the drop-off and then, while business was being conducted in the shop, sprint to their car and be ready to follow our man home.

Nothing at all happened on the first day, nor the second,

apart from a good description of the pet shop owner over the radio from Eddie, looking through his binoculars.

'He's about thirty-five, Tony, and he has no neck. His head, which reflects the light, is joined directly to his shoulders, which are about five feet across. I'd say he was the type to pull up trees with his bare hands. Or, if it was Liverpool, lamp-posts. He has enough earrings to start a market stall and when he dies they'll put his skin in an art gallery.'

Andy listened to this with a sad expression in his eyes. At some point in the exercise we would have to come into contact with this man.

'I'm too young to die,' said Andy. 'Can we think of another Plan A?'

Lunchtime on the third day came and went. At about two o'clock Andy and I, doing the crossword, heard David's voice on the radio.

'Stand by, stand by,' followed by a short giggle.

Those two words always galvanise the brain and bring all the senses up to full function. Giggles, though, were not part of normal procedure, but as David described what he was seeing we began to see why.

'It's a taxi,' he said. 'Peugeot 406 estate. A hearse would have been better. It's got a great long plastic coffin in the back, and the tailgate is tied down with string. The passenger's getting out. He's one of your favourites, Tony, late twenties, average height, heavy build, shaven head, tattoos, earring. Driver's out, undoing the string. I'm getting all this, Tony, don't worry. The camera is rolling. They're lugging the coffin out of the car. It's obviously quite heavy. They're carrying it as if there's a glass of water on top and they're trying not to spill it. Okay, they're in the shop. Film crew are go. Bloody hell, they're straight out again. See you, Tony.'

There had been no business in the shop, and the taxi's

meter was running. David and Eddie had no time to get to their car. I'd already started our van and was moving to our new position on a street corner. We could overlook the shop but they wouldn't notice us. First thing we saw was David and Eddie leaping into their vehicle and setting off with tyres burning in pursuit of the taxi, which had disappeared. They overtook two cars in heavy traffic and shot off into the distance.

Our plan now was to wait for half an hour, keeping watch on the shop, and then drive up as if we were the official alligator collectors. We felt that we couldn't go in straight away without arousing suspicion. Half an hour seemed about right. We had to hope that the real people wouldn't be any more prompt than that.

Andy went around the back of the shop to keep a lookout there, and on the half-hour came back to join me for the snatch. Plan A was scripted and rehearsed. If the owner objected to us, we would say we didn't know anything but were only here for the job. Our boss had paid us. It would be more than our lives were worth to return without the box. If there were any problems with that, he would have to sort them later.

Of course it was a fairly weak plan. All the man had to do was phone his Irish contact if he was suspicious. Even less to Andy's taste was Plan B, the plan of last resort, which was to show our ID to the neckless shop owner and, whatever his muscular protests, confiscate the alligator.

After a very long-seeming thirty minutes, Andy opened the passenger door and got in. I drove to the shop front and parked half on the pavement. Andy was not a happy bunny at this point. I couldn't let him see I was nervous too, so I overcompensated and went for the cheery, have-a-laugh kind of confidence that was guaranteed to make him feel even worse.

I set my covert video camera running in my jacket, then marched in as if I owned the place. I was hoping to get some pictures of our man in his shop with the plastic box, although I expected the shop would be dark, illuminated mainly by the UV lights in the vivaria. It was, and if I got any pictures they would be poor.

There on the floor was the plastic coffin, a box about eight feet by three, made out of heavy-duty polystyrene. Standing by the door to the back room was a young girl, no more than seventeen, who looked like the type you see hanging around bus stations late at night. She was chewing gum that, judging by the amount of meat on her, would probably be all the food she'd had that day.

Next to her, like a housebrick stood against a cocktail stick, was the shop owner. I didn't need to look at Andy. I could feel his shiver from where I was. Ah well. All or nothing.

'Hi,' I said. 'I'm Ali. I've come for the 'gator.' Our man pointed at the box without speaking. I went to one end and Andy went to the other. As we picked it up and Andy started backing away, I examined his face. In that light he looked like one of the walking dead. Such a sight stimulated me into more cracking action.

'Didn't you hear what I said?' I called over my shoulder. 'I'm Ali. I've come for the 'gator.'

The girl smirked and put her hand over her mouth. The rest of my audience was less appreciative.

Andy sighed a deep, mournful sigh and nearly dropped his end of the box, while Ringo No-Neck said, 'I don't give a toss what your name is, just get the bloody thing out of my shop.'

When we'd put the alligator in the van and driven a few streets away, Andy relaxed.

'I couldn't believe you said that, Tony. "I'm Ali, I've come for the 'gator." I couldn't believe it, Tony. I think you must be mad.'

Mad or not, we were both desperately keen to look inside the polystyrene coffin. I drove until I found a piece of waste ground and we stopped. We climbed in the back of the van and gingerly or, indeed, extremely gingerly, slipped the catches on the lid and lifted it up a few inches. Naturally we'd got the wrong end and could only distinguish a section of scaly tail, but at least we knew we had an alligator and not a section of tree trunk.

We decided not to explore any further on our own, fastened the lid firmly, and set off again. We would wait for Eddie's call at the services on the M1, where we could have some coffee and a bun. Andy was in giggly mode now, repeating every few minutes 'I'm Ali, I've come for the 'gator'. With the end-of-term feeling you have after a successful operation, anything can seem funny.

Eddie called to say it had all gone swimmingly. They had caught up with the taxi, followed it to Chesterfield, and filmed the guy getting out of it. Although they couldn't follow him into the flats because of a security door, they had been lucky and filmed him through a first-floor window. Now, in court, there was no possibility of him saying, 'It wasn't me, it was another of the hundreds of reptile lovers who look like this.' We see them at the fairs.

All the academic herpetologists, whether they're on the dark side like the crook Blakey or whether they're eminent world authorities, like the great John Fordham, head keeper at Drayton Manor Park, seem to be six foot four. All the fair-going, snake-buying, alligator-keeping reptile fanciers seem to be five foot eight in both directions and would not be seen dead without a polished head and a black T-shirt decorated with lightning flashes, wolves and swastikas.

Eddie and David were keen to see the alligator so right then they came to the service station. We took the box out of the van, turned it around, put it back in, climbed in with it, and undid the catches. The interior of the van was quite dark and the polystyrene was opaque, so for us to get some light on the job, enough to see the beast's head, we had to raise the lid almost a foot.

Unfortunately this was also enough to allow light onto the alligator's eyes. It was fed up with being imprisoned in a dark cell and immediately made a bid for freedom. I don't know who moved faster, the alligator or Andy, but by the time the mouth had gaped, showing us all eighty teeth, the tail had swished and banged against the box sides and a very loud and angry hissing noise had been made, Andy was on the tarmac and backing away fast.

Eddie and David were not far behind, leaving me – well, I was the senior man, they said afterwards – to try and get the lid back on. I think if we'd been outside the van in the daylight the alligator would have been more determined and we would have been on the front pages of every newspaper in the land.

'Alligator to Go in Burger King.' I could imagine it. 'See You Later, Says Alligator.' Thankfully, the catches went click and we were safe – for the moment. To be on the safe side we wrapped about six reels of insulating tape around the box before heading for Drayton Park.

I rang John Fordham on the way. He asked if the animal was a small seven foot or a large seven foot. I supposed he meant fat or thin. Whatever charges we might bring in contravention of the Dangerous Wild Animals Act, our lad from Chesterfield was not guilty of underfeeding his pet. I said it looked like a gigantic seven foot to me.

When we reached the zoo and the lake, John showed us what was what. He grabbed the alligator by the back of the neck and gestured to us to pick it up by the body and tail, and that was how we carried it, uncomplaining, to its new if temporary home. John had the touch all right. An angry alligator – or a hungry one come to that, and we didn't know when it had last been fed – is physically capable of taking a cow in its jaws if one happens to be in range, and every year there are a number of fatalities in the United States where alligators decide they'd like a leg of man for tea.

We marched down to the lakeside under orders from John, and there was no trouble at all. This helped me decide that David, once he'd found a permanent home for it, needed no help to drive it there.

The alligator would move to a life of palatial luxury at Thrigby Hall in Norfolk. They have a huge tropical pool inside a hothouse, complete with vegetation and basking areas. They really know what they're doing.

John Fordham had it ready in its original box, so they loaded it in the van and David set out for Norfolk. It was a warm day and a longish journey, and they were almost there when the heat in the van became too much for the reptile. He wanted some cool, cool water and he was going to find some. David could hear him thrashing about in the box and, through the rear-view mirror, see the box jumping around.

There was a dog guard of metal bars between the cargo space and the driver, which was enough to keep away an excited Bernese mountain dog, but David wasn't so sure if it was guaranteed 'gator proof. As he drove the last couple of miles to his destination, his glances into the mirror were getting longer than his glances at the road. The box was really hopping now, and the 'gator was getting mad. He was not going to tolerate being in darkness and a confined space any longer and, with a huge effort, he pushed his snout through the front of the box.

David was in a quandary. What could he do if he stopped? He wasn't going in there with eighty teeth. If he kept driving and the thing made its way right out, would he have enough time to make a dash for home before he became the first fatal accident in Norfolk to be caused by a Mississippi alligator?

'Here is the news. Norfolk police are searching for the body of RSPCA inspector David Atkins, missing from a crashed van. An American alligator is helping them with their enquiries.'

Once he'd worked his snout out, the alligator had no problems with the rest of the box, which was in small pieces in a few seconds. Free at last, he started circling, turning around and around inside the van. He didn't like it. It wasn't much bigger than his previous prison cell, and there was no cool, cool water, so the only objects of interest became the human head and the big wide world beyond, visible through the van windscreen.

With about half a mile to go the alligator pushed its snout through the bars of the dog guard, luckily for David to the passenger side of him. The bars bent, but didn't break. David slid his seat as far forward as it would go, and leaned as far as he could towards his window. He decided not to risk changing gear any more. The movement might be taken the wrong way.

Five hundred yards to go. The place was at the end of this lane. The alligator decided he didn't like the passenger side of the van, retreated, and banged his nose through the dog guard in a different place. This was right above the head of David, who now had his chin resting on the steering wheel trying to avoid sounding the horn but also having a care towards alligator bites on the back of his neck.

All he could think of was trying to frighten the animal with noise, so he turned Radio One on full blast. The 'gator seemed to like this, and pushed his snout between another pair of bars with even greater enthusiasm.

At last, the gateway, the drive, and safety. David leaped from that van like a rocket out of a milk bottle, and slammed the door. Whatever else the RSPCA SOU might have in store for him, he was going on no more alligator jobs.

The reptile handlers had a bit of a laugh, saying that alligator bites didn't really hurt all that much, it was the shock that killed you, then they noosed the animal and led it smartly away to its last known address. David, after a close inspection of the bars of the dog guard, decided to redesign it with an increased specification.

(At the time of writing, the investigation is continuing.)

9
―

Whatever Don said, I wasn't giving up on the ivory case yet. I knew someone who might know someone, so I worked a little flanker. I left Don a message saying I had gone snake hunting in Lancashire and set off. Regardless of the success of my hunt, on my way back I intended to call at a pet shop in West Yorkshire run by a close friend called George who, I hoped, might have information about the Egyptian connection.

As far as Don was concerned, this fitted in with my quest for snakes because George, God love him, was our favourite babysitter. Whenever we had something dangerous or special-ised to look after, George would do it.

For some time I'd been assembling a file on Paul Blakey, an obsessive collector and dealer in rare and endangered reptiles, including venomous snakes. This was someone I was keen to make some progress with. I had nothing but hearsay on him from the alligator episode and other stories going back years. I needed some hard evidence.

Knowing I'd be seeing George next day, I contacted Blakey, mentioned the name of one of his customers and said I'd like to buy some snakes from him. I turned up at his house that evening. He was a strange fellow, a tall, gangly, long-haired weirdo who looked like he ought to be lead guitarist in a heavy metal band. Within twenty minutes I'd parted with eighty quid for two puff adders, among the most venomous snakes in the world, which he put in a small plastic tank.

This was all very well for evidence against the man, but what was I going to do with the snakes? By now the nights were starting to get cool, so I couldn't leave them in the car. Their body temperature might fall too low. The only alternative I could see was to smuggle them into my room at the Trafalgar.

Caroline, the one who was married to a crime squad copper, was on reception. When it was quiet she was always up for a long chat but I wanted to get the poor snakes to the room without her seeing them. She was used to me carrying in odd pieces of kit secreted in bags but it was a bit more difficult to hide a twelve-inch-square plastic vivarium.

I draped my jacket over it and held it under my arm. It probably looked even more conspicuous. I asked Caroline for the key to 59.

'What have you got in there, then?' she said. 'More gear for the lady at the Lotus Blossom?'

'Oh, some exhibits I didn't want to leave in the car. They'll be safer in my room.' I had to raise my voice at this point because the two puff adders, already unhappy with the way I drove around corners and further annoyed by the sound of our voices, started to hiss and strike at the vivarium. There was a succession of thumps as they hit the side. Caroline's face was a picture. 'See you tomorrow,' I gurgled, as I walked off, not daring to look behind me.

When I reached the room, I put the puff adders near the radiator. It was a one-and-a-half hour drive from where I'd picked them up and, though they seemed active enough already, I wanted to raise their body temperature to be sure they were comfortable. The puff adders were happy, curled up and resting. I left early the next morning, passing through reception at top speed with the cubic jacket once more tucked under my arm. I had an appointment at the RSPCA clinic in Salford, so I could pop straight down the M61.

My appointment in Salford was with a reptile expert, a vet who was going to give me some advice about a crocodile. While I waited for him to be free, I had a look at the patients in Dogs' Surgical, the recovery ward in the RSPCA hospital where injured strays are looked after until they are fit enough for an ordinary kennel. There were dogs of all sorts and sizes but one in particular, with a broken back leg, decided that it liked me. I walked past it a few times to a great thumping of tail and pushing of face against the bars so I could stroke it.

The nurses there said I must have some special attraction because this little animal was petrified of people. They thought that it had had a very nasty owner who had broken its leg deliberately. One of the nurses, seeing an opportunity, told me that the stray kennels it would go to had had some serious problems lately with disease. Even if it was adopted within a few days, it seemed that every other dog that went there caught something horrible.

I looked at the dog. It was reddish-brown, with a very appealing face, and was only about six months old, but its parentage was in serious doubt. If a terrier had mated with a fox and the result had bred with a lurcher, the offspring might have been something like this but more pure-bred. Somehow there was African elephant blood in the line, because its ears were perfectly ridiculous.

I asked the nurse to call me if the hospital didn't get any takers. I think I knew when I said it that I had just made another lifetime commitment.

I saw my vet, who told me what I wanted to know about crocodiles, then set off for George's place, driving as fast as I could, consistent with the law of the land and the need to avoid hurling puff adders from side to side in a plastic box, towards my very dear friend George's pet shop.

In previous lives, George had told me several times, he'd been in the Paras, a gymnast in the army team, a film stuntman and, for a while, a strongman in a circus. Whether or not all this was true, he certainly looked the part. He was about five seven, in width as well as height, with a shiny, bald head and forearms like anchor chains. He was definitely someone you would prefer to have on your side.

George's soft spot was animals. When he got too old for the physical life he set up a pet shop and, through his circus contacts, went into animal imports. He was in his late fifties and had been in the trade for thirty years. The circus connection led him to zoos, which led him to private collections and specialists. He brought in lions, bears, elephants, reptiles, birds, all sorts. Importing in those days was straightforward once you had the contacts abroad, because there were no restrictions. The Importation of Endangered Species Act and the Dangerous Wild Animals Act were both passed in 1976. Prior to that, the trade was barely regulated at all. If you had the expertise, if you knew how to pack and ship and how to deal with the animals when they arrived, you could build up a thriving business, as George did.

He enjoyed telling me stories of his animal imports, especially the ones that would be totally illegal now. Although he loved animals and would never do anything wrong to them, at that time people looked at the trade in a different way. I think he liked to watch the effect his stories had on me, and the more illicit the better.

I handed over my adders, with strict instructions for him to keep them in the very best of health. When we mount cases like the one I hoped to have against our Lancaster guy, there's nothing like the real hissing, striking animal to impress the courts.

Business completed, I was made to sit down with a cup of tea so I could listen to George recounting an incident when he had set up a consignment of lizards, a common species from India, and as a token of good will the Indian exporter had included a little bonus for his very good customer in Yorkshire, far away. George opened the crate and among the lizards, found a pair of spitting cobras, which can blind you if they spit their venom in your eye.

Nothing worried George. He dealt with whatever life put his way – even spitting cobras. Now his trade was tropical fish and the odd garter snake or gecko for the domestic pet trade.

The first thing George did if you took him a reptile was to give it a good wash. This was quite amusing to watch when it was a crocodile or a venomous lizard. After he had given the animal a thorough scrub with a nail-brush and warm soapy water and rinsed it off, he would hold it up as if he'd been renovating a priceless Picasso.

After I'd listened to several of his horror stories about spiders, birds of paradise and goodness knows what else, and had drunk enough strong tea to float a battleship, I came to the main point of my visit.

George did remember dealing with people in Egypt and was convinced that he had some paperwork somewhere. I was less convinced. For the next hour or so I stood in a corner of the shop watching an orchid mantis stalking a cricket while

George slowly waded through reams of paperwork. I couldn't decide which was the more exciting, George going through his files or the mantis moving at a speed of three inches an hour. At least the mantis was going to get there in the end.

Then, without looking up, George nonchalantly handed me a fax. It was dated ten years before and headed 'Nile Zoological Supplies' with an address in Cairo. It was a price list, in dollars, of animals for export. I skipped through the common species of lizards and small birds but a few things did catch my eye. Baby Nile crocodiles were offered for sale, as well as Nile monitors – both species now classified as threatened or endangered.

I reached the bottom of the list and saw a name. The slimmest of possibilities had become a big fat certainty. There it was, the name on the scrap of paper beside Fat Al's telephone.

'That's him,' I said. 'Amr Saad. The very man. George, you're a genius. What time do the pubs open?'

'Oh, him,' George said, ever the master of composure. 'I used to deal with him occasionally, you know, bits and pieces, but I stopped. You couldn't trust him.'

'Come on, George. This is a big day for me. What do you remember about this Saad character?'

'He was well known in the business. We all knew him and we all agreed about him. He was as slithery as one of his snakes. Mind you, he could get you anything. Anything at all. If it lived and breathed, he could get it, but you only used him if you had to. He was the last resort, because he'd take your money and you were never certain if you'd be sent what you ordered, or if it would be dead, or what.'

'Sounds like my man, George. Come on. I'll buy you a pint.'

There was only one logical way forward. I had to go to Egypt. The fly in the ointment? There was not the slightest possibility of the RSPCA sanctioning such a trip.

On the return journey to Horsham, I worked on my plans. The first objective was to persuade Don, and possibly Don's boss, that there was a potential prize for the firm in progressing the investigation into Egypt. When I arrived at the office I wrote the name of Amr Saad in big letters on a sheet of paper. Underneath I wrote 'Fat Al' and 'ivory' and then put it on Don's desk along with the faxed price list from Nile Zoological Supplies. I pointed to the name at the bottom.

'Bloody hell,' said Don, looking up at me with that old glint in his eye. For a moment he was the Don he once had been, the enthusiastic animal crusader with the sword of justice in his hand. Then reality overtook him and he lapsed into his more recent mode, that of Old Nick's pessimistic defence counsel.

'Forget it, Tony. There is no way they are going to let you go swanning off around the Middle East investigating ivory dealers. Get a grip. This is the RSPCA, not James bloody Bond.'

I spent the next twenty minutes arguing my corner. Don replied with all the obstacles and red tape that would prevent me doing the job. I saw obstacles as in an obstacle race, things you get around or over or under; they were there to make life difficult, not to stop you dead. I was still pestering him as he put on his Harris tweed coat to leave for the day.

'I'll tell you what,' he said. 'I'll go to Nigel Thompson tomorrow. I'll see if I can convince him. All right? Now, if you'll excuse me, I have a date with a Dover sole and a bottle of Chablis. Good night.'

Dear old Don. He would have very little chance with Thompson, Chief Officer of the Inspectorate and something of a sceptic about the SOU. Still, if anyone could do it, Don could. I stayed behind to put everything down on paper in preparation for the morning while the last couple of colleagues followed Don through the door, saying cheerful things like 'No chance, mate' as they left.

Next morning, I presented the file to Don. My strategy was to go to Egypt posing as an importer of ivory and rare species. I would approach Saad first from the UK, and then go out to meet him and, I hoped, his fellow dealers.

Don knew I'd be at him until he had his meeting with Thompson so he came to the conclusion he may as well have done with it. I watched him gather up the papers, stick them into his briefcase and saunter off down the hallway to Nigel's office.

Twenty minutes later Don returned. He never gave anything away by his expression but his words were always to the point.

'There's no chance they'll do it. They will not finance you flying off to Cairo.'

I tried to argue. It made no sense that I'd put all that effort and time and resources into the investigation and then, just when we were getting somewhere, we were going to drop it because it would cost a few hundred pounds to travel to Egypt.

'Sorry, Tony. That's it. The answer is: will not fund it, no can go.'

I would find a way around it then. If all that was stopping me was a few hundred quid, there had to be a solution some-where. For the moment I tried to seem disappointed but accepting of my fate. I started pushing papers around and shuffling files, and almost immediately had the answer.

There, on my desk, was the file on lamping. Men with strong lights, often small searchlights mounted on top of their vehicles, go out at night in search of deer, foxes or badgers. As the animals come out, they are caught in the glare, mes-merised, and make easy targets for the fast-running, lurcher-type hounds that are released down the lamps' beams.

This particular country pursuit was on the increase and animals were being hunted in their thousands. There was quite a large amount of evidence but I had needed specific names, addresses, times, the sort of thing that would stand up in court, so I went, cap in hand, to a quarter where we very rarely trod. As a rule, we were fairly negative with the media. They were always wanting to come with us on operations like dog-fighting raids, but we couldn't allow it if we were to remain an effective covert unit. This time it was me looking for a favour, and I found it at one of the daily tabloids.

The paper ran a story and as a result of the publicity we recruited four or five first-class informants and received high-quality information on a score or more of individuals who were actively involved in this kind of lamping. The venture was a complete success and I was very pleased with the way the reporter had dealt with it.

Would they be interested in ivory? Perhaps I should find out before telling Don. No point in getting him worried. I got on the phone and a few minutes later a reporter was already planning how it could be done. They would pay my expenses if they had the exclusive. Fair enough. Ideally I'd have preferred to keep complete control over all information, but if we weren't prepared to pay the cost we would have to beg rather than choose.

'Don,' I said, a short while later. 'You know you said I couldn't go to Cairo because there was no money. Well, I've got the money. From a newspaper.'

He looked up at me, his head back and one eye half-closed. He got up from his desk, set off down the corridor without a word, came back after ten minutes, nodded, and went back to his desk.

Brilliant. The big boss had agreed I could do the job. No doubt it would be subject to a thousand provisions, but I would deal with those when I came to them. The main thing was he had sanctioned the trip. Now all I had to do was set it up.

An ever-present problem is lack of the most basic resources. We don't have safe addresses, we don't have telephone lines that can't be traced back to us, we don't have anything that other covert agencies would regard as standard. As usual I would have to find a willing volunteer to provide me with what I needed in my new guise as international dealer in rare species. Good old George, I thought.

I did the letterhead, with my name and George's address, on my computer at home. The letter said that George had retired and I'd taken over the business and wanted to re-establish lost contacts. While George hadn't been very active lately with animal imports, I could assure his old friends that I was going to be much more positive. I was interested in fulfilling the UK's requirements for live animals and animal products at the high-value end of the market.

I could have posted it to George for him to send to Saad, but I'd had a call from Salford. Little Big Ears was being turfed out of the ward and would be headed for the stray kennels tomorrow. I said I'd be there. I called at George's on the way and, cursing my stupid soft spot, went to pick up an animal, which, quite unforeseen by me, was to become the world's first Undercover Terrier.

The journey home with her was a nightmare. I put her on the front seat, her plastered back leg sticking out at a strange angle, and set off. She was in a highly nervous state and would pee if anything surprised her. Seeing that nearly everything surprised her, there was a lot of peeing going on. It started to rain. I put on the wipers, which utterly terrified Pegleg Peggy, as she was now known, so more pee was let go.

I put my hand across to her, to stroke her and make her

feel better, which amounted to another sudden movement, only this time she crapped all over the seat. Things calmed down a little after that, until we got near home and she threw up. I put her in a basket next to the Aga, with her pot leg stuck up in the air, and told Denise we were only looking after it until the plaster could be removed. I knew my wife would fall for the little dog, and she did, but I had Plan B just in case. A uniformed colleague was going to collect her, then come back and say the kennels were full and she would have to be put down.

Back on the Cairo case I could only sit back and wait, hounded by the reporter, who was on the phone every day wanting to know what I was doing to make things happen.

I got in touch with my friend David Astley, one of the country's finest taxidermists, who had been out to Egypt to work with the Natural History Museum in Cairo. I knew David was a very keen conservationist and would have had a good look around the wildlife scene while he was out there. He could brief me.

I drove up to York, we talked, and he showed me video-tapes he'd taken while he was there. Best of all, he'd read an article about a naturalist, an expat called Richard Hoath, who featured in the serious Cairo publications about wildlife and was obviously one of the leading authorities. He could be a good point of contact for me. I needed somebody with Cairo experience.

I also needed a reply from Saad. I was getting increasing pressure from the tabloid newspaper and especially from the reporter, Rochelle Stevens. She had done some undercover work for another newspaper, but was fairly new in her job and keen to prove herself. She had sold the idea to the editor and now she wanted things to move fast.

At last I had the call. George, in his usual imperturbable

manner, phoned to say that the new owner of his business had received a reply from Saad, with an updated and much fuller list of mammals, birds and reptiles for sale. I hopped into the car and headed north to send a reply to Saad stating that I was very interested in what he had to offer; I had arranged to travel out to Cairo shortly on a business trip and would like to include a meeting with him on my itinerary. I had to hope that he wouldn't take it into his head to telephone. He might get George on the other end, with me in Horsham.

While all this was going on Pegleg Peggy was, I thought, coming along nicely. As the leg mended, I'd been taking her back to the clinic every so often for a check, which journeys were largely pee-free although she was a martyr to travel sickness. The sales of car upholstery cleaner certainly increased down our way. Just when her troubles looked over and the plaster was about to come off, she suddenly became very lethargic. My local vet diagnosed parvovirus and my heart sank.

This is a very strange disease, unknown in dogs until the mid-1970s but closely allied to cat distemper and possibly mutated from that. It is very unpleasant indeed, with vomiting, internal bleeding, dehydration and worse. Unless treated, it is fatal.

Peggy needed round the clock nursing and treatment. She got it, recovered, and cost me three hundred pounds, which proved to be among the best such sums I've ever spent. There have been various peeing incidents – she's never quite surmounted that instinctive reaction – but she's been almost everywhere with me, often helping me get near to badger diggers, playing her part as Undercover Terrier. I tell them Peggy is my wife's dog and she's ruined it, where I want to train her up as a bushing dog – that is, one that goes into thick undergrowth after rabbits. I ask them what they think

I should do and, as in every walk of life, if you get someone talking on their specialist subject you've got a friend straight away.

With the Peggy crisis over, Saad did his bit for my peace of mind and stayed on the fax. Soon we had everything arranged. Three of us – me, Rochelle, and her photographer, an experienced guy called Mark Reid – would fly out to Cairo, meet up with Saad, persuade him to show us his stock of animals, and try to buy some ivory through him. In the meantime I made contact with Richard Hoath, who was working as a lecturer at the American University in Cairo. He was willing to help and gave me plenty of information. I became confident I could trust him and asked him whether he knew Amr Saad.

Did he know him? Amr Saad was an even bigger fish than I had thought. Not only was he the leading rare animal dealer in Cairo, he was also in with the government officials who issued CITES permits for exporting endangered species. I faxed Saad one more time with our travel details and a promise to give him a call as soon as we got there, then spent the rest of the day checking and packing my kit.

I met the other two at Heathrow. All we had to do was get our kit through the X-ray machine without embarrassing queries from customs, get on the plane, and away we'd go to Cairo and Mr Amr Saad.

10

If I was to deceive the target, he had to believe in me and accept that I was in a position to do him some good. So we had to stay somewhere swish. Three to a room in the Old Bazaar Dosshouse was not going to fit the bill. We settled for the Ramses Hilton.

Our plan was to have a quiet evening together, dinner and a few drinks, during which we'd scout the hotel and work out exactly what we'd do when our man Saad got in touch. Filling in the time after that, until we had the call, would not be a problem.

In the plane I dug out my brochures again. I would go and see the Khan el-Khalili, the fourteenth-century market built by the Turks. I would walk along the street of a thousand goldsellers, I would take coffee with the artists and writers in el-Fishawi, the Café of Mirrors, and I would take a very close look at the carved ivory I was sure there would be in al-Muski market.

To the south of the city were the Sphinx and Chepren's Pyramid. I could visit the intriguingly named Mohammad Ali Mosque, otherwise the Alabaster Mosque, tomb of the great soldier who founded the royal line that came to an end when Colonel Nasser deposed the last King Farouk. I began to hope that Saad wouldn't be in too much of a hurry to find us, so I could improve my education and, possibly, the suntan.

We touched down late in the evening. A taxi took us to the Ramses and we showered, changed, and then assembled in the bar to take a good look around. The meeting place had to fulfil several requirements. It had to be discreet, obviously; Saad must not be nervous about being overheard. It had to be quiet, so our tape recorder could pick him up. It had to be well lit, so that Mark could get his pictures.

Most of the other guests in the hotel were businessmen, not tourists. I was sure they wouldn't be using the pool area much during the day, so I decided we'd set up there. We could easily move the tables so that Mark had a clear line from his covert position on a balcony some distance away.

While Mark went to take a few practice shots and decide on his lenses, I arranged the chairs. Saad would sit here, so that he was facing in Mark's direction. Rochelle would sit there, her audio equipment in a stylish kind of shopping bag, the sort tourists carry. I would sit to the other side and as soon as introductions had been made would get up and go to order some drinks. This would be Mark's chance.

It was all settled. No problem. I went to bed very pleased with myself.

I was up at the crack next day and thought I'd have a look at Cairo. The hotel interior could have been anywhere – Helsinki, Miami, Nairobi or Hull. The air-conditioning kept the temperature at the level decreed by head office, and the double-glazing ensured that the outside world was kept exactly where they wanted it, outside, and silent.

I stepped across the threshold onto another planet. It was only half seven but the temperature was already blasting. It must have been seventy-five degrees Fahrenheit or more, like a hot summer's afternoon back home, and it was made much worse by the pollution. The sun was hardly visible through the clouds of dust and exhaust fumes, and the air tasted of diesel, actually tasted of it.

The noise was unbelievable. If every vehicle at Hyde Park Corner, Elephant and Castle, Oxford Circus and Trafalgar Square all had their horns going at once the cacophony would still be nothing compared with this. Yellow cabs, New York type, were nose to tail with wagons like the ones I was used to seeing full of sheep, only these were lavishly decorated and full of men on their way to work with rags over their mouths to filter at least some of the airborne poisons from the filth they had to breathe.

I noticed one very peculiar thing – I was the only pedestrian in sight – and then another. Above my head, soaring high over the office blocks, was a pair of black kites, the fork-tailed scavenger bird, the street cleaner of ancient cities, now rare in Europe but obviously quite at home here where, presumably, the living was easy.

I headed back to the hotel, and found Mark and Rochelle having breakfast. I had hardly raised the first spoonful of international muesli to my lips before Rochelle started putting on the pressure. Her editor was not the type to send reporters off on an expensive jolly and then sit back to await results. She was on my back, wanting an update that had more to it than Situation Normal.

I looked at my muesli and then at Rochelle. She was eating scrambled eggs and toast in a way that made the words Pay, Piper and Tune come to my mind, so I went back to my room.

I attached the recording device to the telephone receiver and dialled Saad's number.

Nothing. The number was dead. Possibly ET wasn't quite so efficient as BT. I tried again. Still nothing. I rang down for the hotel operator, who went through to enquiries, but she fared no better. Possibly, she suggested, my man hadn't paid his phone bill.

This was news guaranteed to disturb Rochelle's composure and, sure enough, she had a minor flap. What kind of a contact was this who had his phone disconnected? I didn't know, but there was something we could do. I had his address. It was on a fax he'd sent me, which was in my room. We would take a taxi to his address and see what the score was.

The first thing we discovered was that your average Cairo taxi driver does not read English, the language in which the fax was written. Cairo taxi drivers also do not understand the English way of pronouncing an address, so when we said, 'Therr-tee, Rrrownn-derr Sstrreeet,' all we got were blank looks.

Three hours and three taxi drivers later we found what was supposed to be Saad's business premises. If it was, then his front for rare-species smuggling was paperback books, because this was the local equivalent of a branch library, specialising in Harold Robbins, Jacqueline Susann, Jackie Collins and everything else from the 1970s that had a tight-fitting dress on the front cover.

Rochelle was getting distinctly bad-tempered. If I had done my research properly we wouldn't be in this mess. Why couldn't I get right something as elementary as a contact's phone number? Or address, for that matter? How was she going to explain to her editor that he had funded aeroplanes and hotels for three, just so she could write a filler about Arab taxi drivers? If we went back to London with nothing, she would personally make sure that the RSPCA would never get another penny out of them or any other newspaper. Was that clear?

Flapping and carrying on like this was not going to improve matters, but Rochelle needed her flap and I had to be flapped at. I thought a better plan might be to recognise that no investigation is without its hitches and we should go back to the hotel and try faxing Saad.

We faxed him at one o'clock and again at five, but there was no reply. Rochelle was now flapping in what seemed like a determined effort to reach thirty thousand feet, although Mark was displaying all the characteristics of the old sweat – calmness, and a phlegmatic belief that one should conserve one's physical and emotional energies against the day they are needed.

We had arranged to meet Richard Hoath that evening. I'm six foot, but he towered above me; you could say tall and slim, or you could say gangly. With his dark hair perfectly combed back, his silver rimmed glasses and his off-white cotton suit, he could only have been British. He reminded me of Alec Guinness in *Our Man in Havana*, the archetypal British expat in the tropics.

After four years in Cairo, he was perfectly at home there and fluent in Arabic. He was also an excellent naturalist, with a deep concern for the local wildlife, radiating enthusiasm and displaying considerable knowledge. I instantly took a liking to him and knew we would have no problems working together.

That was the good news. The bad news was that concern like his was rarer in Egypt than the rare species themselves. Indifference was the most concerned they got around here, and corruption, cynicism and exploitation were much more common. This attitude extended to other African countries, and illegal traffic in animals across borders was not generally considered worth making a fuss about. And I'd thought things were bad in the UK.

Richard had done some research on Saad and confirmed that he was an official representative on the Egyptian CITES panel. The panels decide policy on regulation and enforcement and, along with civil servants and scientists, always include members from the trade.

I couldn't believe it. Here was a man we believed was an international dealer in ivory and all kinds of rare wildlife, yet he actually sat on the government committee that was meant to stop him doing it. Bloody hell, what couldn't we achieve when we lifted the lid off this one? The first requirement, though, was to get in touch with Saad, which we seemed no nearer to doing than when we boarded the plane.

A few minutes before midnight I went to get my room key and the receptionist handed me a note. There had been a call from Saad. He would be at the hotel at half ten the next morning.

We were breakfasted and at our stations by nine; we didn't want to risk him turning up early and sussing us out. We needn't have bothered. He came at eleven, comfortably late, which I took as a good sign.

I hadn't known quite what to expect. Apart from Fat Al, my experience of Middle Eastern crooks was confined to the movies. Was he going to look like he'd walked off the set of *Casablanca*, or would he be more the PLO terrorist type?

He was very pale-skinned for an Egyptian and spoke perfect English with hardly a trace of accent. He was about five ten, mid- to late thirties, colour of eyes unknown behind large sunglasses. His dark brown hair was closely trimmed and he had a neat beard like some of the sheikhs you see on television at the racing. With an open-necked, light blue striped shirt and dark blue trousers of a thin material, the verdict was: businessman dressing smart-casual to meet his friends. Another good sign.

I showed him to his seat and introduced Rochelle as my associate. I tried hard not to make the accompanying wink too theatrical and he seemed to understand perfectly. He gave me a knowing smile and an appreciative, ever so slightly raised eyebrow, as if to congratulate me on being able to combine business with so much pleasure.

With a little smile back I went off to see about some drinks and left Rochelle to chat with Saad. A swift upward glance told me that Mark was in position, and by the time I was on my way back he was gone. Good man. He'd got what he wanted – what we all wanted – and we were on to the next play in the game.

Rochelle already had Saad going on the art of smuggling rare reptiles. I wondered for a moment if he imagined that the favours she was supposedly doing me might be extended his way. He was certainly turning on the charm and trying to prove what a wizard he was at avoiding the traps and snares that authority set for him.

Saad was keen to take us to his place, and he promised to continue the story in the car. Yes, he would drive us himself, and here was the car, the very earliest model of Datsun Bluebird, which had clearly experienced everything a car could experience and still be in one piece.

This was our chance to see Egyptian driving at close quarters. Rochelle and I looked at each other and felt envy for Mark as we spied him getting into a relatively luxurious Mercedes taxi, ready to follow us.

Saad drove as if it were an activity requiring no more than a small percentage of his attention. While spinning the wheel, torturing the gears, blasting the horn and shouting at all the other drivers on the road, meanwhile negotiating at high speed the most congested traffic on earth and the most complicated route imaginable, he still managed to devote most of himself to telling us about his smuggling techniques.

What he liked to do was hide his rare reptiles among the common sorts and export them from Cairo via different airports to Manchester. At Heathrow there were permanent exotic species experts on the customs teams, but at Manchester you were unlikely to have anyone check your consignments. He dropped a few names, too, dealers in rare birds and so on whom he'd supplied. I knew the names, but not for the reason Saad thought.

I also knew the animals and that gave him confidence. We were like two tradesmen talking about work in the pub, or two lorry drivers in a transport café moaning about the latest hold-up on the M1. We were colleagues, we spoke the same language, we knew the tricks of the trade that others didn't know.

He started to open up about his own special little scam, which was a plan to set up a farm for breeding exotics. Once he had breeding stock he could pass off as his own the specimens his poachers collected in the wild. It was very neat. He could legally be attempting to breed, say, zebra, sand cats, Egyptian gazelles and reptiles, and whether he was a roaring success or not didn't matter. The likelihood of anyone proving that this lizard or that zebra was not bred and reared by the Saad stud was remote in the extreme.

By now we were twisting and turning through the backmost of backstreets. The road signs were no longer in English as well as Arabic. Obviously the infidel was not expected to penetrate this far. I had tried at first to keep a mental log of how many lefts and rights we took, so we could later retrace our route, but it was impossible; we didn't have a prayer of finding our way here again. I also guessed, correctly, that Mark would have lost us by now, no matter how good his taxi driver was.

After forty-five minutes we were in deepest real Cairo, with every square, whitewashed building looking exactly like every other square, whitewashed building. Saad pulled the car over and stopped in a cloud of dust. Some very skinny specimens of the common worldwide species, Football-Playing Boy, were on the street with a flat football. If that was their home strip – a few strands of dirty rag – goodness knows what their away strip was like. An old woman in a black dishdash sat on a step and showed us her complete lack of teeth in a cheery kind of a grin, like the smile the salesman gives you just before he rips you off.

As we walked into a small tenement block, out of the glaring sunlight into the cool dark shadows, I felt a shiver of concern. We'd lost Mark, I was sure. Nobody in the UK, nobody in Egypt, nobody in the world knew where we were, except Saad, an old lady who was probably his grandmother, and a few boys who hadn't noticed us anyway and couldn't have cared less or they'd have been after us begging for piastres.

That was a point. Why hadn't they registered the Westerners in this God-forsaken hole? Why hadn't they come rushing across, asking for a few coppers to mend their football or, as I'd been led to believe, to allow me the privilege of divesting one of their young sisters of her virginity? Could their neutrality be because of Saad? They knew Saad and they knew better than to interfere with him. They knew that I would shortly be fed to the crocodiles while Rochelle would be sold to a brothel keeper after Saad had fully tested her first.

I looked in the gloom for some sign of normality. Saad's name was written in English, in blue felt-tip, on a slip of white card beside the doorbell for apartment 3. When you're feeling as I was then, something as mundane as that can be the most enormous comfort. Mr Saad of apartment 3.

We had no contingency plan in case we were compromised and I was working with someone I didn't really know. Alone, I would have felt more confident. One wrong word, one glance, one mistake with the body language and the situation could deteriorate from excellent to disastrous and, while I was fairly sure I wasn't going to do any of those things, I couldn't be so certain about Rochelle.

This wasn't so much a worry about physical safety; I was sure that I could handle Saad, provided he didn't have too much assistance knocking about. It was more to do with the operation. If we made a mess, there would never be another opportunity.

At one time apartment 3 would have been quite lavish, with its rosewood panelling covering the walls and oak parquet blocks for the floors, but its best days were long past. The immediate physical danger didn't come from Saad but the ceiling plaster, which was hanging off in great loose chunks that looked liable to crown us at any moment.

Saad showed us into a spacious but rather dark room. There were no windows and a dim and dusty single bulb gave us our only glimmer of light. The furniture consisted of a wooden desk with chair and fax machine, a bookcase containing books on animals of all species, assorted cupboards and, curiously, a grandfather clock of some distinction and London make, presumably left over from Empire days but still ticking the minutes away.

Normality stopped there, and we went into the cutting edge of interior decoration with the ornaments on the walls. If you're going to have animal trophies, they're usually stuffed heads on polished plaques. These were heads, but they were just the skulls, bare and white. There must have been coming up to thirty, most of them from the big animals like eland

and kudu, lion and even a hippo, with some from the smaller cats.

Saad disappeared into the next room, and I could almost hear Rochelle's reporter's brain composing copy about butchery and graveyards. I was more interested in his reading habits. I wanted to see how professional he was, how knowledgeable. He had quite a range of books, from the basic kind of identification guide a tourist might buy to take on safari to scientific textbooks. Most important, his books covered the entire globe. He had references to every traded rare species on every continent.

We could hear Saad talking to somebody in the back and a couple of seconds later a young Egyptian man walked through. Saad mumbled something to the lad, who disappeared through the door we'd come in by. Chairs were produced and placed beside the desk. It was time for business.

I felt it was also time we started recording, so I asked where the toilet was and, like a good tourist, took my shoulder bag with me. The equipment only had a sixty-minute recording span so I hoped the next hour was going to be conclusive. There were three connections to make on my – very basic – surveillance kit. The audio recorder had a small nine-volt battery while the video recorder and camera worked off standard batteries. I checked the screen to make sure everything was working, flushed the toilet like they do in the films, and returned to the meeting.

Saad at once began his sales pitch. The fax he'd sent me in England was merely a minimal list of species, a kind of calling card for use when establishing first contact with a new customer. What he really had to offer was totally different and on a much grander and wider scale. He had agents in Tanzania, Rwanda and Hong Kong who had further contacts in all the animal exporting countries. Through this network he could obtain virtually any animal a customer might want.

On the distribution side he had people in Germany, Holland and Spain as well as the UK, so he had plenty of options for ensuring delivery to any European destination. Of course he had contacts in the Egyptian system too, including friends in government circles who could help him if need be. He had recently exported some very rare gazelles using these special contacts.

Finally, he also carried a small stock of frequently ordered species. It was too expensive and wasteful to carry large stocks, he said, but having just a few made things quicker for some customers. He would show us his stocks soon, but we mustn't forget that any species, any species at all, was available on request. There wasn't an animal he couldn't get for the right price.

I felt it was time to make a contribution to the meeting. It had all been Saad's sales pitch so far. We should be doing more than listening, so I told him I was mainly interested in reptiles, that being my speciality, but I could be persuaded to expand into other areas if the prospects looked good.

The lad returned with three cups of sweet Egyptian coffee – you can't have any kind of business meeting without coffee – and Saad said he was sure that together we could make a successful partnership. He went on to give himself more and more credentials. We should understand that here, clearly, was the most learned professor of wildlife and the most artful of dodgers of every country's law and every species of authority, rare or common. Cleverly he slipped in a few little tests, satisfying himself that I also knew a bit about the subject, from amphibians via local birds to the large African mammals.

He asked me who I knew in the UK. I mentioned a couple of people, importers I'd been trying to catch for years, like Paul Blakey. Oh yes, he knew Mr Blakey. He dropped some more names, mostly pet shop owners around London and in the North of England. I was waiting for one particular name to drop, Fat Al's, Kefah Almomani, the Darwen Doner. I was keen not to let Saad know there was a connection between me and Fat Al. Saad was a shrewd cookie. He would check, and Almomani would want to know how I'd got to Saad. Two and two would be computed and these were not the type of guys to believe in coincidence.

When the name did come up I was happy that it was no more than the mention. What I was not happy with was the way time was running out. We'd had the equipment going for over half an hour now, and we had no animal pictures yet. Rochelle glanced across at me and I knew what she was thinking.

'Could we have a look at these animals you've got then, Mr Saad?' I asked.

He stood up behind the desk. The animals, he explained were kept a short distance away and we would have to drive. Blast and bloody hell. My tape was going to run out. I'd been pushing hard for one of the newer systems where you had an automatic on/off switch that kept the system on stand-by, but we were still stuck with stuff John Logie Baird would have recognised.

I explained to Saad that I had been drinking gallons of water like I'd been told by experienced travellers, to avoid dehydration, but all it seemed to do was keep me running to the toilet. Saad accepted this and probably felt sorry for the northern caveman, used to snow and ice and rain and totally unfit for a proper, civilised climate.

Rochelle kept him chatting while I nipped back to the loo to switch off the camera and all the batteries, then once again we were twisting and turning through the backstreets of Cairo, trying to remember the directions and straining to get a glimpse of street names. We didn't have a clue where we were. There were no landmarks or features to tell one street from another, and you couldn't see the skyline because there were always such high buildings and narrow streets.

We were only on the road for five minutes but that was enough to disorient us completely, especially when we pulled up outside a building that was exactly the same as the one we had left. What was this, Blind Man's Buff? Some kind of trick? Had we driven around the circle, through the maze and in and out of the puzzle, only to land back where we had started? Whatever, we were committed.

We followed Saad into the small block of flats and up the stairs. It still looked the same. There was no handwritten card saying Saad at apartment 3, but then he would have removed that, wouldn't he?

Come on, I told myself. You're getting paranoid.

We passed an extremely ancient resident on the stairway. He greeted Saad as a very familiar acquaintance. At the third floor we transferred from stairs to fire escape and mounted the last stage to the flat roof. Here we were greeted by the most amazing sight. The roof was covered in cages of every description − small wooden sheds, wire cages, long runs, wooden-fenced corrals. The size and shape of each structure was unique to it, dictated by the materials it was made from, which in every case had already spent a long and useful life as something else.

Saad went to a shed made out of old doors. The walls were the length of a door on its side and the height of two such doors, with about a foot and a half of rusty second-hand chicken wire providing the ventilation system. On one side the doors had been cut and hinged to make a stable-type entrance. Saad opened the top half and gestured for us to have a look, positively beaming with pride.

I could not believe my eyes. Inside were five gazelles. They blinked in the beams of sunlight, three Thompson's gazelles and two Dorcas gazelles, which must have been two of the last in Egypt because they were almost extinct there. Dorcas gazelles in particular are noted for requiring very little water, because they get what they need from the green food they eat. I wondered what the food and drink was like in this shack.

They are very alike, these two species, small — about two feet at the shoulder — delicate-looking, dainty you might say, with big black eyes and beautiful curving ribbed horns. The Thompson's gazelle has a broad black stripe running from its front shoulder to where the back leg joins the body, dividing its brown back and rear from its white underside.

Both species are extremely nervous as, indeed, their natural life demands they should be. Any sudden movement could have spooked these five and possibly sent them into a blind panic. Trapped in that small space there could have been broken legs, broken horns, wounds and gashes or even deaths. After a minute Saad shut the door and ushered us away to another astonishment.

There, in a little shed on its own, was another African gazelle, an even rarer one, a species on the very brink of complete extinction: a Dama. The latest estimates indicated a total population of maybe fifteen hundred divided between ten or more sub-species, at least one of which, the Morr Dama, had already gone entirely. There were remnants of herds in several Saharan countries like Morocco and Sudan, although this was doubtful since they were under great pressure and hardly ever seen. At any rate, such tiny numbers offered no possibility of a revival, and there were none left at all in most of their traditional haunts. The last real hopes lay with the herds in three particular game reserves in Mali, Niger and Chad, where they could be protected from poachers, cattle ranchers and destruction of their environment – but not, it would appear, from Cairo animal dealers.

I needed to capture this on video. I asked yet again if I could pop to the loo but this time it was no go. Saad only rented the roof space. There wasn't a toilet anywhere. Looking around the rooftop I couldn't yet see an alternative to my toilet plan but I would have to find one somehow. I'd see what else there was up there and try to think of something as we went along.

In the next wooden shed, about ten feet long and made of wire mesh and recycled floorboards, there was nothing to see apart from feeding-time leftovers, in this case seed husks, and some oblong boxes, roughly on the scale of a shoebox. These were sleeping quarters, obviously, and each had a two-inch hole cut in the front. Saad opened one of these boxes and several red-footed squirrels ran out. He opened another box – pygmy squirrels this time, and various others that he named, but I couldn't really see because the shed was dark and they were moving so quickly. If he was telling the truth, he had species of African squirrel ranging from uncommon to extremely rare.

The next cage housed four genets, small predators living on reptiles, insects and mice as well as fruit. They are related to the civet cat, although smaller than it, and the mongoose, and they look something like a cross between the two. There are several varieties, including the common genet that lives in the open plains, but these were the kind called blotched genet, long and sleek with beautiful spotted coats and black and white striped tails. They're mainly nocturnal, at home in treetops, great leapers, and extremely rare in the wild after being hunted for many years for their pelts.

In another cage, encrusted with stale excrement from several different species, were half a dozen little bundles huddled together in the corner. It took me a moment or two to realise what they were. Flying squirrels are not much bigger than our ordinary house mouse but with a flat furry tail and great big eyes. Of course they don't really fly, only glide, but they can do fifty yards. When they're not gliding, their 'wings' – skin-like webbing between the front and back legs on each side – can't be seen very well. They tuck it up so they can scamper up and down trees like any other squirrel.

Four rare sand cats were in a cage the size of a tea chest with a few square feet of run for an exercise yard. Like so many animals in danger, these – slightly bigger than a domestic cat, rather flat-headed and a lovely desert sand colour – have a very limited range. They live among the rocks in the arid parts of North Africa and nowhere else.

Three more gazelles were hidden in a small shack at the far end of the rooftop and assorted reptiles were secreted in small containers all over the place, including Nile monitors, which were being kept in very uncomfortable conditions. They are very agile lizards, with powerful claws for catching and tearing meat, their only food, and they are related to the Komodo dragons – very large monitors, up to ten feet long, but never known to breathe fire or fly.

Crammed in a long narrow cage underneath the three gazelles were about twenty rock hyrax. These are highly peculiar animals, mentioned in the Bible as conies, that look something like a cross between a guinea pig and a rabbit although they're not remotely related to either. In fact hyraxes are not rodents at all but a completely separate family with six member species. Their teeth structure shows similarities with the hippo and rhino, and their brain has common features with the elephant, but they are never more than twenty inches long. In the wild they have to contend with all kinds of predators, large and small, land-based and airborne. Humans want to eat them, use their pelts and sell them into captivity; the others, like the eagles, lynxes and mongooses, just want to eat them.

I couldn't say precisely which species of chameleon Saad had. Eighty-five different ones are known about, half of which live only on Madagascar, not all that far from Cairo as the smuggler flies. The genets would have happily eaten the chameleons if they could have seen and reached them. Chameleons may be one of the slowest-moving lizards but they do have this ability to disappear into the background by changing colour to suit.

I was concerned about the genets and all the other animals being fed and watered properly, but I didn't worry about the chameleons. They have eyes that swivel independently, so they can look in two directions at once, and they have this sticky tongue that uncoils like one of those party whistles with a feather on the end, except about a thousand times faster. And, there was no shortage around there of the chameleon's favourite dish: insects.

Up on that roof, in the hazy heat, with the normal sounds of the city below, this whole business began to feel insane. Or perhaps it wasn't the business at all. Perhaps it was me who was slipping. We live in an age of international conferences on wildlife, held in front of the world's news media in exotic capital cities. We have dukes and presidents and kings and princesses espousing the cause, and we have university dons and leading politicians pronouncing on rain forests, global warming, save the whale and everything else.

Yet in this golden age of compassion it had been proved to me that day that it was possible for an ordinary Egyptian citizen to assemble numerous examples of some of the world's rarest species and keep them on a rooftop in Cairo as if they were chickens in his back yard. While the great and the good make speeches to each other and, over the banquet that follows, discuss the plight of the tiger in Java and the quality of the claret in their glasses, I can walk around a flat roof and in five minutes see more rare animals than an entire conference will see in a lifetime.

Governments might formulate policies to stop the trade, and sit back thinking they've done something, but here we were at the sharp end, where real animals were really bought and sold as if they had no more significance than a tennis racquet or a spare part for a car. Here we were, at the centre of a filthy trade, but it wasn't as you would imagine a criminal meeting to be. There were no shady corners, whispered conversations, threats, glances, strange bulges under jackets.

It was more like we'd met a man who kept a few pets and he'd let his hobby get the better of him. We could have been in a pigeon loft in Hull for all the drama there was. They were animals in cages, and they behaved like any other animals in cages, like Jumbo the pet rabbit and Horace the hamster. The fact that they were the last of their kind meant nothing to them.

Saad said there were purchasers for everything on that roof. Soon they'd be gone and the next lot would be coming in. I needed to get some photographs if I couldn't get video. Time for the trusty sureshot, if only I could get a few seconds on my own. There was no possibility of him agreeing to have pictures taken openly. Somehow I had to get him off that roof.

Rochelle gave me an idea. She was looking flushed and flustered, struggling in the afternoon heat, on the other side of the rooftop ten yards away.

I stepped quickly to her side. 'See if you can get Saad to go find a cold drink for you. Give me a chance to take some pictures.' I wandered away.

Rochelle must have had something of the actress in her

because her brow-mopping and distressed swaying would have been a credit to any professional. Saad quite fancied Rochelle, I was sure – well, we were both sure – and he was there in an instant. Surely he could not resist the chance to win her favour. In two ticks he would be rattling down that fire escape, three steps at a time, in search of a jug of fresh lemonade with ice.

'Rochelle is not well,' he called to me. 'Come, I will take you to the pyramids and we'll stop somewhere cool for refreshment on the way.'

Sod it. I looked around from the rooftop to try to find some distinguishing feature that would lead me back to this place. About three blocks away there was a large satellite dish. I took a mental picture. Perhaps I could find the dish again and use it to get myself back here.

For the rest of the day Saad gave us a personal guided tour around the pyramids. He even paid for us to go in and was most generous, gentlemanly and humorous, especially when persuading Rochelle to take a ride on a camel. We saw all there was to see, but got no further with our investigation. Saad then drove us back to the hotel, dropped us off outside and promised to pick us up the following morning. He was going to take us to the zoo at Giza where he had his main contact.

Mark had already developed his photographs. He had the perfect upper body shot of Saad beside the pool. This was all very well but we also needed pictures of the animals, the getting of which would involve a bit of breaking and entering. The newspaper was planning to run this story as soon as we returned home. A picture of a pleasant-looking gentleman sitting by a swimming pool was not exactly going to thrill the picture desk nor shift masses of copies off the news-stands.

Mark felt that illegal activity, such as said breaking and entering, was outside his remit, and in any case he wouldn't know which animal to photograph. I decided to leave this little expedition for the end of our scheduled week. Other opportunities might arise meanwhile.

Next morning, bang on time, Saad turned up in his battered Bluebird at the front of the hotel and once again we dived into the whirlpool that is Cairo traffic. I am quite sure that the species 'Sunday driver' cannot exist in Cairo. Nobody who drove slowly and carefully could live beyond Day One. Their normal defence mechanism – not looking in the mirror while driving in the middle of the road – which saves them in the UK would assure them of instant extermination in Cairo. The other drivers would barge them off the highway, crush them against walls or drive straight over the top of them.

Saad, in the proper local manner, drove us right across town to the zoo at Giza, which has Egypt's main collection of animals. As we swept through the front gates it became obvious that he was known by everyone, from the woman in the ticket office to the guys sweeping the paths. We didn't have to pay, everybody waved, and we went in a straight line without hindrance to the director's office.

The director was a middle-aged, heavily built Egyptian woman – well, she was more than heavily built – with frizzy black hair and dark glasses. After brief introductions we thanked her and set off around the collection with Saad. It was a depressing experience, and nothing could have made me more miserable than the two polar bears in burning North African sunshine without access to water. The zoo director, who obviously looked after herself very well, hadn't even got the nous to give the bears a pool to swim in – and in that climate. One bear looked decidedly ill. They'd put a makeshift kind of a canopy over it but it was a sick, sick animal and it wasn't going to survive much longer.

Meanwhile groups of schoolchildren were clamouring to

feed the bears with whatever they had to feed themselves —
chocolate, crisps, candy, whatever — and the keeper, instead of
taking the chance to tell them about the bears' natural diet
and how you mustn't give them sweets, was actually encouraging the bear to the front of the cage.

His technique would have been funny if it wasn't so tragic.
He had a carrot, that well-known Arctic vegetable, on a stick,
trying to entice this majestic carnivore towards a child with
a bag of chocolate-coated peanuts. The truly depressing thing
was that it worked. How are the mighty fallen. This magnificent creature, three-quarters of a ton of stealth, beauty and
ferocity in the wild, had been reduced by man to a feeble
beggar of trifles from the ignorant.

As he showed Rochelle and me around the collection, Saad
pointed out animals that he had supplied. He explained the
system to us, obviously trusting us completely by now. I
thought I couldn't be surprised any more by the corruption
and depravity of my own species when dealing with our wild
and innocent companions on the planet. How wrong I was.
Saad surprised me all right. He astonished me.

He had a very productive relationship with that zoo. The
director also sat on the official government board that issued
CITES permits, and had authority, on behalf of the national
government of Egypt, to grant a licence to anyone exporting
or importing animals of endangered species. Saad was on the
official panel representing the traders, so between them they
had the job stitched up. If the director wanted any rare species
in her zoo, Saad would get the contract to supply. If he had
an order from his overseas customers for any rare animal, the
director signed his permit. With huge glee he told us he was
about to pull off his biggest coup ever. He was licensed to
supply two gorillas, mountain silverback gorillas, from the
wild in Rwanda.

This was a difficult moment for me. I already wanted to catch the director, put her in a cage and leave her on an Arctic ice floe to see how she could cope with a complete reversal of her natural surroundings. Now I wanted to punch Saad in the face and throw him to the lions.

I can't have betrayed my emotions because he gabbled on, telling us how he'd already obtained red pandas from Hong Kong and had smuggled, to a zoo in Germany, five hundred lizards of the species *Uromastix*, or Dabb lizard, a heavily built vegetarian beast with a tail covered in spirals of sharp spikes. Five hundred Dabbs – I couldn't believe it.

And he had also sent two shoebills to this German zoo, claiming they were bred in captivity in Egypt. I wasn't quite sure how many pinches of salt to take with all this. Silverbacks? Five hundred Uromastix? Shoebills? It sounded fanciful even for a man of Saad's undoubted resourcefulness.

Shoebills, for instance, have been rare for a long time, and they are now very rare indeed on the Nile, although they can be found in the marshlands of central Africa. In fact, Saad said these two came from Uganda. These great birds, five feet tall, stand in the wet, motionless for hours, waiting for a frog or a fish to come within striking distance. They look like no other bird. From the neck down they will pass for a fairly normal kind of stork, grey, long-legged, but the large head carries the most amazing beak, enormous, with a fierce hook on the end, and in a shape that earns the bird its other name, the whale-headed stork. In fact they're herons, not storks, and how Saad came by them I cannot imagine.

There was no doubt that Saad enjoyed boasting of his exploits. The only question was: how much was he making up? He was obviously an international animal-smuggling crim-inal, but was he the lord of the trade he claimed to be, or just another functionary? Was there a genuine Mr Big we hadn't seen yet? Was Saad another runner like Fat Al, a foot-soldier, doing the front-of-house work for a mastermind who could remain hidden and stay in business after we exposed Saad?

Whatever his rank, Saad was efficient. Before dropping us off at the hotel he passed me a piece of paper. On it, given freely, were the names and addresses of certain rather special traders in the souks, the markets, including several ivory dealers, and detailed directions to an animal market, plus the names of two contacts there.

This was information so vital, and so dangerous to give to an outsider, that I could not help but suspect a trap. Perhaps Saad was being clever in layers. On the surface he trusted us and showed us everything, possibly exaggerating the size of the business and his own part in it. He acted as our courier, our driver, our tourist guide. Nothing was too much trouble if it pleased or helped the important people from England. Underneath he was leading us into a snake-pit.

This was a very lucrative trade, conducted by hard people with no sympathy or finer feelings for near extinct wild animals. Why should they hesitate when it came to their extremely common human enemies? We couldn't expect any mercy from Saad, the director, the possible Mr Big behind them and all the other connections that were making their very comfortable livings from the business we were trying to stop.

We were going to have them arraigned before the law, in a case that would make the news all over the world. Against that, the disappearance of two or three English tourists in Cairo would cause a brief flurry of interest but the local police would soon decide the crime was impossible to solve. I'd heard stories of tourists getting so lost in the depths of the souks that they'd had to pay considerable sums of money to locals to lead them to the edge of the maze. What could the police hope to find in such a place when there was a deliberate conspiracy of silence, probably backed by a few bribes?

It looked like I was going to see the Khan el-Khalili after all, but was I going to find my way out? We had little choice if we were going to continue our investigation; we had to take the risk or give up now.

I knew from the brochures that the Khan el-Khalili is divided into areas by category of goods sold, and there isn't much that isn't available. One part is spices, another carpets and rugs, another silks and fine materials, and so on. Saad now told us that an especially tourist-oriented area is devoted to Egyptian glass and various trinkets and novelties of the sort people buy when they can't think what to get for a present to take home. Incorporated in this area are those little decorative items carved from bone and ivory. Anybody can come and haggle for this stuff, any Brit or American or Japanese, but they don't have the names of the ones who deal big time. We did. We wouldn't be distracted by offers of baubles and bangles. A telephone call from Saad before we arrived would ensure that we were shown the pukka stuff.

I spoke to Richard and he offered to take us to the right part of the souks and drop us off where we couldn't get lost. We would thus have at least one reliable witness to say we had gone in. I asked him if he thought the sun might shine tomorrow, because I hadn't done much for my tan apart from our trips to the pyramids and the zoo.

He laughed. 'The sun doesn't shine in Cairo. The smog won't let it through.'

He tried to dissuade Rochelle from coming along to the souks. She would be pestered endlessly by the Egyptians who did not see many Western women; above all, they were likely to get very excited by a fair-haired woman, a rare event. If she insisted on coming, she must cover herself as much as possible.

The plan was for Rochelle and I to go into the shop indicated by Saad and introduce ourselves. If ivory was produced, Mark would follow us in and take some covert pictures. On this occasion, I was glad to say, I would be able to use the video and sound machinery when I wanted, switching it on before we went into a shop and off when we came out. If we came out, that is. In all our enthusiasm I hadn't forgotten that the whole thing could be one great con trick and we could finish up floating in the Nile.

11

At the crack of dawn, Richard breezed up in his Fiat Uno. He sighed with disappointment when he saw what Rochelle was wearing — a short, thin, sleeveless cotton dress and sunglasses on top of her hatless blonde head.

He'd warned her that she she should cover up, but she hadn't listened, even after an unnerving experience with one of the assistant managers of the hotel. After several peculiar internal phone calls, she'd woken up to find him standing at the bottom of her bed in the middle of the night, pretending to tuck the sheets in.

Driving through the Cairo streets, it immediately became obvious that Richard had gone native. He had refined to perfection the local custom of sounding the horn every twenty seconds and was fluent in the rarefied form of Arabic used between car drivers. He was especially adept at second-guessing the traffic lights, which, in Cairo, are a rough guide to vehicle movements rather than the precise indication that they are in the UK.

After fifteen minutes of this we were at Khan el-Khalili. I'd been in Petticoat Lane on a weekend, but that was like a stroll in the country compared to this. This was the January sales crossed with the Tokyo tube in rush hour. No traffic was allowed in the streets of the market, but the decibels and the dust were more than enough without. It was mayhem, cacophony, a crush of people coming and going in a crazy whirl of colour and noise in the heat and the haze, and every-where there were traders in ivory. Among all the rugs and glass and tourist trinkets and jewellery there was ivory. Mostly it was small, carved figurines but we could also see full tusks, generally made into a procession of elephants linked trunk to tail.

Our first appointment was with a man called Abdel Morem Mohamed at the Reda Bazaar. Richard knew where it was and pointed us in the right direction. As soon as we got out of the car, every male eye – and there were hundreds and hundreds – turned on Rochelle. They stared first at her bosom, encased in thin blue cotton, then at her face, hair, legs and arms, and then back to her bosom. Rochelle flushed bright red, stuck her nose in the air, ignored them all, and kept going.

At first she walked behind me. I was looking ahead when I heard a shout of 'Oy!', followed by a well-known two-word phrase or saying in which the second word is 'off', then by a loud slap. I turned to see Rochelle even redder than before, and a middle-aged Egyptian holding his face.

'He grabbed my tit,' said Rochelle, outraged.

We found Reda Bazaar easily and I switched on the video as we neared the shop. From its window display it was no different from its neighbours and its neighbours' neighbours.

They all had the same kinds of small decorative items, rings, brooches, bangles, earrings, things to put in your hair, in ivory, gold and silver.

Inside was a high-ceilinged room with a fan turning gently, its walls furnished with tall, glass-fronted cabinets full of jewellery. Four shop assistants, young men, stood behind the counter doing nothing. I asked to speak to Abdel Morem Mohamed, the owner. One of the young men disappeared into the back and returned immediately with a man in his early fifties with a round face, a bushy black moustache, thinning hair and a white, open-necked shirt.

I told him I was a friend of Saad and interested in taking some ivory back to England with me. Any friend of Saad's was quite clearly a friend of Mohamed's too, and he would be delighted to show me special pieces. The young man stayed with us, watching and acting as Mohamed's minder. The others were extremely busy making their sales pitches to Rochelle. She was giving a fine performance, interested in everything and nothing, keeping them distracted.

I wanted a clear view for my video camera and we would need the same when Mark turned up, and Rochelle was doing a grand job of keeping her little swarm of bees tightly around the honey pot. I adjusted my shoulder bag position and hoped everything was working. If it wasn't, we wouldn't find out until we were back at base.

Displayed in the shop's cabinets were some very small tusks, only six inches long, plus all the innumerable pieces of worked bone and ivory, but no large entire tusks. I asked if there were any. Mohamed nodded and his minder pulled a stepladder from under the counter, climbed up to the top and opened a wooden cupboard door. I could make out four or five big tusks, probably from a foot and a half to three feet long, but they were too high up and it was too dark to get any video footage of them. I asked him to bring some down and tried to peer more closely into the cupboard. The tusks were stacked upright; there were a dozen or more.

Abdel Morem took charge of the scales and weighed the first tusk his young minder brought. 'Six point two kilos,' he said. That was nearly fourteen pounds, a stone of ivory. He wanted three hundred pounds sterling for that one. I said I'd want more than one and suggested he got out his entire stock and weighed the lot. Maybe we could do a bulk buy? My contacts in England wouldn't want me to mess about with bits of this and that.

If those contacts had been real they would have been thrilled. Within five minutes there were eighteen tusks leaning against the wall. The biggest weighed twelve kilos. Mohamed said he would do me a special favour and let me have them all for nine thousand pounds sterling. I said I was interested at that price if it included delivery.

He shrugged. 'No problem. I have someone at Egypt Air who is responsive to requests for help, and there should be no difficulty at the British end because it will be packed among ordinary goods.'

At that point Mark walked into the shop dressed as a typical tourist. He nonchalantly checked out the prices of some jade jewellery near the door. Taking her swarm of assistants with her, Rochelle immediately moved to the far corner of the shop, ostensibly to look at a particular piece of engraved ivory that she must have examined three times already.

I asked Mohamed to reweigh some of the pieces. 'I want to be sure the calculations are right.'

As he did so I sensed as much as heard a couple of clicks from the camera in Mark's jacket. He shrugged and walked out, a true professional. He had what he'd come for. Work was over for the day.

Mohamed had finished weighing the ivory. 'Would you be interested in anything else?'

'I'm always on the lookout for anything in the animal line.'

He showed me into the back room. With no more fuss and bother than if he was selling me some socks in M&S, he produced a dozen skins from spotted cats, mostly leopard, but also some I couldn't identify. They were fifty pounds sterling each.

I could see why smugglers took the risk. These would fetch thousands each in the UK, and the profit on the ivory would be huge too. Buying it in Cairo at twenty to thirty pounds sterling a pound, you would quadruple your money on the UK market. By spending nine grand in the shop, and another ten or so for the twenty tusks I could see stacked up in a corner of the back room, I'd be looking at about sixty grand profit.

All the tusks were still stained, as if it was not long since they had been attached to an elephant. I played my role of the crooked shyster to the utmost and asked if polishing was included in the price. It might be, depending, was the answer, which I took for a yes if I bought plenty, plus a few leopard pelts.

I felt utterly despondent. Despite every effort to close these guys down, I could still walk into a little shop in Cairo and, provided I knew the magic words – Amr Saad – buy the spoils from a small herd of elephants and the skins of a dozen big cats. And this was just one shop. What could possibly be the point of me, one individual, taking on a task of this scale? How many Mohameds were there? How many little shops in how many bazaars had thirty elephant tusks and a dozen leopard skins? How many elephants and leopards were there in Africa that such a trade could be sustained?

The really depressing thing was that the Mohameds and

the Saads didn't believe that what they were doing was wrong. Of course they knew there were laws against what they did, but they didn't really see themselves as criminals. They were entrepreneurs, taking risks to supply a market with what it demanded. What could be the matter with that?

Such people will never understand the fundamental evil of killing a magnificent creature like a shark so you can make soup out of its dorsal fin. They don't see the sheer horror of killing an elephant so you can make a bangle out of one of its teeth, or a clever little miniature temple for the mantelpiece.

In some cultures people are brought up to think nothing of animals. They are no more than convenient resources for work, food, amusement or decoration. You cannot expect the ingrained attitudes of centuries to change overnight, but you can expect intelligent individuals to see that we who have exploited animals for thousands of years should be protecting them now, when they need us.

I thanked Mohamed for his help. 'I'll be back in touch,' I said. 'I'm very, very interested, but I need to sort out a few supply lines back home to be sure that I won't be sitting on the stuff for more than a day or two.' I winked at him. 'It's not like Egypt over there. You can't bribe your way through the customs and the police. Having this kind of material hanging around would be asking for trouble.'

Mohamed shrugged as if to observe how curious were the ways of the British, and he gave me his business card. Drawing Rochelle away from her fan club was only marginally less difficult than taking a meaty bone away from a Scotch terrier, but I managed and we swiftly wove our way back through the crowds to the drop-off point where Richard was waiting.

Even he was surprised when I told him what I'd seen. It was fairly common knowledge that you could get ivory in

Cairo, but he'd assumed that most of it was still around from the days before the ban. He had no idea they were dealing in such large quantities of fresh raw tusks.

Mohamed had been quite open about his supply routes. He could acquire as much ivory as I wanted. If he could do that, so could others. We discussed for a while the pros and cons of changing tack slightly. If we were to commit to a long-term investigation and actually buy some ivory, we would give ourselves complete credibility and, in a period of, say, six months, we could probably have exposed the entire ivory trade in Egypt and the key suppliers in the rest of Africa.

For the time being, though, we had to take things one step at a time, which meant one expedition, to the animal market of Sayyida Aisha. It only operated on a Friday and Sunday. Tomorrow was Friday and we were flying out on Sunday, so it was now or never.

Richard had already briefed us on what to expect. For some years he had been pressurising the Egyptian government to close down Sayyida Aisha. Very few westerners went there and Richard was well known and often met a pretty hostile reception, so the plan was for him to drive us there but keep out of the way. It would be far more difficult to operate there than in Khan el-Khalili, especially for Rochelle.

'If you thought the trinket dealers were bad,' Richard said, 'wait until you see the animal dealers.'

We decided to split up. Mark would amble through the market like a typical tourist with a camera hanging round his neck. Rochelle, seeing sense, would stay close to Richard near the car, while I would wander off with the video camera and make contact with the two people Saad had listed.

The market was a nightmare, the pet shop from hell. Crammed tightly into crude wooden cages were large numbers of every domesticated species imaginable, from guinea pigs

and budgerigars to rabbits and dogs. Beside the standard kind
of pet stalls, there were seven or eight wildlife dealers. The
noise was almost unbearable. You had the traffic streaming
along the motorway overhead, the dealers shouting and
talking at the tops of their voices, all mixed in with hundreds
of puppies yapping, parrots squawking, finches singing and
God knows what else. As with all markets, people were
shoulder to shoulder, stepping on each other's feet. There
didn't seem to be very much trade going on, but there was
a terrific crowd to see the show.

I had been to scores of these places in Europe, the Far East
and elsewhere, but the more I saw the worse the impact. I
hadn't become hardened – quite the opposite. I became more
and more furious. And this had to be one of the worst I had
ever seen.

Seething but outwardly under control, I approached the first
dealer and showed him the name I was looking for. He pointed
and I pushed my way through the crowd. Perhaps I should
have been better prepared mentally. This was a Saad contact.
This was going to be worse than the others, because it wasn't
tusks and pelts and it wasn't the relatively civilised environment of a zoo. This was a live animal market in Cairo, where
concern for animal welfare seemed to be a fantastical concept.
I should have been ready, but I wasn't.

First, I stopped at the stall next to the one I was aiming
for. It was jam-packed with wildlife species and trophies of
every type. Dabb lizards were in a hutch next to pairs of
Nubian ibex horns. I could hardly have been more shocked if
they'd had Nubian slaves chained up for sale.

There are only about a thousand Nubian ibex in the world,
as far as we know. The males of these wild goats, which live in
the Sudan, Saudi Arabia and Israel, grow the most tremendous
horns, five feet long and semi-circular, way out of proportion

with their body, which is on the small side for a goat. Of course, it was possible that these were the horns of the half dozen elderly male Nubian ibex that might have died that year in among some inaccessible rocky cliffs in the Sudanese desert, but I doubted it somehow.

Next to the horns were Eurasian kestrels (mostly females for some reason), black-shouldered kites (endangered species), and red-footed falcons (very rare). At first I couldn't understand why some of the larger falcons were so subdued. When I looked closer I realised why. Their eyelids had been crudely sewn together.

Falconers generally put tailored hoods over their birds' heads to make them quiet. Here we had someone who thought hoods were too expensive compared to a needle and thread.

These proud and beautiful birds of prey were crammed into messy cages, forty or fifty at a time. Most of them were panting under the extreme heat, and a couple were already showing signs of failing. Such wastage, with several fine birds not making it through market day, was obviously acceptable, like a greengrocer might expect a certain percentage of his lettuces to go limp on a hot afternoon.

Another cage contained hoopoes, cinnamon-to-salmon-pink birds something like the colour of chaffinches but about the size of blackbirds, with striking darker crests barred with black, long curved beaks and black and white wings. They are quite common in Europe and Asia and sometimes visit the UK, although not as much as they used to, apparently: 'The Upupa or Hoopebird so named from its note [is a] gallant marked bird which I have often seen and tis not hard to shoot them.'

This is one Sir Thomas Browne, writing more than three hundred years ago about the birds of Norfolk and referring to the hoopoe's trusting nature, tameness and lack of fear of man, characteristics that got it a bullet in seventeenth-century

Norfolk and a crowded prison in modern Cairo. I saw fifty of them crushed together in a ridiculously small space, so that several were already dead on the floor of the cage, trampled by their brethren, and more would be dead before the day was out.

A small monkey had been forced, more or less doubled up, into a tiny cage. The poor thing had its feet and arms tied together and, like every other animal in that market, no real cover from the blistering heat. It looked up at me with uncomprehending eyes. I couldn't do anything for it, any more than I could for the fennec foxes in the next tiny crate. As if their quarters were not cramped enough already, they had to share with a load of very prickly Egyptian hedgehogs.

Fennecs have the smallest bodies and biggest ears of all foxes. They are superbly adapted to the heat of the desert. Their internal systems operate so that they excrete the absolute minimum of fluids and their enormous ears act as heat exchangers. They're nocturnal, the same colour as the sand and can live miles from the oasis because they don't need to drink. They acquire moisture from the blood of the small mammals they eat, although, if they do come to the oasis, they will not decline a few juicy dates.

Stacked in a corner were three sacks of what, at first glance, looked like baking potatoes. They were Kleimans tortoises, a species on the brink of extinction. These were classified as Appendix One by CITES – that is, no trade allowed at all, across borders or otherwise – yet here they were, hundreds of them, like so many King Edwards bound for the chip shop. There might only be a few thousand left in the wild, so how many market days would it need to see them off entirely? They were twenty Egyptian pounds each, about four pounds sterling at the time. Back in England, you could ask, and get, five hundred pounds a tortoise or more.

Next door was the stall of one of the men whose names I had been given, Abdul, specialising in reptiles. He had hundreds of tortoises stacked in sacks like his colleague, plus a desert monitor several feet long and — how much more astonishment was I going to be presented with in an hour? — seventy or so baby Nile crocodiles about a foot long.

Like the tortoises, these crocs are classified by CITES as Appendix One — no trade at all — yet here he was with dozens and dozens of them. And what were the purchasers going to do with their crocodiles? They might be sweet little babies now, but they were going to grow, to eighteen feet if they lived long enough, which might be fifty years, nobody quite knows. So how did they get here in such quantity?

I knew the basics of their life history. They were my very first research project, after listening to Uncle Tony on the couch all those years ago. Uncle Tony. It was his fault I was here.

In the wild mother crocodile lays her eggs, about sixty of them, in November and digs them into the sand. Then, with virtually no sustenance, she lies on top of them for three months, keeping them at an even temperature and protected from predators such as monitor lizards. When the February rains are finished she wanders off the nest and lies close by, keeping watch while the sun finishes the job of incubation.

The first baby out of the shell raises a bit of a stink about being buried, and then the next and then the next. Mother hears and starts digging. She can take about twenty hatched young and half-hatched eggs in her mouth, and she carries them quickly to a pool nearby. There she shakes her head from side to side, allowing water to flush the partially hatched babies out of their eggs. She needs several trips, but must make them fast because the hatchlings' cries will bring monitors, fish eagles, genets and herons, all anxious for a meal.

For a few weeks, mother and father croc (who has somehow heard the news and also turned up) look after the babies in a quiet backwater. Father will have several families and he will leave this one to go to the next when, somehow again, he hears about a new hatching.

After a while the parents lose interest and the babies are free to make their own way. Not many survive this process. If the eggs aren't plundered from the ground, or the hatchlings aren't taken while waiting their turn in the mouth ferry to their nursery pool, the growing babies face the same predators again as they try to cope with life without parents. Out of sixty eggs, only one or two will make it.

Hatching is in February. We were in Cairo in November, looking at crocs a foot or eighteen inches long. They could not have been caught in such numbers from freedom in the river. No collector, however avaricious, is going to try to take newly hatched babies away from mother croc, who is big enough to take an antelope in her jaws. So how do the scum get them, and what happens to them when they get too big for the fish tank? I made a mental note to ask Richard later.

There was also a selection of chameleons, most of which looked as if they wouldn't live out the day, as well as many venomous snakes. There were Egyptian cobras (especially dangerous beasts whose bite rapidly destroys your red blood corpuscles and sends you to meet your Maker in short order) and horned vipers (desert specialists, identifiable by the spike above each eye like the horns of a little devil).

Abdul wore a multi-coloured dishdash and a black fez. He wasn't a big chap, only about five foot six, but he had very long, muscular arms like a gorilla's. I asked him about Kleimans tortoises. He said he could supply as many as I wanted; in fact, any species of bird, reptile or mammal indigenous to the country could be provided by the following week. Like Saad, he liked to play the great man and now, seeing my tourist video camera, he put on a show for the folks back home.

He picked up two of the horned vipers, which are deadly, although you linger longer than if bitten by a cobra, and held them between his teeth. He picked up a scorpion in one hand and a venomous spider in the other and posed for me while I ran off a few feet of tape. I had a wild idea that I might record something sensational, but no.

I decided to buy a desert monitor for sixty Egyptian pounds (twelve pounds sterling), as well as one of the sickly chameleons. I had a double reason; to get in with Abdul, and to make a token gesture towards liberating his animals. I really wanted to buy the monkey from next door and some of the birds, but I had nowhere to take care of them and these were not the sort of thing most westerners would be buying to take back.

I hadn't been able to work out why there was such a demand for species such as black-shouldered kites and Eurasian kestrels until Richard told me. Even so, I don't think I'd truly believed him before now. These superb creatures were bought as status symbols. They soon died because their owners didn't know how to feed them or keep them properly. It was quite typical for a black-shouldered kite, which eats only meat, to be fed with budgie seed. When it starved to death, so what?

I'd grown used to the fundamental hopelessness of our crusade, but now I was overwhelmed by it, in my stomach and my heart. I couldn't see how I could achieve anything positive here. I didn't think the newspaper exposé, no matter how dramatic, could possibly have any effect this far away. Here at the rubbish tip under the motorway intersection, where birds of prey were given no more regard than a spray of mimosa, how many people gave a damn about what middle-class England glances at over its Sunday breakfast?

I gritted my teeth. All I could do was what we always did in these situations: be professional, get the evidence, pass it on to the powers that be. I noticed Mark in the background snapping off a couple of frames. I was confident that I'd recorded most of it on the video and decided to call it a day. We'd only been there an hour, but a bunch of people were already getting too interested in what we were up to. Even though I had the name of another contact, it was definitely time to leave. I would see Abdul another time, perhaps.

Mark and I made our way back to Richard and Rochelle, waiting on the outskirts of the market. As we drove off, I swapped horror stories with Richard. He wasn't the slightest bit surprised at what I'd seen, but was somewhat amused that I'd actually bought two reptiles. I asked him if we could go into the desert to release them. He said I was being a pain. Why didn't I do what the Egyptians did? For instance, when their baby crocs got too big for the sitting room, they dumped them in the sewers or the city water system.

'Richard,' I said, 'I do appreciate your local knowledge, but I want my prize specimens to have a chance of survival at least as good as a snowball in Hades. Now, if you'd like to give me the small satisfaction of a futile gesture, drive on.'

In thirty minutes we were into the eastern desert. Somehow I had imagined an endless expanse of dunes, an oasis of palms shimmering in the distance, a mirage or two, maybe a line of nomadic tribesmen crossing the void with their camels and wild horses. This was more *Steptoe and Son* than *Lawrence of Arabia*. Residents of Cairo obviously drove to the edge of the city with their scrap and, as soon as they passed the last house, dumped the lot, including the car. It was one great disorganised, haphazard scrapyard. Perhaps someone would come along with a bulldozer and push it a bit further out when more land was needed for houses.

Off the main road we found a small, dusty thicket of coastal palm, which would do nicely for my ceremonial gesture. How long my escapees would last I didn't know. They would probably be caught and back in the market by next week.

The monitor was first to go. I placed him on the sand and he froze. This was my luck. I had bought the world's first agoraphobic, institutionalised monitor lizard. I gave him an encouraging prod with my finger, then another, then talked to him about freedom. He got the idea and scurried under a rock.

The chameleon was more difficult. He would not let go of me. The more I tried to get him to climb onto a bush, the tighter he gripped my fingers. This went on for twenty minutes, until the chameleon suddenly saw the light. He let go, walked off as if I had never been there, and climbed up the branch. Three minutes later you could hardly distinguish him from his newly adopted home. All the yellow of his previous colouring had gone and his green now exactly matched the foliage.

Rochelle and Mark were waiting in the car. I'm sure they would have preferred to have gone straight back to the hotel for a nice cool shower and a decent meal, but they had patiently humoured me.

Our one remaining objective was to get some footage of the rooftop collection, which was probably going to be the most difficult part of the whole operation. Tomorrow was Saturday, my last day in Cairo. Eat, drink and be merry, I thought, for tomorrow we get caught on a roof by Saad and the heavy mob.

We all got together that evening for a farewell meal. Richard wanted to take us to an excellent vegetarian restaurant he knew, which caused a few grumbles from some of the team, but it turned out to be a brilliant place. The selection of Egyptian dishes was mind-boggling and the range of tastes, from stuffed vine leaves to sweet curries to exotic fruits to all kinds of things we couldn't place precisely, was sufficient to satisfy the most confirmed carnivore. It was a nice way to round off the whole trip.

Before we finished for the evening I tried, with the aid of Rochelle and Richard, to locate Saad's rooftop on the map. We managed to narrow it down to within a few streets and hoped that would prove to be good enough. On the previous visit I had noticed that the fire escape, like all good fire escapes, ran right down to the ground. There should be no need to break and enter after all.

I was up before sunrise next morning. I ordered a taxi from reception, showed the taxi driver my map and, to my surprise, he nodded and set off as if he knew exactly where I wanted to go. Compared to my experience so far, the traffic this early was calm. Imagine the rush hour in Paris; that's how quiet it was.

It took the driver less than a quarter of an hour to get me to the dropping-off point, about three blocks from the big satellite dish. When I explained that we would now have to wait for sunrise, my taxi driver, who spoke some English, was perplexed. Why did I want to hang about here? What had daybreak to do with it? It was no good trying to tell him and I didn't want to anyway, so I used the universal explanation – a small wad of notes in the local currency.

My plan was very uncomplicated. I was going to walk rapidly to Saad's fire escape, run up it in silent order, quickly shoot off a few photographs as soon as it was light enough, and return at top speed to the waiting taxi.

Few people were out and about at that time of the morning. If I were to be challenged, I would do my Stoopeed Eeengleesh act, shrug my shoulders and wander off. It was unlikely that anyone would physically try to stop me leaving

The worst scenario would be if I stumbled across Saad. All

I had prepared was a pretty feeble line about thinking he might be up there feeding the animals and wanting to meet up with him one more time before I was leaving on a jet plane.

If he didn't swallow that I would flannel and get away in the confusion. Providing he was unarmed, I had no worries about dealing with Saad man to man, although violence might have jeopardised the article.

At last the darkness began to fade. As soon as it was light enough I was setting a new all-comers' record up that fire escape, partly because of the urgency of the operation and partly because it was coming away from the wall and might throw me into the street at any instant. My actions were designed to look deliberate, as if I had every authority. There was no furtive glancing around. I went straight up to the rooftop.

On the roof I wandered about, calling Saad's name but not too loudly. That way, if he did materialise things wouldn't look quite so bad. I took a quick look across the city. Cairo seemed to be pretty much asleep. The odd stray dog gave a token bark. Vehicles were moving, but hardly any pedestrians. Right. To it. Now or never.

I took a few general shots and then opened the gazelle shed and fired off a couple of frames. One of the Thompson's gazelles was lame, its foreleg swollen and infected. Sorry, mate, can't stop. Let's hope Saad will see you right.

Most of the animals were asleep, so it was difficult to get any decent photographs, but I did my best in the circumstances. Five minutes was long enough and I was on my way back down, managing to reach the ground without the fire escape falling on top of me.

The taxi driver was still there. Phew. For a change everything had gone smoothly. I was back at the hotel, showered and down for breakfast before Mark and Rochelle surfaced.

After breakfast we had a long debrief on everything that had happened. Both of them were extremely pleased. Mark had developed most of his photographs and had some excellent results. Rochelle was confident that it would make a great story and, perhaps even more important for her, would impress her new boss and secure her position at the newspaper. I felt happy too, as far as it went, although in terms of actually achieving something to protect these endangered species, I was less convinced.

We flew out of Cairo that day. I'd spent six days in Egypt. I know it is a fascinating country and I'm sure it is a beautiful one, but I was not sad to see it disappear behind the tail fin of the jet.

Back in England I had half a day off and then it was back to the desk chains, typing up reports, putting all my notes together in coherent form so we could see exactly what we did have on Saad, and giving debriefs to Don and the Chief Officer of the Inspectorate, Nigel Thompson. I also assembled a report on tactics and operational requirements for Egypt. If in the future colleagues had to work in that part of the world they would have insights into what to expect and be rather better prepared than I had been.

Although an outsider might not have realised it, Don was pleased with the way things had turned out. I knew him and could tell when the grumpy old sod was having a good time. He agreed completely that it had been a huge mistake to rely on the newspaper to fund our trip out there. The real cost to us was having to hand over control of how the material was used. Looking at my co-ordinated notes it was obvious that Saad had to be one of the biggest dealers in the world. The RSPCA had lost the opportunity to expose him through the proper official channels, and all for the price of an air ticket and a few nights in a hotel.

Nigel Thompson and everyone else agreed – now – that next time we would deal with matters in a different way. Of course this made me feel much better, didn't it? But the story would be splashed all over next week's Sunday instalment of the paper. Saad would go to ground, pop up somewhere else later and carry on as usual, unless we could get a proper package together and put it in the right people's hands.

My first move had to be to Darwen, to see if I could get Fat Al arrested for selling me that ivory tusk. The trip met with zero success. The reception from BB was hostile, not strictly speaking towards me but towards Fat Al, now clearly her ex. She hadn't seen him for the last week and a half, thank the Lord, and if she ever wanted to speak to him again she hoped the only way would be through a medium.

He had been a bad boy. He'd ripped her off, got her into huge debt with catalogue companies and American Express, the kebab business had folded and, to top it all, he'd moved in with a 'young bit'. I made my apologies to BB and left in search of Fat Al's new squeeze. It took me two days to find her, a woman in her mid-twenties with four kids aged between six months and four years, each one a different variety of the species. Her view of portly Jordanian kebab slicers was remarkably similar to BB's. He had moved in with her but the debt collectors and the police were hard on his heels. After a week he took all the cash she possessed, several hundred pounds, and disappeared.

A call on the local CID confirmed everything. Not only had he ripped off his two former girlfriends, but the list of other creditors was growing by the minute. He owed between ten and fifteen thousand pounds that they already knew about, and then there was the rest of the iceberg. The police put an international marker on his name but after a few more days of intensive investigation the trail went cold. He had gone back to Jordan, and that was that. We couldn't get him out, because fraud, theft, ivory smuggling and drug dealing apparently wouldn't add up to 'offences serious enough to warrant extradition'.

Without Fat Al our own case was seriously weakened. We needed evidence that endangered species were being brought here and that there was international trade that could be shown to contravene CITES. Despite our best efforts and anxious wishes we had to leave it to the newspaper. With no Fat Al, we could add nothing further to the case.

As if that wasn't bad enough, the major Cairo-based part of the investigation also threatened to end in disappointment, if only because that is the way such things generally end. We investigate, make a report, and hand over our conclusions to the proper authorities in the country where the offence took place, also copying the file to the country's embassy in the UK. Sometimes this results in action. More often we get a well-phrased letter thanking us most profoundly, expressing horror that such an evil could exist in their country, assuring us that everything possible is being done to stamp out this disgrace on their name, and faithfully promising that, once eradicated, the practice so brilliantly exposed by Her Majesty's RSPCA will never surface again.

Richard to the rescue. Richard Hoath in Cairo made sure he received a copy of the article, which, as we might have guessed, had not been followed up by the Egyptian media at all. But as luck would have it, the regular quarterly Cairo CITES meeting was taking place a few days later.

Moments before the meeting Richard handed the article to the CITES chairman, a government official who had proved trustworthy in the past. Richard said his eyes almost popped out in joy. He did a little dance of glee. This was what he had been waiting for, a chance to expose Saad and his partner in crime, the dreadful woman who was director of Giza zoo.

The chairman let the meeting proceed as usual, with CITES licences being issued willy nilly to Saad, the excellent representive for the import/export trade, then at a choice moment, he produced his copy of the newspaper, read out the relevant parts about the director, and asked her if she could explain herself. I would have given six months' salary to have been there. Saad nearly fell off his seat. The zoo director came over all faint and had to be escorted out into the fresh air.

Then the chairman read out the piece about Saad, his roof and his close relationship with the indisposed director. Within days the director was fired from the CITES panel. She would never again have anything to do with permits and endangered species, and her position at the zoo was under investigation. Saad was also dismissed from CITES and subsequently arrested by the Egyptian authorities. He was charged with dealing in endangered species and, using the information we had provided to the Egyptian consul, convicted and imprisoned.

The really resounding effect of the investigation was on the Egyptians themselves. The Director General of the RSPCA wrote to the Egyptian embassy, as was normal practice, and received the usual kind of reply; the difference was that this time they meant it. We began to hear about raids by Egyptian environmental officers on the animal markets and ivory traders.

The animal market was closed down. It did reopen some months later, but in the meantime impressive quantities of endangered species were rescued. There were several hundred Kleimans tortoises, a number of Dorcas gazelles, Nile crocodiles, Nile monitors, all sorts of other creatures, plus leopard and ocelot skins and over sixty elephant tusks. None of the animals went to Giza zoo.

The Egyptian authorities, for the first time ever, allowed

themselves to be assisted by Richard Hoath. Esther Wenman, head of the reptile house at London Zoo, set about a rehabilitation project that is still continuing. The tortoises were in such a poor state that they couldn't be released immediately into the wild. They were dehydrated and infested with parasites, and many carried long outstanding untreated injuries. They were taken into care and looked after until they were in a fit state to go on to the project. A special area in the Sinai Desert was found and several hundred tortoises, some fitted with radio trackers, began making their slow journey back to a life in the wild where they belonged.

The operation caused a chain reaction in the Egyptian government. The environmental departments became far more pro-active than before, making further raids on the markets and dealers. Although things are still far from perfect in Cairo, the impetus generated by the job dramatically improved both the Egyptian and the Cairo local governments' views towards endangered species. We made a difference. The police are still raiding. Things can only get better.

12

If I thought I'd had enough for the moment of desert dwellers, CITES, venomous snakes and other tropical exotica, I had another think coming. After the heat and the flies I was quite looking forward to a few wet English mornings sitting in a gorse bush trying to catch badger diggers, but it was not to be.

It all began with a lady called Liz Blow. Apart from being a very professional television researcher and producer, Ms Blow has the doubtful distinction of being just about the only person from the media that I have come to trust completely.

Liz was working freelance for Yorkshire Television and was interested in making a programme about people buying and keeping exotic animals, with a particular angle on how easy it was to obtain them on the illegal but more or less open market.

We had – and, as I write, still have – this situation in the UK because of weaknesses in the Dangerous Wild Animals

Act, which seems to have been drafted largely to protect people against the possibilities of injury from escaped tigers. It pays very little attention to the animals themselves. Local authorities are responsible for administering and enforcing the legislation and that part that deals with the welfare of exotic species generally gets a low, low priority. In my experience, if anyone does come up before the courts charged with offences related to this act they are dealt with so lightly that it is hardly an inconvenience, let alone a deterrent.

With this background we were always looking for opportunities to highlight the problem, so Liz Blow's phone call was most welcome. She explained who she was and told me her purpose. Her first question was whether I could get her any snakes?

'I went to this backstreet pet shop,' she said, 'in Bradford. It looked rough and dodgy and run down, and the owner looked the same. Mind you, the animals were all well kept – hamsters, gerbils, fish, all the usual. All neat and tidy in their cages.'

'The fish were in cages?' I said.

Liz ignored me. 'I told the man I wanted a pet snake.'

'What kind of snake?' I asked her.

'Be patient and you'll find out,' said Liz. 'I told the man snake. He said he could get me grass snakes, and he had slow worms already there. Slow worms, I said? I don't want slow worms, I want something with a bit of oomph. The man looked at me, like he was summing me up, and asked me how much I was ready to pay. Fifty quid, I said? A hundred? He was tempted, I could see that, but he kind of closed up on me. No go.'

'They won't sell unless you're known. You have to be one of the brotherhood. Usually, anyway,' I said. 'But I think I can maybe get you some. Any particular species?'

'Just make them poisonous, Tony. And thanks.'

What else could I say? Yes, yes, yes. I could see a double coming up. One, we could get publicity for the inadequacies of the Dangerous Wild Animals Act. Two, I could get heavily into my old mate, Paul Blakey. He'd slipped away from me the last time, when I bought those other two puff adders that, eventually found a home at London Zoo. I had put a case together against Blakey, without him knowing of course, but he somehow managed to bamboozle the police with his detailed knowledge of species and sub-species, so they never went as far as charging him. There the matter had rested — until now. He seemed the obvious choice for a hit.

I checked that George was at home and willing to receive two venomous snakes, then I rang Blakey and reminded him about the puff adders. Being one of the less cautious brethren, he seemed happy to deal and offered me a pair of diamond backed rattlesnakes. I drove north that night, met Blakey at Charnock Richard services next morning, and delivered the snakes to the studios in Leeds.

Liz was delighted at first, and called her pair of biters Bremner and Hunter, after the great Leeds players of her youth. They were filmed, but they turned out to be rather unexciting on the small screen. Liz wanted drama, and the snakes were not playing. She also wanted some real action, real evidence, secret cameras, that sort of thing. She had come to the right place.

I rang Blakey again to see if he had anything more interesting for sale. Yes, he had loads of interesting stuff, various different reptiles as well as snakes. Best thing would be to come up and look. He'd moved recently and was living in a bungalow outside Morecambe.

Perfect. I took the rattlers to George and came back to give Liz a briefing session on undercover work. I showed her the covert jacket camera and explained its limits – battery time, tape length. I put it on and showed her where and where not to stand, so the lens got a clear view. It was silent in operation but it was always best if any interested parties were diverted in some way, so I asked Liz if she would help out with this part of the action. She was very pleased to have a contribution to make. Her cover was that of my girlfriend, quite fed up with my obsession with snakes rather than herself. She was to occupy Blakey with her grumbles and give him the come-on while I did the necessary.

I didn't expect any trouble. Even if things went wrong Blakey was not the violent type, unlike some I'd had to deal with. I was confident Liz couldn't come to any harm and so was happy to have her along.

It was a cold January night, pouring with rain, which was a slight problem because the jacket camera was liable to short out if it got wet. As we drove along I went over the plan again, concentrating especially on the legal problems of being agents provocateurs. At all costs we had to avoid what they call 'inciting the offence', by which I particularly meant asking for a specific reptile. Obviously we had to show interest or we wouldn't be there, but we had to keep it general. We had to let him make the offers, and we would respond.

We stopped a few hundred yards short to switch on the camera, then drove up to his front door. It was a weird place to be going to see snakes. All the bungalows on the avenue were nicely kept, with neat gardens and painted fences and little ponds with fountains, clearly the sort of estate that people retired to. Blakey, the six foot four beanpole with the long black heavy metal hair, must be regarded as the neighbourhood eccentric, I thought, even if the neighbours had no idea they had a snake collector in their midst.

I'd told Liz what to expect so she managed a lightly fanciable smile when the apparition came to the door, looking like he'd stepped off the cover of a Black Sabbath album. I wanted to ask him if he would please come to our village show in the summer and enter The Pet Most Like Its Owner competition. Blakey and a black mamba would walk it.

He was the laid-back type and beckoned us in, explaining that he was mid-game in Doom and at a ticklish moment. He'd never reached this far before, so we wouldn't mind waiting, would we, while he carried on? He took a few moments to explain about the massive arsenal of cyber weapons he had collected, then settled in his chair and began zapping everything in sight, bouncing up and down as he killed and killed again down the long corridors of Doom.

This was bad news for us. I only had thirty minutes of videotape, and so far all I'd filmed was a refugee from an eighties rock band turned cyber-killer, front view and back of head. I had two choices. I could go to the bathroom and turn my camera off, in which case I would have to repeat the exercise to turn it on again, or I could take the initiative. Like all good managers I delegated the task and, after a whisper in her ear, the lovely Liz went sidling up to Blakey, saying she didn't know which was worse, men who were daft about reptiles or men who were daft about computer games. Why didn't he come and talk to her while he let boring old Tony look at his nasty snakes?

Blakey, more than energised by the thought of a tête à tête with Liz, suspended his game immediately, as, I think, most men would have. I know they say that power tends to corrupt and absolute power corrupts absolutely, but it didn't seem to be the case with Liz. She could get any man to do whatever she wanted but she used her power selectively and for good causes, and remained thoroughly nice with it.

He took us across the passage to a spare bedroom and ushered us in. We stopped dead. The walls were lined, from floor to ceiling, with vivaria; there must have been fifty or sixty. He had the radiator turned up for the residents' comfort, and there was a strange noise that it took me a moment to work out.

'Crickets,' I said.

'Yes,' said Blakey, giving me a wink. 'Food for venomous snakes. They escape and get under the floorboards. I could try biological control and let a few snakes out.'

Liz took this as a good opportunity to do her fearful school-girl act and grabbed Blakey by the arm. He didn't mind in the slightest.

The wink and the remark were a bit of a test for me. Blakey, like all of his kind, was proud of his knowledge, and he would never miss a chance to score off someone less well informed. He didn't score with me. I knew what the crickets were for. Venomous snakes don't eat crickets, but lizards do, and snakes eat lizards.

The problem Blakey and other snake keepers always have is how to find enough lizards to feed snakes that won't eat anything else. The answer is to buy in or breed mice and rats. They take a baby rat, say, and rub it on a lizard, which passes on its scent. This is enough to fool the snake into believing the rat is a lizard, so it will eat it. These small, delicately lizard-scented suppers are called, in the trade, pinkies. When Blakey made his snake food remark I crooked my little finger at him to show I knew the real story, and he gave me a slight nod of approval.

Liz was still gripping his arm like he was Saint George and she was the maiden tied to the rock waiting for the dragon to stroll by. I could see him calculating his chances but he decided that, for the moment, business came before pleasure.

With Liz in tow like the reluctant bride, he showed me some
spitting cobras and asked me if there was anything special I
would like to see. I told him I'd like to see everything, then
make my mind up, so we moved on to some more cobras, the
Egyptian variety this time.

I happened to know a bit about this snake through the extra
reading I'd done for the Cairo trip. I thought I had a chance
to get some of my own back on Liz, who was, in my opinion,
slightly overdoing her willingness to leave me to seduce the
hairy beanpole.

'See this one, Liz?' I said. 'Egyptian cobra. Latin name, *Nuja
hajc*, right, Paul? Grows to six feet. Used by Cairo snake char-
mers in their street performances, God rest their souls. Also
known as the asp.'

'The one that Cleopatra . . .?'

'The same. Nobody knows for sure that the Cleopatra story
is true, but it is a fact that the ancient Egyptians used the asp
as a means of execution. They liked it to bite you on the
breast.' I looked meaningfully at Liz and she stuck her tongue
out 'The condemned man ate a hearty breakfast, then they
put an asp down his shirt and that was that. They called it a
merciful death, so goodness knows what the alternatives were
like.'

'God, I hate snakes,' said Liz, shivering with real feeling.
'And I hate men who think they're funny.'

As we went along the banks of vivaria, seeing puff adders,
more diamond-backed rattlers and various kinds of cobras and
vipers, there was plenty of evidence, but whether we were
gathering it I didn't know. The tanks were steamed up, plus
they had strip lights that made for reflected UV, so altogether
the filming conditions were not promising.

Blakey mistook my technical gloom for lack of interest in
his collection and decided to gee everybody up by showing

the greatest prize among all these rare and – in the UK – illegal animals.

'I know what you'll like,' he said. 'Come and look at this. I'll bet any money you've never seen one of these.'

He was like a schoolboy, looking through the keyhole at the French mistress kissing the gym teacher. He was almost hopping in his secret pleasure.

On the floor in a corner was a large vivarium, a yard across, with a plywood sheet over the top. He took the plywood away, like the magician revealing the missing damsel he'd just put twenty swords through.

'There. Have you ever seen one of those before?'

I hadn't. In fact, I had never expected to see one. I knew what it was, though.

'Good Lord above,' said Liz. 'What is it? It looks like a baby dinosaur with bubblewrap for skin.'

'Beaded lizard, Liz. *Heloderma horridum*, am I right, Paul? Pacific coast of Mexico only. One of only two venomous lizards in the world, the other being the closely related Gila monster, also Mexican, which you will surely have heard of.' I neglected to add that I knew the beaded lizard was CITES Appendix One and very much endangered, both by slash and burn agriculture destroying its habitat and by collection for the prestige pet market.

It was a truly remarkable animal, very impressive indeed. Your first impression was, as Liz said, of a miniature yellow and black dinosaur covered in blisters. It had a black head, shaped something like a pit bull terrier's, with those blank little eyes that looked through you rather than at you and didn't care a toss either. The black tail had yellow bands and, all over, everywhere, were these little bubbles, the beads that gave it its name. It was over two feet long.

Blakey was like the proverbial cat with the Cornish clotted.

He had every right to be excited – I certainly had never seen anything like that lizard and I was sure Liz hadn't – and, being in this state, he could not resist boasting, as it happened straight into the camera.

'Quite right, Tony. Beaded lizard. Smuggled in from Mexico, and about four years old. Could grow to three feet, Tony. What would you say then?'

'Tony,' said Liz. 'You're not buying that. You are not. If you put a three-foot dinosaur with acne in our sitting room, I'm moving out. Then you can see how the beaded wonder keeps you warm at night, instead of me. Where's the poison come from, anyway?'

'From glands in the lower jaw,' said Blakey. 'And it's not really for sale.'

'Not really? Is it for sale, or isn't it? You're not wasting my time are you, Paul?' I was desperate for this to be our purchase. It would make great television and, therefore, a very big point on our side.

'If it was for sale,' said Blakey, 'if, mind you, it would be a grand.'

'I'll give you nine hundred, cash, tomorrow.'

Liz hadn't forgotten her part. I knew she would be as desperate as I was to get hold of the beaded lizard, but she was undercover. She had to be convincing.

'Tony. You're not spending nine hundred pounds on that thing. We're supposed to be going to the Canary Islands, you said. I'm warning you. It's me or the dinosaur.'

'We'll think about it, Paul,' I said to Blakey. 'I'll call you tomorrow.'

'No, he won't, Paul. We are going to the Canaries. Mr Blobby over there can go to hell.'

'I think I'll get back to my game,' Blakey concluded. 'I'll see you out.'

'I'll phone you. About midday,' I whispered out of the corner of my mouth, with a nod and a wink, putting my arm around Liz, who responded with a sharp elbow in the stomach.

'Well,' I said as we drove away. 'Congratulations to Dame Judi Dench. That was some performance.'

'Never mind that,' said Liz. 'How much money can you get out of the hole in the wall?'

As soon as we arrived back at the hotel, we ran the video. The first fifteen minutes were fine. Excellent quality. You had a really good view of the back of Blakey's head. Luckily the snakes had come out reasonably well too, and Mr Blobby was a star turn.

Liz got on the phone to the lawyers at Yorkshire to see if she could safely buy the lizard without compromising the possibility of successful prosecution, agents provocateurs and all that. They eventually called back to say that on the one hand it might be compromising, but on the other hand it probably wouldn't be.

I called Blakey. No answer. I tried several times through the evening and again the next morning. Something like that always makes you anxious. You begin to have doubts about your cover and whether your man has done a runner. Of course I did reach him in the end, around midday, and told him that I was going to have that beaded lizard, girlfriend or no girl-friend. I had the money (courtesy of Liz's and my plastic combined), and I'd be there in twenty minutes.

Liz sat in the car, supposedly sulking, while I collected the vivarium. I was, genuinely, as enthusiastic about it as Blakey. It was one of the most remarkable animals I had ever seen or was ever likely to see. If I could deal with the case properly I could think about reintroducing it to its homeland in Mexico, and I could watch it wandering off to find its old desert burrow. Fanciful I know, but it was one very fancy animal.

We took the beast to be filmed in its box by Yorkshire TV, then I moved it on to my good friend George. When I arrived, I didn't tell him what I'd brought. I wanted to see his eyes pop out of his head, fall in the vivarium and be eaten by the beaded lizard, and it nearly happened. George was over-whelmed with delight. He grabbed it by the neck and lifted it up.

'This is the bees' knees of lizards,' he said, ever the poet, as he started stroking it like a puppy dog. Next was the old wash and scrub routine, which brought the lizard's colours up a treat. I could see a kind of faraway look in George's eyes.

'No, you can't keep it,' I said. I knew what he was thinking. In his mind, he had already designed a massive compound for the animal and made plans to bring over a mate. He was going to breed beaded lizards.

'It's going back to Mexico,' I said. 'Look after it, but don't fall in love.'

Next time I popped by for another look at my favourite lizard, George had constructed a small corner of Mexican desert with rocks and sand and lots of heat, and the lizard was looking extremely fit on a diet of raw egg.

We were ready now to move against Blakey. He was not a registered holder of dangerous wild animals, so all his snakes were illegal. None of the vivaria had locks, and neither had the bedroom door so anything that escaped would be able to slither and slide its way around until it found a route out into the streets of Morecambe.

The sooner we could close him down and seize his collec-tion the better. The problem was that we didn't want to inter-fere with Liz's TV schedule. If Blakey was arrested and charged before the programme went out, that would put the mockers on it because any broadcast then would be about a matter that was *sub judice* and so itself illegal. This may seem a trivial worry against the possibility of spitting cobras wandering down Morecambe sea front, but if it hadn't been for Liz we wouldn't have been anywhere in the case.

Added to that we had a big, big concern with the local authority. We had to go through local authorities because they were written into the legislation. We could not sit on all this evidence, and, if we wanted to get Blakey, there was only the one way. I said to Liz that it was down to her to persuade the powers not to act until her programme was transmitted. I told her I thought I would have no chance but that she might have a slim one.

'Feminine wiles, you mean?' she said.

'Just so,' I said. 'You'll have to use them on our man.'

'What if it's a woman?' asked Liz.

'In Lancashire?' I answered. 'Nay, lass. It'll be a man.'

It was. Warren (not his real name), Liz and I went to lunch – on Liz – in a Lancaster hotel. I didn't say much. I sat and watched as Liz twisted the poor fellow around her little finger. She wore a tight silk blouse with rather a lot of the buttons undone. When she leaned forward confidentially and put her hand gently on his, my only uncertainty was if he would be able to finish his lunch before his eyes could be collected off the tablecloth for feeding to the lizards. He had no hope. In the face of Liz's glories he would quite happily have agreed to a nuclear strike on the Town Hall if she'd wanted one.

We had four weeks to get everything organised, and now we ran into another problem. Warren, although bewitched by Liz, wanted to run the whole project himself. Needless to say I wasn't keen on having a pen pusher, no matter how committed, running an operation like this. It was my territory. I was experienced. I knew about snake handlers, vets, transport, police and all the rest. Also I had no politics to worry about, no committees of councillors anxious to deflect a little limelight onto themselves.

Warren wasn't too bad, though. If I could keep a close eye on progress, we would be all right. Then he mentioned a certain snake expert, whom he would be bringing in on the project. This was disaster. I knew this man. He was a contact of Blakey's and had a shady side. Blakey, one of the UK's leading snake dealers, had been supplying him for years. If he was told about our project, I knew the first thing he'd do would be to ring Blakey up and warn him.

I banged on and on about this to Warren and did persuade him in the end. We wouldn't use this man. We didn't need this man. Good. Warren, not without considerable difficulty, managed to take out a search warrant under the Environmental Health Act. I faded into the background while my colleague from the Far Al surveillance, Paul Goldston, took over the job from our side, liaising with Sue Taylor. I'd worked with Sue before and knew she was bombproof and highly capable. Not unnaturally, the police wanted to leave the snake part of the op to us. They would be there to force entry if necessary, to make arrests and to ensure there was no breach of the peace. Everything looked fine. We were ready.

Two days before we were due to strike, Warren proved that my misgivings were well justified. Despite his pleas, his boss had insisted that the aforementioned herpetologist be brought in.

There was nothing I could do. I knew that the entire operation was blown apart, but had to hope against hope that it wasn't.

On the morning of the raid I took the briefing in glum mood at 07.15. Trevor Knowles, another ex-forces recruit to our unit, had been watching Blakey's house since 04.30, and he reported no activity. We had environmental health people at the briefing, Sue and other police, Paul and uniformed RSPCA. There was to be no attempt that day to take away the snakes. Some zoo people were coming the following day for that.

Once the expedition had gone I settled down to wait at the police station, out of the way. I didn't want to be seen by the mistrusted snake expert, who was being picked up en route as snake identifier. I didn't want Blakey to know who I was because I was already vowing that there would be a next time. Most of all I didn't want to watch such a clear-cut op come to nothing because of people who knew nothing about the job.

They came back at 08.45, minus the expert, their faces long as fiddles. Blakey hadn't been there when they arrived at the bungalow, and they had been about to enter the premises force-fully when the swaggering sod turned up as if by magic, putting on this innocent, who-me act. Of course he would be delighted to co-operate with the police and the RSPCA, anything at all he could do, sorry you've got the wrong house this time but I do hope you catch the swine.

He showed them the spare bedroom. In a corner was stacked a pile of empty vivaria. Sue and Paul were certain that he had been tipped off and had cleared the place in a hurry.

In the depths of despair I tried to salvage something in a long chat with Sue. We decided on two angles of approach. She would pursue the herpetologist, attempting to prove a link between him and Blakey that could lead to a charge of perverting the course of justice. I would try and find the collection.

Over the next fortnight I trawled the herpetological world for a hint or a word. Nobody knew anything. Everyone had heard about the raid, but that was it. I paused for a while to reconsider the position and to see what might be done about my old friend, the beaded lizard. I consulted Esther Wenman, head curator of the reptile house at London Zoo, who did not say what I wanted to hear. My lizard had been out of Mexico too long. In captivity all that time, in close proximity to all sorts of unfamiliar and foreign species, he may have picked something up, a disease perhaps, which could spread among his fellows in their native land. I would very probably be doing more harm than good by releasing him, and it was not a risk that Esther could recommend.

Instead she offered to contact colleagues at Zurich Zoo who were developing a breeding programme for endangered species that she thought my lizard might fit into, so that's what happened. If it didn't get back to the wild, at least it would be doing something for its species' future.

Back on the snake trail we suddenly hit it lucky. George rang me to say that he'd heard a whisper that Blakey's collection had migrated south, to Surrey somewhere, and that a man called Ramsden was acting snake keeper. No sooner had I put the phone down than the RSPCA regional control centre in London called. They'd had an anonymous phone call from a woman who had seen Liz Blow's TV programme, which had been broadcast nationally by that time. Although it had concentrated mainly on the beaded lizard, my covert footage of the snakes in their vivaria had been shown, and this was what had triggered the call. This woman said she knew that a man, name not known but at such and such an address in Sutton, Surrey, was keeping poisonous snakes in his garage.

We only had to check the electoral register. His name was Ramsden, Ian Ramsden.

To set up the operation we needed to collect together a group of people with the right expertise who also could be trusted. I was determined there would be no leak this time. My first meeting was with the local RSPCA inspector, James

Lewis, and the police wildlife officer, Peter Harris. Peter had spoken to the environmental health office and made sure that Ramsden was not licensed to keep venomous snakes. We still needed to be sure that a substantial number of snakes was being kept in the garage, then we had to start assembling our experts. We would be looking for a short-term home for the snakes, and we would also need transport to get them there, someone with real authority to identify them, someone to move them from the garage to the transport, a veterinary surgeon to see to the health of the reptiles and, preferably, an army of doctors standing by with snakebite antidotes and maybe a priest to administer the last rites if they didn't happen to have the right one with them.

This was a real concern. For example, Blakey had had five young saw-scale vipers in his bungalow, and the anti-venom situation with these was (and still is) confused, partly because the venom varies from sub-species to sub-species. Even so, when you see how widespread they are, found throughout the world and always common in these habitats, and when you note how many people they bite – they account for more of these incidents than any other family of snakes – you wonder why nobody seems to have taken a hold on this issue.

The adults are not big, maybe two, two and a half feet long. Our young ones were less than a foot long, but they are highly poisonous and exceptionally aggressive at all ages. Their other name is carpet snake, because the patterns on some types look like Persian carpets, but saw-scale is a more fitting name because of what they do just before they bite you. When annoyed, which is not a difficult state to achieve, they double up, back and forth, into a sort of coiled horseshoe shape with the head in the middle. By rubbing sections of the coiled-up body together, the skin, which has special scales called keels, makes a noise, a blend of coarse glasspaper on hardwood and bacon sizzling in the pan. If you ever hear this sound in anger from a free saw-scale you have probably had it, because the next thing is an extremely fast, springing leap up from the coiled body, and the strike.

I always enjoy telling police officers this kind of thing. It's funny how they are quite willing to face up to a Saturday night drunk with a broken bottle in his hand, but show most of them a little snake and they have quite a different attitude. Not PC Harris, though. He was still keen.

At three the next morning I was sneaking around Ramsden's garage with Paul, trying to see what was inside. There seemed to be a good number of vivaria, because we could see the glow from the lights. Even if it wasn't Blakey's collection – which we were sure it was – it was still worth a raid.

The rest of the plan soon fell into shape. George, good old George, fitted up a room at his place, ready to take the proceeds of the raid, with proper locked and labelled tanks, locked doors and warnings. We needed an internationally renowned snake expert, so I went to my good friend John Fordham at Drayton Manor Park, who knew more about venomous snakes than almost anyone on the planet. Interesting character, John, tall, thin, white-haired, and a complete enthusiast. And, for a hobby, he bred wolves. He had one in his house as a pet. Most importantly, he was totally trustworthy.

John knew of a firm called Proteus, which specialised in reptile rescue and had purpose-built vehicles fitted with secure heated tanks. So transport was booked for the day, although we didn't yet tell them from where to where.

Next we recruited the vet, a young man called Steve Divers who was making a reputation for himself in the treatment of snakes, especially in surgery. Then we made our arrangements

with the police, got the warrant, sorted out our own personnel – Trevor Knowles was going to organise – and finally
we booked the ambulance.

I had to be there this time, undercover or not. I was the
only person who could say if those snakes were Blakey's.

The morning came and, after the briefing at the police
station, we all moved close to Ramsden's place but stayed out
of sight while Trevor and a police sergeant went knocking on
the door. We didn't want our massed ranks to make Ramsden
overreact. We didn't know him. He could flip, he could panic,
and the result could be urgent calls to fly in anti-venom to
Sutton hospital.

In fact Ramsden was badly shaken by the arrival of the
police but by the time the garage was opened and the rest of
us had arrived he was taking things in his stride. He was especially impressed that John Fordham was there, one of his idols
apparently, and he was all for going back to the house to get
a copy of one of John's books for him to sign. Business first,
we said, firmly. I had a quick look to satisfy myself that we
did indeed have Blakey's collection, then retired into the background. There was a massive amount of stuff here, maybe sixty
snakes, and the fewer people there were around the better.

Ramsden and John Fordham agreed on the identification of
each snake while Trevor videoed it. Things were going nicely
when, without any warning, Ramsden thrust his hand into a
vivarium and grabbed an Asian spitting cobra and waved it
about to show how domesticated it had become under his care.
'It won't hurt you,' he declared to a garage instantly empty of
people. He didn't mean any harm, but after that it was decided
that Ramsden might as well take the risks and be nominated
as the one to move the snakes into the Proteus tanks.

Although Ramsden was most accommodating throughout
the proceedings, I can't say anyone warmed to him particularly.

Steve the vet was collecting evidence of poor and downright bad treatment of the animals, and it became clear that charges of cruelty would be brought as well as those of illegal keeping.

Many of the snakes looked thin and undernourished, and there were some without water. Steve said that by the state of the water bowls they hadn't had any for days, and this was the laziness of a man keeping snakes like a baby anaconda, which lives in swamps, and a water moccasin, which is an aquatic species of pit viper that eats fish and frogs. All animals need water, but to keep a water dweller without it is criminal cruelty.

After about two hours the snakes were all loaded and the convoy could set off for George's. We kept the police informed, in case of accidents, but we arrived safely with no trouble at all. We took the special containers out of the Proteus vehicles and into George's new snake parlour and awaited another dangerous part of the operation. Trevor, Paul and I were there, and George had brought along an old pal, Pat Fletcher, to watch and advise. Pat was an elderly gentleman who had spent many years in India with the army, and he had studied snakes out there to such an extent that he became a well-known expert and snake handler and went into zookeeping when he left the forces. George called him the Master, but it was fairly clear that this level and volume of snake handling called for the reactions and certainty of movement of a younger man than Pat.

George assembled his range of snake hooks. Normal people go and buy these essential tools in two types. First there's the metal pole with the right angle on the end, which you use to press down just behind the snake's neck so you can grab the body in your hand. Then there's the metal pole with the swan-neck end with which you pick up the snake at its middle point, whereupon it will balance and hang there, not moving (it says on the instructions).

The snake hooks we had that night were more various altogether. There were small ones made out of wire coat-hangers, large ones made out of golf clubs, and everything in between, but not a single hook was of a proprietary brand. Every one was home-made.

George moved the snakes, individual by individual, to their new homes. Few of them were in very good moods, and it required all of George's concentration to complete each task successfully.

I confess I was distinctly worried when, as a sign of respect, George asked Pat if he'd like to transfer this little puff adder. Pat needed no second invitation and was selecting a small snake hook straight away, one of the ex-dry-cleaner adaptations. He had the little monster hooked with no bother, but as it was travelling through the air it fell off, hit the floor, and struck out. It missed Pat's ankle by a fraction as we all took an instinctive step backwards. I assumed it would have another go at Pat, not miss this time, then set off for its freedom. George would have to catch it while Paul and I tried to do something for Pat, although at his age I wouldn't have thought he had a lot of chance with a puff adder bite.

I don't know how much of this thought process I went through at the time, because Pat moved like lightning. He had that snake rehooked and in the vivarium in one swift movement and we all felt the fear subside.

That was the remarkable thing about Pat. We RSPCA lads were none of us soft or lacking in fibre, but when a poisonous reptile is about the old jungle instincts take over. All you want to do is climb the nearest tree as fast as possible. It says something for Pat that he could overcome these baser instincts and save his own life and possibly someone else's too.

By the end of the evening some of the snakes were definitely not pleased with us. They'd had a long day, and they didn't like it. Every time anybody walked past the vivaria, snakes would strike at the sides. There was a three-foot-long glass case with spitting cobras in it, and the front had venom running down it like rain on a window.

It had been a long day for me, too, but as I drove home I was highly pleased. Ramsden would have been charged and bailed by now, so he'd have been on the phone to Blakey, and Blakey would have been on the phone to the so-called expert who had warned him. I looked forward very much to their court appearances.

'A court heard today that an illegal collection of fifty-eight poisonous snakes was discovered in tanks in an unlocked garage at a suburban semi,' said the report in a national paper. 'Ian Ramsden, thirty-four, unemployed, who lives there with his wife and children, denied thirteen charges of causing animals unnecessary suffering. He was also accused of keeping dangerous reptiles without a licence.

'One of the snakes, a saw-scale viper, was described by an expert as "the most dangerous snake known to man". The prosecutor told magistrates: "In preparing for the raid, officers found that they were not sure if an antidote would be available if they were bitten."

'The snakes are now recovering in zoos. The case continues.'

London Zoo had taken most of them off George's hands, and Thrigby Hall took some, but it was a year before we found a home for every one. It was suggested we should put the homeless ones down but I would have seen that as a failure. To rescue an animal from a Blakey or a Ramsden and then to kill it does not seem either moral or logical.

While all this was going on, Sue had been pursuing the expert, but to no avail. It was fairly simple with modern phone records to prove that he had called Blakey at the relevant time, but there was no way of proving that what he had said had perverted the course of justice.

Blakey himself was found guilty on six counts of keeping dangerous wild animals without a licence. The magistrates fined him fifty pounds on each count. I didn't know whether to laugh or cry.

13

'Anybody here heard of a chap called Verril?'

No racing commentator would have had time to describe my rate of progress across the office to the desk occupied by team member Martin Wilson.

When he casually mentioned Verril in that laid-back voice of his I was there so fast, snatching his report from his hand, that he must have thought he'd named the Devil himself – which, in a way, he had. Verril had been my Devil almost since I started with SOU ten years before. I hadn't heard of him for a long, long time.

There wasn't much in the report but what I did read was priceless. According to the local uniformed inspector, Verril now lived in a lovely Sussex village, was head keeper on one of the major estates, and was bringing his old mates down from the North to indulge in their favourite sport, the brutal killing of badgers.

I knew something of this estate. It had quite a reputation

for gamebirds, pheasants of course but especially partridges. It was a prestigious shoot, one of those where the clients pay really big money and arrive from mainland Europe in helicopters. When they have a good day they tip the gamekeeper so heavily that he doubles his salary.

The Sussex Downs are ideal partridge country and perfect too for badgers. According to the report the estate was several hundred acres, very large for this part of the world where land is so expensive, and a fair proportion was woodland. Badgers would love it. Nice gentle hills for them to dig into to make their setts, and lots of pasture to maintain their chief item of diet, earthworms.

Martin said he'd been in touch with the local naturalists' badger group who had confirmed that it certainly was densely populated with badgers. 'But they haven't done a proper survey. Mr Verril, apparently, won't allow them access.'

'What a very strange thing, Martin,' I said. 'Fancy an inveterate badger digger not being nice to the local naturalists. I think he'd tell David Attenborough to get lost as well.'

Martin had also acquired a jewel, a gold nugget, an answer to our prayers: an informant.

Eric was a village lad, a farmer's son of fifteen who, like most village boys of his age, had tried his hand at all the country sports. When the estate was short of beaters Eric was on Verril's list of contacts who could be called upon at short notice if a regular beater dropped out. It was easy money and enjoyably earned, strolling along, thrashing the undergrowth with a stick, kicking the great fat, hand-fed pheasants into the air and driving the faster, wilder partridges towards the waiting guns.

At the end of the previous season Eric had been invited to a beaters' day, a chance for the local lads to thin out the population of cock pheasants, always too many for breeding purposes or to be kept in expensive food over the winter. Eric fancied himself as a bit of an artist with his old Russian under-and-over twelve-bore. He'd accounted for many a woodpigeon and rabbit over his young years and he scored very well on the cock pheasants, which was noted by the older men around him. It was this undoubted skill with a shotgun that had given him the beginnings of his ambitions in gamekeeping.

He didn't see farming as glamorous enough. Instead he admired the life of Geoff Verril, head keeper of a fine estate, a position of some note in any rural community. Eric was not alone in his views. Many of the local youths put Verril on a pedestal. In their eyes he had everything. He lived in the best tied house in the village, had a top-of-the-range Land Cruiser, came and went as he pleased, had four underkeepers to do all the hard work, and was in charge of his own personal arsenal – shotguns, .22 rifles, deer rifles.

Socially he exploited his position to its fullest extent. He had his own space in the pub car park and his own seat in the tap room, a window seat, facing the road so he could keep an eye on passing traffic in case any strangers were in the area. Gamekeepers are professional watchers, permanently on the lookout. It's in their blood. They miss nothing, gamekeepers, which is why it's so damned hard to catch somebody like Verril. You're up against a pro who's at least as good at obser-vation – and covert surveillance – as you are.

This season had seen things move on for young Eric. He had spent all his spare time during school holidays and week-ends doing donkey work on the estate. His intention was to get on the good side of the keepers, and it certainly seemed to have worked when he had confirmation from his school that he had been put onto the estate for two weeks' work experience.

His eagerness and enthusiasm impressed all the underkeepers but the man with the power was Verril. He was the guy who hired and fired. In theory it was the job of the agent but in practice everyone knew that such matters were the head keeper's decision.

By the end of the first week Eric hadn't even set eyes on Verril. As he was getting his things together to go home on the Friday, one of the other keepers took him aside. Verril had arranged a bit of recreation for Saturday evening and, because Eric was a known and trusted lad and had shown such promise in his first week, he was invited to come along. He was told to be at the shooting lodge at seven o'clock. He never thought to ask what the entertainment was, nor did the possibility of some kind of test cross his mind. He didn't really care anyway. It was a chance to rub shoulders with the great man.

The lodge was only a ten-minute walk from his house but he'd never been there before because its main use was as a luncheon room where the shooters adjourned for their simple repasts of salmon, venison and caviar, all served with the correct wines. Verril was there now with two strangers, men with Northern accents like Verril's. They had spades, guns, three terriers and a lurcher. As before, this lurcher was not one of your greyhound-based mixtures, the sort gypsies use to run down rabbits. Verril liked lurchers with solid fighting stock in them, preferably Staffordshire. If one of the old bear baiting dogs from medieval times could reappear, it would probably look something like Verril's favoured type.

Eric was deeply traumatised by the sickening events of the next two hours, digging badgers out of the earth, and he was exhausted by the effort of pretending he wasn't. The story was blurted out to his father that night, through his tears. Initially the boy refused to return to his work experience. His dad said keepers didn't have to be like that. Eric could still be a keeper without being a badger digger; it wasn't a necessary qualification. In any case Eric could do more good from the inside, particularly if he was in touch with us, so that's what happened. His work experience developed into a part-time keeping job and now we had a fifth column, a spy behind enemy lines and, knowing what we did about Verril, a very brave one.

From what the boy told Ian it seemed that Verril's reputation for violence and temper had been firmly re-established in Sussex. Not only was he a man with style and position. He was to be feared as well.

The Sussex Downs were bang on our doorstep, which meant that, for once, I could be at home with my family and do the job. I could put in the kind of surveillance time the operation needed without long-distance commuting, hotel bills for Don to moan about, or restraints of any kind. I could do the job properly and, boy oh boy, did I want to do this one. It didn't take me long to persuade Don to assign me the necessary time and resources.

It would be Martin Wilson's role to pose as the kind of gentleman who would be highly acceptable in the sort of pub I guessed there would be in the Sussex village where Verril now lived. I knew Verril of old. He would be spending many an hour in the pub, holding court and establishing himself as a local kingpin. It would be no good for me to start to go in there regularly, a stranger with a Northern accent. I would stick out too much and, even if he didn't spot me himself, Verril would soon realise we were on his trail again.

'Okay, Martin,' I said, after I'd given him a rundown on Verril and our previous encounters. 'Get your cavalry twills and your Oxford brogues out of the wardrobe and start having lunch at that pub. Twice a week should be enough. Be extremely careful about what you say and do. I'm not having a word of this job getting out. This is our chance to nail one of the biggest bastards we'll ever come across, so make sure your profile of him has everything. And I'll see you at half past four in the morning.'

This was the start of my part of the project, which was to assemble a complete picture of the estate and Verril's activities. We would need such a report before we could have any consultation with the police leading to direct action against him. I knew it would take weeks of creeping about the estate at dawn like the Apache scout of my boyhood, only this time it was for real. I had to find out everything I could about how the estate was run and Verril's routines, and I had to do it without spooking him or leaving any sign of my presence.

My aim was to set a trap for these people. Obviously I had to be familiar with the terrain, which in itself was extremely difficult. I couldn't contact the landowner, who might be turning a blind eye to Verril's badger activity or even actively encouraging it. The decision to enter private land was never taken lightly, but sometimes it was necessary to commit the technical offence of trespass to stop a far more serious crime. I was a trespasser, and if I was stumbled across by any of the keepers or, worst of all, by Verril himself, at the very least it would blow my cover and possibly it might blow a lot more. Verril could even shoot me and claim afterwards that he thought it was a raiding fox after his pheasant pens. It would be a difficult defence to disprove. I would be dressed for subterfuge, and who could blame a gamekeeper for doing his job?

The season was early spring and it became light at about six o'clock. The idea was for Martin to get me onto the land in the dark. I would wait there for dawn, make a rapid recce as far as I could, and get out before Verril's normal day began. By doing this methodically, section by section on a grid, I would gradually draw a picture, literally, of the whole estate and identify the locations of the badger setts.

The personal risk increased like compound interest. I would surely get away with it once, twice, three times, maybe even ten times, but when I looked ahead and saw thirty, forty, fifty times I couldn't see how I was going to continue to have the luck to beat a man of Verril's abilities. Whatever else he might have been, Verril was a top-class gamekeeper, with all the experience and acute senses that requires. Plus he had a staff of four, and there were the possibilities of a chance observation by somebody from the village. Either he'd find me and expose me, or he'd get my scent and disappear like he'd done before. But there was no other way and I could only hope that, this time, the gods of badgers and all wildlife would be able to help me enough.

On that first morning, when Martin arrived at my home I was already fully dressed and kitted up. I was head to toe in DPM (Disruptive Pattern Marking) camouflage – smock and trousers with the noisy Velcro replaced by buttons. I had black army issue boots, green and brown gloves and a face veil. Underneath all that I had my radio and, in various pockets and a small bergen, I carried binoculars, Ordnance Survey map, sketch book, compass, video camera, Maglite – a near indestructible American torch with a red filter for covert work – and a mobile phone for comms back-up. This was undulating country, and there would be lots of radio blackspots.

It was only a forty-five-minute drive. Martin would drop me off and then wait at a public car park not too far away, a popular spot for taking the views across the Downs. Thank goodness for the profession of sales representative. Whenever we wanted to sink into the background, all we had to do was put on a collar and tie and take a few files and computer print-outs with us in the car. Martin could snooze until it was light, look at his papers, listen to the radio, eat a sandwich, drink a flask of coffee, enjoy the panorama, and nobody would take a blind bit of notice. If only my part of the job was as easy.

I had selected the drop-off point for the first section and, twenty minutes before our estimated time of arrival, I lay prone on the back seat. I did not exist. The only person in the car was Martin, who gave me a commentary as we approached. About four miles short I switched on the radio, did a comms check and put on my gloves and face veil. I was sweating cobs because he had the heating on full blast, being in shirtsleeves while I was fully dressed for a cold dawn.

Martin began his countdown approaching the drop-off point, which was immediately before a sharp bend in the road. There was nothing behind or in front. Three hundred metres, two hundred metres, one hundred metres, fifty metres. I had my hand on the door handle. As he eased his speed right off I opened the door and rolled out onto the grass verge, pushing the door to but not letting it click. If anyone had been watching it would have looked like a cautious driver had slowed for the bend, that was all.

All this palaver was very necessary. Gamekeepers are often about at night with their guns, and so are poachers who would certainly wonder what was going on if they saw me and talked about it in the pub.

It takes twenty minutes or more for night vision to kick in. I lay motionless in the grass, hoping no cars would pass by. Hearing Martin's voice in my ear I spoke briefly back. Yes, thank you Martin, the grass is soaking wet with dew and it is quite chilly out here. Have a nice time in the car park.

The sweet fragance of the blossoming hawthorn filled the air. Don't cast a clout until the may is out, I said to myself. Watched pots never boil. Don't let the sun catch you crying. After twenty minutes of this and other meaningless ways of filling empty time, no cars had passed and I was beginning to make out the shape of the hedgerow next to the road.

Time to go. It took me five minutes to get through the hedge, moving very slowly and carefully, desperately trying not to leave a sign of my penetration into enemy country. I looked for vehicle tracks, but there weren't any. This meant I had to cross an open stretch of grassland that, if I wasn't meticulous about where I put my feet, would leave a trail as visible as footprints in the sand. On long wet grass you leave marks that a child could see. On short wet grass you can still betray your route to the practised eye so, if you can't wait until it dries off a little, you go around the boundary rather than across the middle and brush out your footprints as you go with a leafy branch.

I was confident of travel without trace. I also felt that if somebody was about this early, moving on the land, I'd spot them before they spotted me. My weakness was that I had no current knowledge of poacher activity on the estate. There was bound to be some. Every estate has poachers. If it so happened that poachers had been around recently the keepers would have made a response. They could be waiting in ambush somewhere, or they could have set little devices of varying degrees of ferocity. Knowing Verril, I wouldn't put mantraps and live shotgun cartridges past him.

After years and years of watching animals and sneaking around other people's land I had built up a kind of sixth sense tuned in to normality, like a personal combination of radar and sonar. I could pick up signs of something amiss. Normality is the right blend of smells, sights and sounds. If there's anything wrong, if a part is missing or there's something extra that shouldn't be there, the sixth sense notices and flashes a light in my head.

It was still dark but everywhere was the faint sweet scent of spring, of growing grass and opening leaves, with the

stronger, more specific aroma of wild violets coming through
from time to time. Occasionally a blackbird told me it knew
I was there, with its 'ping-ping' warning to watch my step.
Every few metres I stopped, crouched down and listened.
Nothing. Still nothing. I reached my first cover, a clump of
blackthorn bushes. Deep inside – a painful process – and
keeping low, I waited for the dawn.

I feel at my most alive doing early-morning reconnaisance.
It's like having your ears syringed and the equivalent done to
your eyes, nose and spirit. Everything is tuned up to its keenest
level, everything is clearer, sharper, more distinct. The focus
is perfect. If Verril dropped a pin half a mile away I would
hear it.

There was no breeze. Everything was still. The world had
stopped at the boundary between night and day then . . . here
came the dawn and with it the first sound of movement. It was
much nearer than half a mile – thirty metres, I would have
said. Two fairly heavy bodies were walking steadily and carefully from my left towards my blackthorn hide-out, which suddenly didn't seem quite such a marvellous concealment as before.

The natural reaction to a sudden noise is always to turn
your head, snap, towards the sound. That could easily give
you away so the trained person, however difficult it might be,
makes himself turn his head so slowly it seems to take an
eternity. This is what I did, not exactly looking forward to
discovering the source of the disturbance.

Two roe deer stepped out from a willow coppice and walked
towards me. Their breath was clearly visible in the cold
morning air as they walked right past, near enough to touch.
I gave them a few minutes to get well away before I moved
out. I didn't want them sounding the alarm.

And so to work. Methodically and painstakingly I videoed
and sketched the small area I was surveying. I gave myself

until half past seven then I called it a day and retraced my steps, checking behind me every few metres for mistakes and unwanted company. Back in the hedgerow I called Martin on the radio and asked him to pick me up. This was another well-rehearsed routine, with Martin leaving the rear nearside door ajar and the interior light switched off. I counted him down to my exact position in the ditch while he slowed to walking pace. I leaped in, held the door shut and lay on the back seat until we were well clear of the area.

Back in the office, in my normal clothes, I sorted out all the equipment, went over everything in my mind, made notes and pieced together the video and the sketch map. This episode, with minor variations, was repeated over fifty times during the next six weeks until every block on the grid was filled in. Contrary to expectations, both mine and everyone else's in the office, my luck had held. The badger gods had smiled and I was through it all without being discovered — as far as I knew.

I now had four six-inch-to-the-mile OS maps stuck together on the wall, with a complete picture of the estate with its six entrances, some gated. I knew every road, track, path, wood, ride, coppice and badger sett, including four that appeared to have been dug in fairly recent times. I knew where his pheasant release pens were, where he stored his grain and where he kept his vehicles.

I was pleased to find his anti-poaching devices too, around his pens. Poaching standards must be dropping, I thought, if these are expected to catch country people. Fine fishing line, above deer height but right enough for a walking human, would detonate a blank, black-powder cartridge if it was pulled. I thought any decent poacher would have expected such things and found them, as I had. Maybe Verril wasn't up with the latest technology. These trip lines were old hat.

He should have kitted himself out with a few infra-red rays and pressure pads if he wanted to catch the real top men.

For the action plan I'd identified vehicle entry points, RV – rendezvous – points, emergency RV points, lying-up points, places for holding resources and back-up, observation posts, everything. All I needed was opportunity. I needed a badger dig. I was ready to go.

Towards the end of my mapping programme I had had a long meeting with Martin. He'd been doing a good job. His profile of Verril included photographs, details of the vehicles he used, family members, associates and a full range of activities off the estate.

Martin had also been in touch with our informant again. Eric had told him that Verril and his cronies were periodically digging up four setts, which confirmed my own observations. The cronies were not local, but old pals from Ribblesdale. Like most long-term badger diggers, Verril practised a kind of cynical crop rotation and conservation, not wiping out a sett completely but leaving a few animals to keep the population going and ensure that he would always have lots of fun to offer when his mates were able to come down again.

'It's the usual problem, Martin,' I said. 'Time and place. Unless we know which sett, and when they'll dig it, all our other work is just material for the filing cabinet.'

'Eric will find out which sett.' Martin was confident of that much, anyway.

'Can he also find out when the others are coming down from Lancashire?'

'Don't know. I can only ask.'

It was a while before he had an answer but after several tiresome weeks had gone by – how we wished Verril would get on with his badger digging – Eric let us know that our man had two friends coming down from the North sometime

over the next month. They would be staying for the weekend
and go on several digs but he didn't know which setts. Eric
could not be more precise, sorry.

It was patently obvious that we were unlikely to find out
from Verril when the digs would be. It also looked important to capitalise now on Eric's information since we didn't
know when, or if, we'd have another chance. The only way I
could see around the problem was to try and extract something from the pals in Lancashire. Perhaps I could find out
the date from that end.

I could see another big hotel bill on the horizon, so I went
to see Don and explained. After all this work we were so nearly
there. Surely my boss and his boss and his boss's boss would
not let the ship be spoiled for a ha'porth of tar?

Don said okay, I sighed my relief and rang Vince Graham,
the chief inspector in that area. He was delighted to hear that
I was back on the Verril trail.

'Anything, Tony, anything at all. What can I do to help?'

'Somewhere up there Verril's old mates are still knocking
about. I want to find out where they go, so I can go as well.
I'm desperate to find out when two of them are coming down
here for a badger party.'

'Well, there's one called Dobson, still up to his old tricks,
but never so's we can catch him. Then there's Trueman, and
the raving idiot they call Crocodile, although I think he's out
of it now.'

'Crocodile?'

'Fruit cake. Dundee. Crocodile. Get it?'

'You are a mine of information, Vince. Now, can you find
out where they drink?'

'I already know where they drink. At least, I know where
Dobson drinks because it's the next village to me and I can't
go in there on Thursdays and Fridays. It causes an atmosphere.'

'I bet it does, Vince. Right. I'll be with you tomorrow, Thursday. And could you see if anyone can fit me up with a van. British Gas. Norweb. Anything like that.'

Vince not only got me a van with North West Water written all over it. He also found me a set of contents – tools, barriers, orange flashing lights, the lot – and some overalls with logo. My cover story was in the van. I only had to say I was working over such a way on Thursdays and Fridays and it was nice to drop in at that pub for pie and chips and a couple of pints on my journey home.

For the next three weeks, every Thursday and Friday saw me leaning against the bar having my first pint of Thwaites draught bitter, sitting at a small table near the dartboard for my pie, peas and chips, and getting as near as I could to Dobson for my second pint and subsequent alcohol-free lagers. I can't stand alcohol-free lager, but this was in the line of duty.

Dobson came into the pub on the dot of eight o'clock and stayed until about ten. He was generally a bar stander, not a sitter, so it wasn't too hard to listen in on his conversation. For the first two weeks we didn't speak ourselves. I chatted to the landlord, if anybody, but I tried not to be too sociable because it's extremely difficult to eavesdrop while having a conversation of your own.

On the third Thursday Dobson and I exchanged brief pleasantries. I was thinking that if I didn't get something soon I'd have to push the issue and try to extract the information directly, a very dangerous game that could ruin the whole show. This episode of the long-running saga *Get Verril* was becoming frustrating and depressing and beginning to look like another wasted effort.

To make matters worse, on that third Thursday evening Dobson went and sat in a far corner of the bar with one other chap, whom I gathered was a local pig farmer, and talked very

earnestly about something I couldn't catch. It wasn't possible
to saunter casually over there and lean against the wall, so I
had to put up with an evening of nothing, lubricated by
delicious alcohol-free lager.

I always waited until Dobson left then departed myself
about twenty minutes later. It came to nearly ten o'clock. He
drained his pint and, as usual, put his glass back on the bar
as he turned to go.

'See you tomorrow,' said the landlord.

'No you won't,' said Dobson, on his way out. 'I'm going
down south this weekend to see a mate. Next Thursday I'll
be in.'

On the outside I maintained my taciturn, serious demeanour. On the inside I was laughing, cheering and punching the
air. Patience and tenacity had paid off. As long as we kept
luck on our side, we were on for the big one.

I kept my grinning and chuckling for my own car and the
long drive back to Sussex after returning the North West
Water van to Vince. There was a lot to do. We had a day to
set things up. One day only. If Dobson and, probably, his mate
Trueman were driving down tomorrow night, they could be
out on a dig first thing Saturday morning. We had to be in
position, somewhere on the estate, all kitted and commed and
ready for whatever they might get up to. The only sure bet
was that they would go digging. We didn't know which sett,
what time or, come to that, which day.

The problem with exercises like this is that always, *always*,
people fail to do what they are supposed to. They will do
something else instead. Probably nine out of ten set-ups fail
because the intelligence is wrong in the first place, or the
targets do something we haven't predicted. If we were going
to win, we needed the very best organisation, some excellent
guesswork, and a big slice of luck.

I phoned Martin on the mobile, and also Trevor Knowles. Trevor was one of the world's best organisers. He'd been a sergeant in army intelligence, then he was a uniformed RSPCA inspector for eight years. He was brilliant at logistics and at sifting through facts and figures to make them into a picture. Incidentally he was also excellent at foot surveillance, mainly because, as a barrister once put it, he looked like Postman Pat. No one would ever suspect him of being a covert agent.

We met in the office at seven thirty and started to develop our plans. A team was despatched north to carry out surveillance on Dobson and Trueman, to confirm when they left, what they were travelling in and what gear and terriers they had with them. All of that day was spent in the office, making plans, going over them, finding faults, plugging holes, making sure everyone knew exactly what they had to do. We kept in close touch with the police, who left us to run the operation and, as usual, offered us first-class support. We could have whatever we needed, from helicopters to dog handlers and as many officers as we wanted.

It turned out there were six setts on the estate. Of the four that were dug regularly, one was a favourite. This was the biggest sett and it had easy access for the Land Cruiser or other 4WDs they would be using. The size and complexity of the estate was the problem. We didn't have the resources to cover every eventuality. All we could do was stake out the most likely sett and keep a close watch on Verril's movements between home and estate, so that if he came in on a different route through one of the other five entrances we should know which of the setts he was headed for.

To do this we would have Martin in his public parking space overlooking the Downs, from where he could watch two of the entrances. For each of the other ways in we had to have a car with two SOU officers positioned a fair distance from their assigned gateway. When we received the word that Verril and pals were on their way, these vehicles would set off. To avoid being noticed, they hoped to pass Verril on the move as he reached his chosen entrance. It all sounded a bit hit and miss, but it was the best we could do.

We would have police air support of course, but they had to be careful not to get too low and obvious, and they didn't have long-distance imaging equipment that was sophisticated enough. There was nothing for it but close personal surveillance.

Our last problem was how to find out when our targets were setting off. Verril's house was in the middle of the village, overlooking the green and the main road. It was very exposed, no cover anywhere, in a community where everyone knew everyone else and where keeping an eye on everyone was a way of life going back centuries. Verril, embarking on his illegal day out, would be even more watchful than normal and no strange vehicle could be risked doing anything other than driving once straight through the village.

I had a cunning plan, naturally, and I was especially pleased with it because, having so many officers on this job, the boss had to come along and be part of it – and very early in the morning too. It was a one-off kind of cunning plan, unfortunately. We would be all right for Saturday and probably Sunday, but it was non-repeatable after that. If this operation didn't succeed I'd have to think of a different plan for next time.

We were pretty tired by the end of our last briefing session, when I went through the whole operation from start to finish. I detailed each individual's responsibilities, made sure that everyone was fitted up with the correct radio frequencies, and covered every little thing right down to checking that accommodation had been arranged for any seized terriers, vets had been put on stand-by and sustenance had been provided for hungry RSPCA officers.

Our real weakness, however comprehensive our planning, seemed to be locating the men once they had crossed the boundary into the estate, into Verril's own territory. He knew the land intimately, far better than I did. He might even get as subtle as seeming to head for one sett then diverting to another once he was on home ground. He had been badger digging for more than ten years to my knowledge and he had been pursued, by me and others, for at least eight of those years. He'd be taking no risks. He'd be feeling secure and confident, but he wouldn't be careless. Neither would we.

With all that over, we waited for the phone call that would tell us we were on. It came at about seven o'clock. Dobson and Trueman had left in one vehicle and were heading south on the M6. With them they had two terriers, a lurcher and miscellaneous gear. ETA about eleven, depending if they stopped off. We felt sure they would have eaten before leaving and would only stop for fuel, so a drive-past at half eleven would be enough to confirm their arrival. It was. There was the car, a white Volvo hatchback, in Verril's driveway. Phone calls to the police chief inspector and Trevor Knowles triggered the job as 'live'. We were off and running.

I went to bed but couldn't sleep. This was the biggest operation of my life, involving – for us – massive resources. Everybody had given me total support, without question. Everyone was depending on my basic plan and my conviction that Verril, Dobson and Trueman would be digging badgers this weekend. From our information it seemed perfectly obvious. From the amount of scrutiny and discussion it had had, my plan must have been watertight. But that didn't stop me going over everything in my mind, trying to find the little leak, the loophole, the tripwire. The trap was ready to be set, but would it be escape-proof?

14

At half three on the Saturday morning Martin Wilson picked me up. I was kitted out as in the recce phase of the operation, plus I had a camera with a long lens, 500mm. I had also packed an image intensifier, a few biscuits, some high-energy drink and some mosquito repellent. We were expecting a fine day. Everything metallic or otherwise reflective, even zips, was masked with black tape and lenses were covered with nylon from a pair of tights.

By four I was on my own, in the dark. Martin was away to his lookout point and I was two hundred metres from Verril's favourite sett.

Everywhere is green and white through these intensifiers. Trees and grass look like there's been a hard frost, but you soon get used to that. I made my way slowly towards the laying-up point, trying to envisage the general scene in front of me. I was looking for a thick clump of gorse I remembered as being there, a place where I could be completely hidden yet near enough to see when the men began digging. I wouldn't be able to see them on their way here — I'd have to rely on my colleagues for that — but I would see them arrive.

The sett was quite well concealed too, in a coppice of hazel and willow. Beyond the coppice was dense mixed woodland. A narrow track ran between the gorse bushes and the sett and on, deep into the wood.

I settled into my gorsey den and waited for the dawn. There was nothing more I could do. Ideally we should have been operating in pairs but we were too few to afford such luxury. In the past we had tried to overcome this by using uniformed police and RSPCA inspectors, but they'd no training in field-craft or surveillance in a rural context and we found out that it simply didn't work. We would have loved to have highly trained, specialised police or army units, but they wouldn't waste their valuable resources on catching mere badger diggers, so we had taken a decision to do without. Our policy was: muddle through on our own.

I watched the countryside come alive with the dawn and thought of my boss, Don Balfour. He would be getting into position now with Eddie Carlyle, our shaven-headed Scouser, dressed up in fluorescent jackets and disguised as traffic census takers. We'd persuaded the highways people to lend us some survey warning triangles and a few cones, plus authentic highways census forms, matching clipboards and a vehicle with a flashing roof light. Don and Eddie would be taking it in turns. Their car would be parked across from Verril's cottage, and while one man kept a lookout for activity in the rear-view mirror the other would be doing his census charade. Soon I expected to hear Don's call sign and those of all the rest of my colleagues as they took up their positions.

Time to check my kit. Very slowly and carefully I made

sure everything was functioning. I always kept pieces of equipment in the same pockets so if I needed a torch or my small binoculars, while I was lying under a bush and wanting to stay silent, I knew where they were. It seems to go without saying, until you forget to do it. It was six o'clock.

'Traffic census in position,' said a voice in my ear with a strong Liverpool twang. 'Road signs deployed. Confirm we can see Verril's Land Cruiser in the rear-view mirror. No sign of movement as yet.'

Radio checks were done between all units to establish that Trevor Knowles, our co-ordinator, up on a high point on the Downs, had comms with everyone. So. The trap changed status. With no fuss at all it had moved from 'ready' to 'set'.

Seven o'clock came and went and there was still no activity around Verril's house. Maybe they were going to dig on Sunday. Maybe they'd been on the whisky last night and stayed up late, and they were having a lie in.

You don't know how slowly time can pass until you do a job like this. I tried to keep my mind occupied, going over the plan, assessing the various possible outcomes, using my SAS training to build up a series of 'what if?' scenarios, but there is a limit to anyone's ability to discipline the brain. It will shoot off at random, and that's probably a good thing, but I enjoyed watching wildlife anyway so I was quite used to sitting in hides for hours waiting for some bird or animal to appear. I was reasonably well equipped for the long wait.

We were supplied with a limited amount of entertainment over our radios, as the boss got himself really deeply into his role and started complaining about the terrible amount of traffic there was passing through this tiny village at such a ridiculous hour. He was making detailed notes of each vehicle that went through and getting increasingly annoyed about them. A couple of residents going to the village shop for a paper said it was about time the local authority did something, and Don heartily agreed with them.

Don didn't seem to want to take his turn on the rear-view mirror and it was Eddie's voice again, coming up towards eight o'clock, that reported the first movement.

'Verril is out. He's opening and closing doors on the Land Cruiser. I can't see exactly what he's doing but it looks like he's getting ready to go somewhere.'

This sort of information always cranks my alertness up a notch and makes me run mental checks on myself, on my mental state, to be sure I'm prepared for the task. All was peace and quiet around me. Surely I'd be able to hear voices or dogs barking when they started getting close. More time passed, and more. The Don Balfour Irate Citizen act began to pall.

Those bastards in the house had got up late, I bet myself. I imagined they'd had five or six more hours in bed than me, and had enjoyed a long, hot breakfast. They were sitting now, in a nice warm kitchen, eating sausage, bacon and eggs. Then they would read the paper, have another cup of coffee and a smoke, and discuss what they might do on their holiday weekend.

'Stand by, stand by.' At last. That Scouse accent and Eddie's coolness in operations made the call sound so matter of fact. We'd been waiting hours for that call. I'd been waiting eight years for that call. I'd been in my gorse bush since half four and now it was half past ten. All around the estate SOU officers were turning ignition keys and clunk-clicking and psyching themselves up for the job. I had no key to turn. I couldn't do anything but wait. Eddie came on again.

'Three men outside the cottage. I can't see what they've got with them. There's a hedge in the way. I can only see their heads. Verril is bare-headed. The others have flat hats. It looks like they've got wax jackets on but I can't see any spades or tools, or any terriers. I can hear car doors. Engine. Here they come. Bloody hell, they're in the Volvo. They're going badger digging in a hatchback?'

He had a point. It was hardly the ideal vehicle. What were they up to? Why were they leaving the Land Cruiser in the driveway? It would be just our luck if they were going into Chichester. That would be it. A few Saturday lunchtime pints and a meal at the Chinese.

All the call signs went out in the hope that they might still be heading for some entry point on the estate. I waited. Fifteen minutes went by, twenty minutes, and no one had seen the white Volvo. We'd lost it. After all this time and effort, we couldn't even keep tabs on a car for fifteen minutes. And I thought our weakness was keeping tabs inside the estate. God, we'd lost them at the first opportunity, on the open road.

I began to get that awful slipping feeling. The operation was sliding away from me. Nobody was taking charge. Who was supposed to take charge? Me, of course, damn it, except I couldn't co-ordinate two men on a tandem from where I was.

'Trevor. I need to find this bloody Volvo. Contingency plan for lost vehicle. Do it.'

This meant physically checking all the entry points to the estate. I heard as each call sign acknowledged, but nobody came up with anything. My slipping feeling became a plummet. I was in an express lift going down and down. What were the bastards doing? They could be going anywhere, doing anything. Whatever it was, it was the opposite of what we wanted. We wanted these men to go digging badgers. They had to go, one more time, the last time of their lives. I had to tell myself to be patient. There was no point in trying to guess. There were no advantages in supposing or imagining.

Two more hours went by. We were getting desperate. They could have had their sport and be in the pub by now. I got on the radio.

'Trevor. Initiate helicopter fly-past. Ask them to stay high and make one pass only. Let's hope they can spot a white blob in the middle of all this greenery.'

It was easily the fastest thing to happen so far. It can't have been more than three or four minutes before a blue and white police helicopter went over at about two thousand feet, followed almost immediately by a result. The helicopter police radioed Eddie, the person nearest to the sighting and, as it happened, the nearest to my gorse bush. The police had a copy of my map, like all the others, and they could see that the white Volvo was no more than half a mile from the position I had marked as mine.

It was down there, down the track. The car, and therefore presumably Verril and his mates, were a ten-minute walk away down the track in front of me, the track that divided the wood and led me straight to the target. I had no setts marked in that area. They must know one I had never found.

'To all mobiles. Return to your positions. I'm going to take a short walk down a forest trail.'

It was not so much a short walk as a long, curving crawl. In as big an arc as I could I set off to find out what was going on, carrying all my gear and having to pass through dense undergrowth, brambles, thorns. Brer Rabbit might be at home in the briar patch but nobody who has a heavy bergen on his back can be. It all requires enormous concentration and field-craft. You only have to set off a roosting woodpigeon or alarm a blackbird and the whole forest will know you're there.

Certainly such a sound to Verril would be the equivalent of a station tannoy announcement, so you make a little progress, you stop, you check, you make a little more progress.

Always the danger is that you'll suddenly stumble into the open in front of your target.

Not this time. After about twenty minutes I saw white paint ahead. Creeping cautiously forward I could see only the car. No people. I crawled right around it. Still no people. I looked in the car. Nothing but the usual mess and a couple of old wax jackets. There was the track the car had come up on, and a pathway beyond which looked like their most plausible route.

Keeping the path within easy distance I carried on in creepy-crawly mode. It was not long, maybe another twenty minutes, before I heard the sounds of canine and human activity. Then I saw them.

The men were little more than twenty yards away. Through the thick foliage I could see all three of them and I stared hard and long through my binoculars, which are a great help towards giving exact descriptions of people and actions later. Verril was wearing a camouflage shirt with fawn trousers. The second man I recognised as my friend from the pub, Dobson. He wore a blue denim jacket and jeans, and the other, Trueman presumably, a dark blue sweater and light green trousers.

Dobson was carefully poking a metal rod into the ground, like the kind of thing farmers use to put up a temporary wire fence. After a few experimental prods he found what he wanted: the badger's tunnel. This was the spot. Trueman took up a spade and began digging furiously.

A gun was leaning against a tree and I could be sure there would be more guns not far away. A young terrier, a puppy really, a small, squat black one with a lot of Patterdale in its family, was tied to a different tree and barking in mad excitement. Another, a longer-legged, dark and brindle Patterdale terrier cross, was in a decidedly more quiet mood. It was covered in mud, licking itself and taking no interest in proceedings.

This dog had obviously already been down below and had been wounded in a fight. He who fights and runs away lives to fight another day. Fair enough, but it wouldn't exactly earn a gold star in the terrier men's eyes.

Verril joined in the digging. I could hear the ringing of the spades as they hit hard chalk, and then the muffled sound of frenzied barking from another terrier below ground. This one, no doubt fitted with a small transmitter on its collar, must have found a badger and driven it into a chamber with a dead end. Badgers will tend to retreat rather than fight, until cornered. They will then fight to the last, but only if there is no other way. Their preferred option is to dig their way out of the dead end.

Above ground, Dobson – obviously the expert at underground detection – was looking closely at his terrier receiver, a neat little box of tricks sold openly for use with ferrets catching rabbits. The receiver gives out a beep to the signal from the terrier's collar transmitter. The louder the beep, the nearer the terrier is to the box. These devices also have a depth gauge so, between the two types of data, the men could position themselves directly above the badger and know how much digging there was to do.

I imagined the scene beneath the surface. Brock would be excavating with all his might but would be continually distracted by the terrier, barking and making occasional decoy attacks. It was a race to the death. This was why the men were putting so much effort into their spadework. The ground was stony. If they took too long Brock would dig his way out and be away down the tunnel maze and the whole business would have to be started over again.

Another possibility was that the terrier would lose patience, get the red mists and go on all-out attack. The dog might be extremely game, completely fearless even, but attacking a badger like that, in its own underground home, had only one possible outcome. Defeat for the terrier was certain. Perhaps it would be killed, perhaps have its jaw ripped off. It was unlikely to come to its senses soon enough to avoid horrible injuries.

Dobson got down on his stomach and listened with his ear to the ground. Verril was taking a breather. Trueman was shovelling like his life depended on it, rather than the badger's, then I noticed the lurcher. It was a large, sandy-coloured animal, like a big fox on stilts, mooching around the woods looking for something interesting to sniff. This wasn't Verril's. This was a hunter/chaser, a greyhound cross, not a battler. I could have imagined it in a pack, running down antelopes in the desert. It was a real danger to me. Any loose dog represented a massive risk of compromise but this one was purpose-made for trouble.

Quickly I tried to give a situation report. Brilliant – I was in a radio blackspot. I transmitted five times with no response. This was near disastrous. Information given out at the time, logged and recorded, always makes much better evidence than statements recalled later.

I looked at my back-up, my mobile phone, and the display told me I had no signal. It should be called Marconi's Law. If communications can let you down, they will. I cannot remember an open-air operation without some sort of comms problem. Here I was, a cricket pitch from where three men were digging into a badger's sett, and I was cut off entirely. It was the perfect moment to call in the cavalry, but the cavalry's call sign was unobtainable.

I snapped off a couple of long shot photographs then went onto video. This didn't work either. I was trying to video badger diggers twenty yards away and the blasted camera kept auto-focusing on the nearest leaf.

Decision time was fast approaching, and so was the lurcher. It was coming straight for me. I crouched lower into the under-growth and kept as still as possible. The lurcher sniffed up and down the track like a bloodhound. I hadn't actually been over that part, but it was sensing something. It came closer and closer, sniffing and snuffling. I tried to remember that statistic about dogs and their noses. How many hundred times was it that they were more smell-sensitive than humans? At this point, I told myself, I should not be too worried. It wouldn't want to come into the gorse bush. I didn't represent any food interest. I wasn't a bitch on heat. I was just a foreigner. My fate now depended on how the dog had been trained. If, as was possible, it had been taught to hate everyone except its owner, I'd probably had it.

I started going over my compromise drills in my mind. The mainstay was one where I would claim to be a soldier on escape and evasion exercise, and I had an army contact who would verify this to anyone calling him. While I was telling Verril all this, I would leave my radio on open transmission – not that I expected it to do a lot of good in this blackspot.

If it became clear that my story wasn't washing today I would give out a coded signal. This would tell my colleagues that I was in it, up to an irretrieveable depth, again assuming they heard it on working comms, whereupon I would run like hell to a prearranged spot, the nearest emergency rendezvous. Given that Verril decided against dropping me in my tracks with his first barrel, I could expect to be picked up within five minutes of reaching it. If I wasn't I would run to the next RV point, wait another five minutes, then make for the road, where a car could collect me.

It was beginning to look increasingly as if at least one of these routines would shortly be tested for real-life effective-ness. The lurcher came up to within an arm's length of me and stopped. It stared straight at me, its ears pricked and its tail swishing. This was one extremely suspicious dog. I doubted whether it could see me properly, if at all. I was wearing my face veil and every part of me was disguised in DPM, but it certainly knew something was in that bush, and by God it didn't like it, whatever it might be. I was the abnormality, the extra something, that made the dog's sixth sense – like the one I was so proud of – switch on that flashing light.

Every dog owner will have seen a dog's reaction to an animal noise on the radio or television. It will look at the set and listen with its head tilted first to one side, then to the other. It can't quite make out how an inanimate box is able to squeak like a mouse or squawk like a seagull. This was what the lurcher was doing now, staring at me and listening with alternate ears in an attempt to make sense out of something very puzzling.

I cursed myself for not bringing a few dog biscuits and my little catapult. This was my way of getting rid of loose dogs. I could spray a few Spratt's Ovals around. If they didn't like the biscuits and I was really desperate, a Spiller's Shape diamond fired from the catapult to ping it on the nose would usually work. Okay, so I hadn't thought of everything. The unfortunate thing was that a small lapse like that could be very costly indeed. If I was discovered by this dog, the reactions of three badger diggers with guns would be unpredictable to say the least.

The lurcher bared its teeth and gave a low grumble, which turned into a solid growl, which turned into loud, non-stop barking. I saw the three men stop and look to see what the noise was all about, but the badger was their priority for the moment and they carried on with their digging. Now Verril was bent over I could see his famous knife, the US Marines

K-bar. I hoped that it would be staying in its sheath today.

I tried hissing at the dog. That sometimes works but it didn't this time. I told it to clear off, trying to think of all the different commands that it might be used to. No good. Since I didn't have my catapult, maybe I could throw a pebble at it. No good either. No pebbles. Nothing but leaf mould.

It certainly was a tenacious hound. The more I tried to get rid of it, the more alarming its barking became. I was really concerned now. Slowly and carefully I raised the binoculars to look at the men. There was no curiosity or particular care on their faces. They glanced round occasionally, that was all, until Verril turned and shouted at the top of his voice, Effing well shut up, you effing so-and-so.

The digging was the thing. They must have been nearly through. Verril was going at it like a demon. Still the dog barked at me. It seemed like for ever and in reality it must have been more than five minutes, which was a long time to have a dog barking at you in those circumstances. Verril's irritability got the better of him and he threw the spade to the ground, stomped over to the big old oak tree where his gun was leaning, picked it up and set off towards me and the dog.

I had three choices. I could stand up, say who I was, tell them they were surrounded and advise them to give in gracefully. I could stand up and do one of my compromise drills. Or I could get down as low as possible, stay as still as possible, flatten my face into the leaves and hope for the best. I decided on the last approach. While hoping for the best I couldn't help a few thoughts of the worst coming into my mind, including being shot with a twelve-bore. I remembered the words of Ken Connor, veteran of the SAS, who once gave us a course on observation in rural areas. He'd said that the most dangerous weapon we could be faced with was a shotgun. Thanks, Ken.

I tried to work out what I'd do if I was shot. As long as I didn't get a fatal head wound I had a good chance of surviving. There was the police helicopter. They'd pick me up – provided my blasted radio worked. What would I do if the pellets busted my radio and my phone?

Verril was three metres away, cursing and blinding, What the effing hell's wrong with you. My heart was pounding so loud I thought the dog must be able to hear it. I was forcing myself to take very shallow breaths, all the time praying that I hadn't let my jacket ride up or let a handkerchief poke out. Every movement of a Verril boot, every rustle of clothing, was amplified in the most intricate detail. He was standing beside the dog, which stopped barking but kept up the growling. By the sound, it was growling directly towards me.

Verril was in touching distance. I could see the cracks in the brown leather of his boots. I could see the soil in his lace holes. There were fresh droplets of blood splashed on his trousers at the ankles, and the metal of the gun barrels' ends shone in the sun. If I was him, I thought, I'd assume there was a fox or something hiding in the bush and I'd let off a barrel. So, I thought, if I see the ends of the barrels moving up I have to do something. The training told me to shout and stand up slowly. A shout and a movement in my current position might make him even more likely to fire, but I didn't see what other options I had.

I watched the barrel ends. They moved two inches and went back again. Jesus wept. It's amazing what you think about at times like this. I actually tried to decide which bodily part could best withstand the blast of a twelve-bore at close range. In the event, there would be only one choice. I should have to present Mr Verril with my backside.

The urge to turn and see what was happening was very nearly impossible to resist. Why was Verril taking so long?

Why had this suddenly become so much more important than the badger digging? I felt the pulse on my temple start to pound. Go on, make a move, do something. I can't bear it any longer.

The decision, when it eventually came, was clear and firm. Verril concluded that there was nothing in the bush, that the lurcher was wrong, and valuable badger time was being wasted. He grabbed the dog by the collar and dragged it away, cursing it for its stupidity. The dog pulled and struggled to get back to me, barking and making a big fuss. I heard Verril kick it, with accompanying obscenities, and tug it along even faster.

As they reached a little bend in the track that took them out of sight for a moment I could move and get myself up and be able to watch the activity at the sett. Verril tied the dog to a tree and, in case it had any ideas about more barking and disturbance, he gave it another kick. The lurcher got the message and settled down, its head pointed in my direction. Verril leaned his gun against another tree, said something to his mates, presumably berating them for bringing such a stupid effing hound with them, then threw himself at the digging.

They were all at it, hammer and tongs. They were only a few short minutes away from their moment of triumph, the moment when they exposed an innocent wild animal to dire punishments for being guilty of nothing. The three men were getting more and more excited, urging each other on to dig faster and faster. If ever proof were needed of the power of adrenaline, here it was. I could have emerged from my hiding place and had a picnic and they wouldn't have noticed. They were in a frenzy, and the mad, out-of-control atmosphere was increased to fever pitch by the hysterical barking of the terriers, the one underground and the Patterdale tied up nearby.

The climax was reached. Shovels were thrown aside as Verril pulled something from the sett. I only caught a quick glimpse of a black and white muzzle but it was unmistakably a badger. The men moved behind a spoil heap, a pile of earth made by the badgers when they excavate their home. Trueman and Dobson became spectators while Verril cast himself as master of ceremonies, introducing two terriers into the programme, the one that had been below, a reddish gingery little dog with a Lakeland kind of look about it, and the brindle.

I couldn't see exactly what was going on but from the movements and sounds it was obvious that the terriers, in the light and on open ground, were doing as they liked. What they seemed to enjoy most was having a kind of tug of war with the badger as the rope.

The men watched in noisy approval. It was a scene of utter depravity and, when they'd had their fill of it, Verril assumed the role of executioner. He'd brought a pickaxe handle with him to use as a club, and that's what he did, raising it above his head and bringing it down several times with crazed ferocity, following the blows with the more precise coup de grâce, the deadly thrust with the K-bar, after which there came the casual wipe on the creature's coat.

There was no more time left. I had to get people down here and have these men arrested, even if it meant revealing myself to the enemy. There was still no signal on radio or telephone. No one could hear me. I made a transmission in any case. Strike, strike, strike, accept one! I gave the details of what I had seen. I knew it was hopeless really, but there was a faint chance that they could get my message even if I couldn't get a signal from them.

The badger was dead. Trueman walked to the oak tree, picked up Verril's shotgun and set off, diagonally away from me, towards the Volvo. Now I had to be in three places at once, one where I could watch Trueman, two where I could watch Verril and Dobson, and three where I could make a successful radio transmission. I decided that number three should take precedence and began backing slowly through the gorse. This was particularly nightmarish. Earlier on, I had been decidedly nervous about what Verril might do. Now, if he knew I had witnessed his awful deeds, what chance could I possibly have of getting out unscathed?

The few minutes it took me to get out of sight and earshot were sheer purgatory but at last I was away and doing something. I ran to what I thought would be a high point. Nothing. I ran again. Nothing. Comms, blasted comms, curse them to hell. It took me twenty minutes before I found somewhere the radio would work.

I got through to Trevor and called the strike. Without stopping to give any details of what I'd seen, I asked for the helicopter and the strike team of about twenty police and RSPCA, including dog handlers, to be deployed. They had a detailed plan to follow. Trevor told me the helicopter would be up in five minutes. I told him I was on my way back to the dig.

I should think I was about two hundred metres from the scene of crime when Trevor called me to say the helicopter was delayed for another ten minutes. How nice it was to know that comms were working again around here. Okay, I would have more time to spot exactly what the men were up to. At least I would have if there had been any men there. They were gone. Not a trace. I had no idea what they were doing or where they were doing it.

I moved twenty metres to my right, to a slightly elevated position, and did a thorough scan with the binoculars. I saw the white fertiliser bag first, then the three men. There they were, with all four dogs, moving deeper into the wood. Trueman and Dobson were carrying the bag between them, making heavy weather of it. This must be the body of the badger. They were going to dispose of the evidence. What lengths they went to. Why didn't they bury it at the sett? Who, I wondered, was going to dig up a badger and notice that it had head wounds caused by a blunt instrument and a knife wound as cause of death?

Time was pressing again. If they managed to bury the badger without me seeing it was going to be my word against theirs and their word would be very well worked out. It was not uncommon for diggers to take dead foxes along with them, which they had kept in the freezer, as evidence that they were only after Reynard, not Brock. Now we'd reached this stage, after eight years of trying, I was absolutely determined that Verril was not going to slip through my fingers. I would maintain my professional stance as much as possible, but a certain amount of caution was surely going to have to be thrown to the winds.

Support would come, I knew, but it was my job now to pursue and watch. I expected them to be on a high, like a sports team after a big win, and so not to be over-cautious. They would be feeling energised and satisfied after their disgusting triumph. With a bit of luck, if the dogs kept in front of the three men and I didn't make too much noise, I'd be able to follow them and keep them in sight.

Of course I had to be careful not to slip into over-confidence myself. I had a good deal of evidence. After eight years I was on the point of success. I felt on a high, too, but I still had the last few hard yards to go.

They were making a lot of noise, crashing through the undergrowth, dragging the fertiliser bag, with four very lively and agitated dogs running around, looking for more excitement. Not once did they glance back, but I stopped every ten metres to watch them through the binoculars. I wanted them in view, but at a distance so that if they did turn round I could stop dead and have a good chance of not being observed. I checked my compass and, with my knowledge of the estate, reckoned we were heading for the pheasant release pens. I gave this information to Trevor, hoping it would help the police get to the men.

Sure enough we came to the pens, and there I watched Verril stuff the fertiliser bag under some brambles before heading off deeper into the woods. I needed to see inside that sack, and I needed to video it and take some stills without losing touch with my quarry, who, thankfully, were still making plenty of row. I dragged the fertiliser sack out from under the brambles. It was heavy, very heavy, too heavy. The weight told me what to expect.

Bracing yourself is one thing. Finding two dead badgers is another. The white stripes on their heads were stained bright red with their own blood, and their bodies were still warm.

I quickly photographed them, realising that here were both a boar and a sow, perhaps a breeding pair. The anger cannot be described. How could a man who lived among nature, who must have come to gamekeeping with some sort of interest in wildlife, who spent his working time on a beautiful estate like this – how could a man become a torturer and a butcher of innocents? Even if you took away the humanitarian, emotional aspect, how could a man, the envy of every young lad in the village, risk throwing his whole career away? And how could a sane, normal human being believe that there were two more men of the same mind who would travel hundreds of miles to execute, by the most cruel methods, wild animals who had done no harm to anybody? If it was beyond ordinary comprehension, my job now was to see that the world did comprehend, that people did understand the presence of cruelty and evil in their midst.

I dropped the bag and moved on. I had to get to these men before they killed anything else. I could hear them, maybe two hundred metres in front of me, but I couldn't see them.

The helicopter came over, with Trevor in my ear wanting to know where the men were. The helicopter couldn't locate them. I took a fluorescent jacket out of my bergen, waved it and put it on. The helicopter police said they could see me but not the men. The white Volvo was still parked up. Martin Wilson, Trevor Knowles and twenty men were making their way towards me.

'Follow me,' I radioed to the helicopter. 'There's no point in me hiding now. Just keep your eye on me and my jacket.' I rushed through the woods, smashing through whatever was in the way of a straight line to my target. The helicopter had no thermal imaging gear. We were working on eyesight.

I broke out of a thicket and saw Verril, Dobson, Trueman and the dogs, there, thirty metres away. They obviously could hear the helicopter now, hovering low over them, but they couldn't see it yet through the forest canopy.

'Stop! Police!' I yelled at them.

They ran for it, not realising that, on the ground, there was only one man chasing them. If they'd turned and run straight towards me, back into the woods, they would have had a chance. Instead they broke cover and ran into open pasture. The helicopter swooped down and hovered a few metres above them. The noise was fantastically loud. The men froze. The dogs were in total panic. I walked slowly towards Verril, looking him in the eye. His face was pure white.

'Is that fear, Geoff?' I said. 'Fear, and terror, like a badger feels?' I don't think he heard me.

A police sergeant and two RSPCA colleagues came out of the trees to my right and climbed the fence between the wood-land and the field. The helicopter dropped a metre or two.

Every branch and leaf was waving about as if we were in a hurricane.

'Stay where you are,' came a voice from the loudspeaker. 'Stay exactly where you are.'

The sergeant was here now. He put handcuffs on the three men, who made no show of resistance. Their whole demeanour had changed. A few minutes ago they had been happy little murderers, cocky and confident in the world they knew and where they felt in control. Now they looked exhausted and drained. That was precisely the way I felt too.

I had no sensation of victory. I didn't feel like I'd won the cup. I didn't even feel pleased. My uppermost emotion was a horrible, empty regret that I'd been unable to stop them killing two fine badgers, and that I'd had to watch them killing one while I gathered evidence.

15

——

More police arrived and took the men away. I trudged back to the dead badgers and gave the bodies to Martin, who took them to the veterinary surgery, then went with Trevor to the sett and left him to do the scene-of-crime work. It's a great rigmarole, but like much meticulous, routine, fairly boring admin-type work, it is of the utmost importance. Many cases are lost because of sloppy scene-of-crime work.

The classic error is cross-contamination, where someone might – in this case – examine a terrier away from the scene then go back in inadvertently taking forensic evidence with him, like a badger hair or a bit of congealed blood. You have to prove conclusively that there has been no cross-contamination, and this was Trevor Knowles' job. He was made scene-of-crime officer, and he stood outside the taped-off area with his clipboard and notepad.

He made a detailed sketch map of the scene, with all the key points numbered on the map and on the ground. Two other officers who had not been involved so far went into the taped area and began calling back the evidence. Trevor logged everything: badger hairs, blood spots, dog hairs and the signs of human disturbance, obviously, but also the badgers' spoil heaps from normal tunnel digging, their latrine pits, their piles of old thrown-out bedding and their paths to and from the sett, all signs of active occupation.

We had to be able to show not only that Verril and his mates had done it, but that they knew what they were doing. Badger diggers almost always pretend ignorance. Badgers? No, your worship, we didn't expect no badgers, not no-how. We were looking for rabbits/foxes/buried treasure/the pot of gold at the end of the rainbow.

As the evidence was called Trevor logged the numbers and the various bits and pieces of forensic were handed to a police exhibits officer. Gradually the whole area was combed. Trevor was delighted. He thought he had the job tied up, tight as could be, with buttons and bows on it.

Meanwhile, partly to avoid any possibility of claims of cross-contamination, I was at the surgery. We had a vet called Richard Edwards, a local man who was a member of a badger group so very interested in this case. We were going to deal with the dogs first. I had videoed them at the scene but now they had a full clinical examination and treatment for their injuries.

All three terriers, even the Patterdale pup apprentice, showed signs of having been to ground. They had mud in their eyes and the conjunctivitis that always causes. They only need to go down once for it to start affecting their eyes. Their hair was also thick with soil and there were blood spots, and samples of these and the dogs' own blood and hair were taken for analysis.

The lurcher was more or less okay apart from a little

bruising, presumably from where Verril had kicked it. The pup had no further injuries beyond the sore eyes, but the ginger-red terrier had its lower jaw and lip ripped. The worst off was the brindle Patterdale. It had been in some battles and all its mouth and jaws were torn and slashed by opponents' sharp teeth.

After they had been treated the terriers had one further small trial to go through for the sake of the case against their masters. The vet gave them an injection to make them throw up. The vomit was examined and badger hairs taken from it, which would be matched against the two dead animals. All four dogs were taken in by the RSPCA and new homes were found for them.

The badgers' post-mortem examinations confirmed my verbal evidence. They had been violently beaten with blunt instruments before being stabbed through the heart. Verril's American issue K-bar was found to have traces of matching blood and was the correct size to have made the fatal wounds We had a very solid case.

I interviewed Verril's two sidekicks at the police station later that afternoon. I had a detective constable with me, mainly because the CID are much more experienced than we are at interviewing criminals, although we do have extensive interview training, but also to make sure there were no mistakes made with the rules of evidence.

These two men said nothing except, 'No comment.' It was the usual tactic when you had somebody completely trussed, roasted, carved and plated. There was no point in them co-operating, so they said, 'No comment,' all day long and, at that time, before the change in the law, there could be no inference of unwillingness to reply to a question. It was their right, and they took it.

I put up with this for five minutes, left them and changed

over to Verril. It was a very weird experience. He obviously hadn't yet realised that I'd been watching them all that time and, when I told him I'd seen everything, he caved in immediately. Well, sort of. He admitted to it all but, true to form, claimed it was an accident.

'An accident?' I said. 'Come on, Geoff. You'll never get me to believe that. You might, just, get a magistrate to believe, possibly, that there was the faintest chance that the first badger was an accident. But two of them? You are joking.'

'Accident. I wasn't expecting badgers. I was expecting foxes. Accident.'

Within a week of his arrest and long before the case came to court Verril was fired from his job and evicted from his house. The owner of the estate had been horrified to hear about what had been going on. He even had the water and electricity cut off to get Verril out quicker, which made social services jump about a bit because, villain that he was, he still had a wife and young children.

Six months later, in court, despite the overwhelming evidence, the three of them pleaded not guilty to a heap of charges that, couched in that legal way, had a strangely formal, civilised tone compared to the reality of what the men had done.

Counselling and procuring the wilful killing of a female badger. Disturbing a badger. Causing a dog to enter a badger sett. There were twenty-eight charges altogether levelled against the three of them, and all the media, local and national, followed the case.

Crowds of naturalists and wildlife protesters gathered outside the court, waving banners. 'Digger scum kill for fun.' 'Jail the badger killers.' It showed the depth of feeling when such vile and inhuman behaviour is brought to public notice.

Most of the prosecution's case was my evidence and we all had a week of tension going through the mangle of the law. Special protection had to be given to the accused men when arriving and leaving each day, else the massed battalions of wildlife groups and badger societies would have had them strung up from the nearest lamp standard.

Verril said he had 'only' been digging for fox cubs – which is a filthy but legal pursuit – and had been shocked when the terriers found a badger.

The prosecution lawyer gave a little smile.

'Mr Verril,' he said. 'You are a gamekeeper, are you not?'

'Of course I am.'

'Would you say you were a very poor, below-standard game-keeper, unable to do a proper job? Mr Verril?'

Verril had seen the trap but hadn't yet worked out a way of avoiding it.

'I don't think that's for me to say.'

'Oh, come, come, Mr Verril. Your modesty is admirable, but surely a man who has been a gamekeeper for as long as you have, a man who has never been out of work, a man who has been put in charge of four other keepers on one of the country's most prestigious shooting estates, such a man must at least be halfway competent, wouldn't you say?'

The magistrate intervened to ask if the point of all this would be arriving shortly.

'Absolutely so, your worship. The point is that, while it is true that foxes do sometimes live in old and disused badger setts, an observing human does not have to be a wizard of country lore to tell whether a sett is in full and current occu-pation by badgers. The accused here today are all countrymen, born and bred. They have been involved with gamekeeping and hunting since ever they were old enough. For Verril and his two companions really to believe the sett had been deserted and left to foxes they would have had to be blind and probably drunk as well.'

Verril then said he had had to put the first badger out of its misery because it had been badly wounded in fights with the terriers. He admitted hitting it with the pickaxe handle but that was a reflex action, in surprise that a badger had come out of a foxhole, and the knife had only been to make sure. The animal was already dead before he used the knife.

Going on to the next charges, Verril maintained that exactly the same thing had happened with the second badger, and the other two men said they had had nothing to do with it. They were only watching, appalled and disgusted.

The vet who had examined the bodies, Richard Edwards, took a different view. He said the badgers had been subjected to a serious and prolonged attack with a blunt instrument and that both the male and the female victims would have been fully aware of their ordeal. There was the most severe haemorrhaging, which showed that their hearts had been pumping throughout. They had both died of knife wounds, by stabbing to the heart with a weapon similar to a US Marines K-bar.

Much to our astonishment, the accused men called a veterinary surgeon in their defence. Even more astounding, this vet said that the knifing of the badgers wasn't cruel as death would have been instantaneous.

There was a very unfortunate hitch in among all of this. Our vet had moved from his old practice and set up on his own and, somehow, the badgers' corpses had been left behind in the freezer. Some well-meaning person had done a freezer clear-out and the bodies were gone.

This meant that Verril's vet could bang on about how he couldn't examine the bodies and how unfair it was that opinions could not be expressed from both sides with equal authority.

We sat there wondering how on earth a fully qualified and experienced vet, who had presumably come into the profession through his love of and interest in animals, could stand up and speak on behalf of these three lowlifes.

On the last day of the four things began to go against us. The stipendiary magistrate started kicking out the charges on technical points of law because the defence hadn't had equal access to the evidence. It was a bad time for me. It was a bad time for all of us in the unit but Verril, in a way, was my life's work. I had him where I wanted him, I knew beyond the faintest shadow of a doubt that he was as guilty as hell, and I was sitting in a British court of law, the source and spring of all justice, watching the bastard slip away from me.

By the time the magistrate had finished with his legal adjudications on the charges there were only three left per man: digging for a badger, killing a female badger, and killing a male badger. To our immense relief he found them each guilty of all three. He didn't remand them in custody, which was a pity, but adjourned the summons and deferred sentencing pending social services reports.

A month later Verril was given three sentences of three months, unfortunately to run concurrently, so he only served three instead of nine – the very least he deserved. He was also made to pay costs of more than two grand. The others were each given three lots of two months, also concurrent. It wasn't anything like as much as they deserved, but it was some sort of justice. I had, after all that, put my man away.

The magistrate also made a statement in which he paid tribute to the Special Operations Unit and to my work in particular. Speaking about the last day of the operation, he said, 'That Chief Inspector Saunders was prepared to put himself at risk to discover these offences is of great credit to him, and his work in this matter I highly commend. He has spoken of his regret at being unable to save the two badgers' lives. I would say to him, sometimes a sacrifice is necessary for the greater good.'

It's always satisfying to be appreciated, although I'd rather he'd mentioned the fifty dark mornings lying on the cold, wet grass.

As he was being taken down, Verril spoke to me. 'Does this mean I can stop looking over my shoulder?'

'Think about it, Geoff,' I said. 'Think about it. You've got plenty of time.'

POSTSCRIPT

Geoffrey Verril lost everything as a result of his conviction. His wife and children left him and he was shunned by all who knew him. He will never work again as a gamekeeper.

On the plus side, he has given up badger digging. We know this because he said so, and because we keep an eye on him. We're delighted because it means that, on average, seventy-five fewer badgers a year meet a cruel, brutal and early death. This is Verril's own figure, produced when I went to see him in prison. It wasn't a social call, needless to say; I visit all the men we've succeeded in convicting in the hope of persuading them to give us information on others in the same line.

Verril told me he'd been digging at least once a week for eighteen years, and that he always got one or two badgers. He was in his mid-thirties at the time of his sentence. Given a normal life expectancy, that's a lot of animal lives saved.

Verril, we know, is only one digger in hundreds. Faced with

that scale of animal cruelty, people like me might wonder what the point is. How can we ever win?

I believe one person can make a difference, because even one life saved, one cruel act avoided, is worth any amount of my efforts.

And, like the young woman said about the starfish, for those badgers, I made all the difference.

Tony Saunders continues to serve as Chief Inspector in the RSPCA's Special Operations Unit.

INDEX

The RSPCA

The RSPCA (Royal Society for the Prevention of Cruelty to Animals) is the world's oldest and best-known animal welfare organisation. It was established in 1824 to prevent cruelty and promote kindness to animals and is a charity supported entirely by voluntary donations.

The Society's inspectors, regional staff and volunteers work around the clock to help animals in distress. During 2000 the RSPCA received one enquiry every 19 seconds, investigated around 127,000 cruelty complaints and successfully prosecuted more than 1,000 people for ill-treating animals.

The RSPCA's Special Operations Unit is crucial in the fight against organised and commercial crime involving animal cruelty. RSPCA undercover operations have led to convictions for cock fighting, dog fighting, illegal slaughter, live transport abuses, trading in endangered species and wildlife crime.

RSPCA animal hospitals, rehoming centres and clinics, together with its network of volunteers, receive and treat companion animals, equines and wildlife. A total of 96,000 unwanted animals were found new homes by the charity during 2000.

Campaigns aimed at improving animal welfare are run on an international, national and local level and the Society carries out extensive educational programmes among young people of all ages.

For further information about the RSPCA's work or to make a donation, contact the Enquiries department by telephoning 0870 33 35 999, emailing webmail@rspca.org.uk or visit the Society's website on www.rspca.org.uk.

To report animal cruelty or seek advice contact the national helpline on 0870 55 55 99.